AMTRAK
America's Railroad
TRANSPORTATION'S ORPHAN AND ITS STRUGGLE FOR SURVIVAL

Railroads Past and Present

H. Roger Grant and Thomas Hoback, *editors*

AMTRAK
America's Railroad
TRANSPORTATION'S ORPHAN AND ITS STRUGGLE FOR SURVIVAL

GEOFFREY H. DOUGHTY, JEFFREY T. DARBEE, AND EUGENE E. HARMON

INDIANA UNIVERSITY PRESS

This book is a publication of

Indiana University Press
Office of Scholarly Publishing
Herman B Wells Library 350
1320 East 10th Street
Bloomington, Indiana 47405 USA

iupress.org

© 2021 by Indiana University Press

All rights reserved

No part of this book may be reproduced or utilized in any form or by any means, eletronic or mechanical, including photcopying and recording, or by any information storage and retrieval system, without permission in writing from the publisher. The paper used in this publication meets the minimum requirements of the American National Standard for Information Sciences—Permanence of Paper for Printed Library Materials, ANSI Z39.48-1992.

Manufactured in the
United States of America

Second printing 2022

Library of Congress
Cataloging-in-Publication Data

Names: Doughty, Geoffrey H., author. | Darbee, Jeffrey T., author. | Harmon, Eugene E., author.
Title: Amtrak, America's railroad: transportation's orphan and its struggle for survival / Geoffrey H. Doughty, Jeffrey T. Darbee, and Eugene E. Harmon.
Description: Bloomington, Indiana: Indiana University Press, [2021] |
Series: Railroads past and present | Includes bibliographical references.
Identifiers: LCCN 2021020580 (print) | LCCN 2021020581 (ebook) |
ISBN 9780253060631 (hardback) |
ISBN 9780253060648 (ebook)
Subjects: LCSH: Amtrak. | Railroads--United States--History. | Railroads and state--United States--History. | Passenger trains--United States --History.
Classification: LCC HE2791.A563 D68 2021 (print) | LCC HE2791.A563 (ebook) | DDC 385/.220973--dc23
LC record available at
https://lccn.loc.gov/2021020580
LC ebook record available at
https://lccn.loc.gov/2021020581

On that first trip, when I was led by the hand into the green sanctuary of a Pullman drawing room and saw spread out for my pleasure its undreamed-of facilities and its opulence and the porter holding the pillow in his mouth while he drew the clean white pillowcase up around it and the ladder to the upper and the three-speed electric fan awaiting my caprice at the control switch and the little hammock slung so cunningly to receive my clothes and the adjoining splendor of the toilet room with its silvery appointments and gushing privacy, I was fairly bowled over with childish admiration and glee, and I fell in love with railroading then and there and have not been the same boy since that night.

E. B. White, "The Railroad," *Essays of E. B. White*

Contents

ix	Foreword
xi	Preface
xiv	Acknowledgments
xviii	Authors' Note
3	Introduction
13	Part One: This Is What We Had
43	Part Two: Creating a New National Network
91	Part Three: Where Do We Go from Here?
165	Part Four: The Road to the Future
181	Epilogue
187	Appendix 1: Tracking Amtrak
223	Appendix 2: Amtrak Presidents and US Secretaries of Transportation
224	Bibliography
226	Index

Foreword

The public need for transportation such as that provided by Amtrak is a given, and by learning and respecting the past, we can only strengthen future outcomes in meeting that need. Policy is a leading and key ingredient for moving public transportation forward and for formulating ongoing policy. Up to the creation of Amtrak, government's policy was to allow the free market to provide for passenger transportation by road, rail, and air. This changed with the collapsing rail network in the Northeast in the 1960s, forcing a shift in thinking about government's role.

The debate about Amtrak continues: Is public funding justified? Money is not about how much is spent but how wisely it is spent. Proving the wisdom of expenditure can be very challenging for an organization that exists more in a state of flux than in one of stability and is influenced by political opinion and erratic financial support. One must always recognize the realities of the transportation business—safety cannot be bought. Human and material assets require ongoing maintenance and eventual renewal, and both are immune to, and cannot be invalidated by, the influences that have always affected Amtrak.

Organization and culture are derived and formulated from what leadership experiences, so as you read this book you can draw your own conclusions about the presence or absence of value in an environment of ongoing change. Raw truths without self-serving agendas are expressed throughout. The authors have done an excellent job of describing and evaluating the reality of Amtrak's 50-year life—something I conclude should be called "lessons learned."

Ronald L. Batory,
Administrator for the Federal Railroad Administration, retired.

Journeys have value in themselves
and are not just a device for saving time.

E. B. White, "The Railroad," *Essays of E. B. White*

Preface

Until the mid 1950s, most people still traveled long distances by rail. Railroads ran all across America, reaching almost every city and town of importance and many that were not. People often had relatives employed by a railroad or knew someone who was. As children they put pennies on the tracks (despite parental warnings that this would cause a wreck) and waved at engineers who waved back. Passenger trains took them to camp in the summer and to distant towns and cities to visit relatives. For generations people often associated train travel with a happier and simpler period of life, and in the fullness of time, passenger trains became embedded in the national psyche. These were "the days when arrival of a train was an exciting event and every little boy was going to be an engineer."[1] No other form of public transportation has such a following.

Train travel also offered young people the benefit of socialization. Parents confidently launched their offspring on a trip in the custody of a Pullman conductor who would deliver his charges safely to their destinations; a solo journey on a train was often a rite of passage to adulthood. As essayist E. B. White observed about occupying a Pullman car's upper berth: "The old act of drawing one's pants on and off while in a horizontal position did much to keep Man in a mood of decent humility. To tuck in the tails of a shirt while supine demanded a certain persistence, a certain virtuosity, wholly healthful and character-building."[2]

Business and industry depended upon passenger trains and enjoyed their comfort and sophistication, enhanced by prestigious names such as 20th Century Limited, Broadway Limited, Capitol Limited, Denver Zephyr, Super Chief, and City of San Francisco. Vacation and leisure travelers, too, were drawn to trains such as the California Zephyr, Empire Builder, North Coast Limited, and Silver Meteor. It was a time when railroads took pride in their trains, courting passengers with safe, clean, comfortable cars staffed by friendly and courteous employees dedicated to their careers.

Dining aboard a train was treated as a special occasion—initialed tablecloth, china, and silverware were standard, hallmarks of a railroad's pride of service. *NYC photos, Geoffrey H. Doughty Collection*

Overnight train travel frequently included an eagerly anticipated dinner in a rolling restaurant featuring a generous menu. Railroads saw dining cars as both an obligation and an important part of their public image. Tables were set with elegant monogrammed china, silverware, glassware, and linens, carefully arranged on a white tablecloth typically punctuated by a floral arrangement. Traveling aboard such a conveyance could be counted on as relaxing, reliable, and enjoyable. Trains transported us beyond the borders of our own worlds and were memorable in part because they were a great way to meet other people. Perhaps this is why so many of the older generation have fond memories of passenger trains.

Two generations and part of a third have grown up never having experienced the pleasure of the well-run privately operated passenger train. To these generations, Amtrak is the standard of passenger rail travel, and what the traveler finds today is by no means all bad. Amtrak has its problems, but its people are doing their best, often in difficult circumstances, and more often than not rise to the occasion and deliver a superior product. Still, this book has been written with a sense of regret about Amtrak's continuous struggle for survival. It will be abundantly clear that the authors think Amtrak, flaws and all, must survive as part of our national transportation system.

As your grade school report card might have once said of you, Amtrak "needs improvement." A nation's strength is often measured by its transportation resources, including its railroad passenger services, and while our society has generally improved its standard of living, our standards of comfortable travel have not kept pace. Amtrak got off to a difficult start mostly because of how it was conceived, the tepid support it received from the rail industry, and the seriously flawed leadership it was given. This book offers insights into the problems Amtrak faced then and still faces, but it starts by exploring the unstoppable post–World War II travel trends that forced the creation of a nationalized railroad passenger system. That history illuminates the need for a balanced national transportation policy that heretofore has been lacking.

As the reader will soon realize, the book is also about leadership and explores steps that could be taken to strengthen Amtrak and ensure its long-term survival. These recommendations go well beyond just "more money" and are set forth in Part Four. The story of Amtrak is much like a jigsaw puzzle with pieces that at first glance do not seem to fit together. But they do fit and make a complete picture. They are important in understanding where Amtrak came from, what it became, and what it might be. Although it is unrealistic to expect a return to the glories of trains past, surely we can find a way to make better the trains we have.

While serving as the Burlington Route's president between 1932 and 1949, Ralph Budd said of his road's passenger service, "By making rail travel attractive enough, we have an opportunity to enlarge our passenger business almost indefinitely. A completed trip, if it can be looked back upon with pleasure, should and will encourage another trip."[3] As Amtrak begins a new era providing train travel to another generation, that goal is not beyond reach.

Preface Notes

1. "Railroad Stations on the Block," *Berkshire Eagle*, August 22, 1956, 22.
2. E. B. White, "Progress and Change," *One Man's Meat* (Gardiner, ME: Tilbury House), 28.
3. "Top Passenger Officers Talk Over the Market," *Railway Age* 125, no. 13 (September 25, 1948): 46–47.

Acknowledgments

Writing about railroads and the history of the industry is a daunting undertaking; the complexity of the industry makes it so. In some ways, it resembles pulling a thread on a sweater; as it unravels, there always seems to be more, and one finds it is all interconnected. Those interested in the industry's history will find it is compartmentalized and one compartment leads to another. Add in the human element and another dimension complicates it further. As a book about rail passenger service, Amtrak, and transportation policy, the tale necessitated a team effort. Pulling together the myriad voices necessary to create such a project required the assistance and support of a cross section of people knowledgeable on the subject—talking with people who knew people. Fortunately, there were plenty who were willing to help. As it turned out, the authors knew more people than they thought, and they all knew each other—it was a club. This usually comes with age but also from working in the industry. The following earned our gratitude beyond words for their willingness to help.

Thomas Hoback, founder, former president and chairman of the Indiana Rail Road, was of invaluable assistance in contacting people connected with Amtrak and the rail industry. Tom was the project's spiritual leader, as it were, giving the authors free rein to write the story as they felt it should be told. Over the years, he has become a valued friend, and both his advice and his hospitality are greatly appreciated.

Getting started can be the biggest hurdle. Among the first contacts was William F. Howes, a close friend who has often provided sound advice and detailed information. His experience as vice president of passenger operations at the Chesapeake & Ohio/Baltimore & Ohio, as well as a director of the Pullman Company, made him an essential resource who did not disappoint. Anyone who writes about railroad passenger service needs to have Bill Howes on their team.

William C. Vantuono helped the authors get their bearings. He invited them to his office at Simmons-Boardman Publishing for several hours of pelting him with questions. As editor of *Railway Age*, he has a perspective on the rail industry and its politics that cannot be challenged. His responses to questions, perspective, and his ongoing assistance have been invaluable.

A well-spent afternoon was with another good friend, David DeBoer, who was employed by the Department of Transportation (DOT) when Amtrak was pieced together. An expatriate of the New York Central, Dave guided and helped form questions to ask of others.

Robert VanderClute, another former New York Central refugee, was a vice president of operations for Amtrak. He joined in 1971 and witnessed the problems the fledgling company faced. As an experienced railroader and a good friend, he lent his views about Amtrak's formative years and provided perspective on its operations.

For any student of railroads, meeting a railroad president is a big deal, and spending time with one in an informal setting is humbling. The authors did this with three former Amtrak presidents, and the fruits of their interviews are detailed in this book. Paul Reistrup, David Gunn, and Wick Moorman graciously welcomed the writing team into their homes, answered unlimited questions, provided perspectives on transportation issues and politics, and shared thoughts about what Amtrak should and should not be. They were candid and forthright and made the authors wiser as observers of the railroad scene. For all of this, especially their time and advice, they have earned a deep measure of gratitude.

Tom Downs was Amtrak's fifth president. The authors could not converse with him face-to-face but were amply rewarded through many long and in-depth telephone conversations. His observations about the role of government in transportation, Amtrak's problems, and what Amtrak could have accomplished were insightful and invaluable and made the book richer.

The authors are also deeply in debt to Clifford Black, former chief of Corporate Communications for Amtrak. Cliff's perspectives on Amtrak, and its leadership in particular, came from his twenty-nine-year career, and his observations about the company became important additions to this book. Cliff and his wife Jeanine provided unmatched hospitality and gave more than generously of their time and interest.

Having recently retired as Federal Railroad Administration (FRA) administrator, Ronald L. Batory graciously consented to write the foreword. His perspective on the rail industry and government's role in transportation is without parallel.

Barbara Mooney, who prepared tables, and Christopher Swan, who prepared the map of state services in the appendix, lent their skills to the book; their advice about including these in the book was greatly appreciated.

Patricia Quinn of the Northern New England Passenger Rail Authority, Mike Franke, former vice president of Amtrak's state-run operation in Indiana, and Robert Zier provided valuable insight into the trials and tribulations of state-sponsored programs. Each told of their challenges, successes, and failures with great candor.

Anna Francis and David Hulsey of Indiana University Press have been the acquisitions editors for the project; they led the writing team by the hand through the maze of publishing requirements. Along with IUP's David Miller and Stephen Williams, their guidance has been invaluable.

H. Roger Grant gave guidance and support in completing the manuscript. His advice and comments were a great aid.

The authors are also very grateful to the committee that oversees the Richard C. Overton Research Fellowship of the Lexington Group, a grant from which helped in the production of the book.

The authors also drew on the expertise of many others who saw the book as a worthy endeavor and whose help they gratefully acknowledge: Arthur Bauer (intercity rail consultant), Peter Benoit (Senator Angus King's office), Rollin Bredenberg, George Chilson (Rail Passengers Association), US Senator

Susan Collins, Peter Espy, Nick Fry (Barriger Library), John Gray (Association of American Railroads Senior Vice President, Policy and Economics), Bruce Heard, Don Hofsommer, Kevin J. Holland, Bob Johnston, US Senator Angus King, Laura Kliewer (Director, Midwest Interstate Rail Passenger Commission), Robert Krebs (CEO, BNSF Railway, retired), David Kutrosky (Managing Director, Capitol Corridor Joint Powers Authority, retired), David Lipari (Marketing Manager, San Joaquin Joint Powers Authority), Marc Magliari, (Public Relations Manager, Amtrak), Joe McHugh (Amtrak Vice President State Services; Government Relations and Corporate Communications), Kari McLain (City of Pittsfield, MA), Kevin McKinney, Sharon Negele (Indiana State Representative), Jason Ortner (Director, North Carolina Department of Transportation Rail Division), Rob Padgette (Managing Director, Capitol Corridor Joint Powers Authority), David Randall, Britten Richards (editor of the Amtrak legislation), Steve Roberts (President of RailPac), Daniel Rust, Victor Ryerson, Ira Silverman, Katie Trout (North Carolina Department of Transportation Rail Division), Michael Weinman (PTSI Transportation), Benjamin Wilemon (BNSF Railway), and Mayor Stephen Wood, Rensselaer, Indiana.

We are also indebted to Alfred Music, Jaime Lee at Conde Nast, and Sam Fox at ICM Partners for helping navigate the permissions maze and allowing use of quotations and illustrations from their publications.

Boundless thanks also to the Amtrak employees and passengers, and others, who shared their stories and opinions.

The many interviews and conversations that enhanced this book increase the chance that someone may have slipped through the cracks and gone unthanked. If so, apologies are in order. Any errors in the locations, times, or other facts are solely the authors'.

Last, but certainly not least, Pamela, Nancy, and Irmis have more than deserved our love and grateful appreciation for their patience with this major distraction over two-plus years of work.

Authors' Note

This book was undertaken shortly after it was proposed in late 2018. In-person interviews began the following January and continued until the coronavirus pandemic struck in early 2020. This interrupted our ability to do in-person interviews but did not slow other research or the task of composition. It was difficult to assess the virus's long-term effects on Amtrak at first. Now, we see it dramatically disrupted the company and threatened its survival along with that of other modes of passenger transportation. Ultimately, we chose to discuss the future of Amtrak under normal conditions, so most of what we recommend cannot occur until the pandemic subsides, and then only if a failure by Congress to provide emergency funding and major changes by Amtrak management in the fall of 2020 do not end up killing the patient.

In the meantime, the state of Florida is proposing three hundred miles of new highways costing $26 billion.

AMTRAK
America's Railroad
TRANSPORTATION'S ORPHAN AND ITS STRUGGLE FOR SURVIVAL

A well-driven train moving smoothly and strongly over a well-laid roadbed offers a traveler advantages and conveniences not to be had in any other form of transportation.

E. B. White, "Progress and Change"

Introduction

On May 1, 1971, America's railroad industry, anxious for relief from financially debilitating passenger services, embarked upon a radical new concept, in the United States at least, for providing intercity railroad passenger transportation. A new quasi-public entity, the National Railroad Passenger Corporation (dubbed "Railpax" but later changed to the less awkward "Amtrak")[1] represented nothing short of a revolution as more than a century of privately run passenger trains came to an end. People who traveled by and depended on trains saw this change as a hopeful way to breathe new life into a moribund service.

This was not just a change in how trains were operated. It created an immense and complex superstructure of people, property, and practices and marked a decisive moment for federal and state governments that had always considered even a hint of nationalization as a form of socialism. It was a sudden lurch from a private business to a national service, a step taken out of desperation to relieve railroads of the deficits driving many toward bankruptcy.

The railroads did not all agree with this solution, however. To some, passenger service was a strain that could be tolerated, while to others, it was a more serious financial drain that demanded relief. Still others wanted nothing to do with Amtrak despite their financial stress. Its creators hoped that "rationalization" of routes, a reduction of the network to what was thought to be a sustainable core, would improve service and make the trains worth traveling again—an early Amtrak slogan that in itself was a piquant comment on the state of America's passenger trains.

For the railroads, there were few options. Amtrak would resolve their passenger deficit problem but was fraught with complications once the federal government and partisan politics became involved. Viewed by many as too fragmented to be effective, and considering the opposition it faced and the managerial problems endured in its early years, it is astonishing that Amtrak survived it all.

Passenger Service, Regulation, and Taxation

Passenger service on the nation's railroads had long been viewed by government as a civic obligation. For generations, railroads had been viewed as different from other transport modes. The foundation of this attitude lay in the nature of the industry: railroads performed and paid for their own research and development; they owned and maintained their own infrastructure, maintained control of their trains, and had their own accounting methods, operating rules, and labor regulations.[2] Unlike the trucking and airline industries, rails' financial reporting, setting of freight and passenger rates, and operations were extensively regulated by the states' public utility commissions and the federal Interstate Commerce Commission (ICC) through myriad and complex regulations developed over decades.

Oversight of railroads gained momentum at the dawn of the Progressive movement following the election of Theodore Roosevelt in 1904; in 1905, he asked Congress to increase and expand regulation of railroad rates by the Commission to discourage "gratuitous malfeasance."[3] Later provisions by successive administrations gave the ICC powers to change and suspend rates, and in 1913, in the belief that railroads were overcapitalized, the Railroad Valuation Act gave the ICC the power to determine their value, including "original cost, depreciation, present value, and the value of all grants and gifts received by the railroad."[4] After government control during the First World War, the railroads were returned to their owners in 1920, and the Transportation Act passed that year, granting the ICC control over securities, new construction, and abandonment of trackage.[5]

During this period, federal and state funding of road construction began to have an impact on both passenger and freight rail operations as private cars and the unregulated trucking industry competed in the short- and medium-haul markets to the railroads' detriment. In the meantime, the railroads' labor brotherhoods maintained their strength and something of a stranglehold by keeping increasingly outdated work rules in effect that artificially inflated the cost of operations.[6] In the days of Teddy Roosevelt, the railroads clearly had a monopoly in freight and passenger transportation. By the close of the Second World War and into the 1950s and 1960s, however, as highway and aviation competition intensified, that situation no longer existed—but the ICC continued to regulate the rail industry as though it did.[7]

In New York Central Railroad's 1957 Annual Report, the railroad was not shy about detailing its complaint about regulation by state and federal agencies.

> The regulatory authority of these agencies and commissions usurped the power of railroad managements from making many of the vital decisions which management normally makes. Government bodies have jurisdiction over the passenger train service we operate; they tell us what trains we must run and they set the fares which we can charge. Too often some commissions refuse to grant

us permission to discontinue service which has been deserted by the public, refuse to allow us to charge compensatory fares, or delay such decisions beyond reason. Yet these same commissions grant a reasonable rate of return to other public utilities which they regulate.[8]

The New York Central (NYC) and its affiliated lines once operated the largest volume of intercity passengers, mail, and express in the nation, so the company serves as a good example of the facility costs—just one component of overall costs—the railroad paid to operate its passenger service. John S. Gallagher Jr., NYC's director of Passenger Research, estimated that in 1940 the system operated 7,315 unduplicated route miles of scheduled passenger service in eight states and Canada, serving 1,380 stations.[9] By 1956, the railroad had eliminated most of them but more than 400 remained active.

The cost of the station operations was enormous. In a report by NYC's Legal Department, the company's district engineer estimated the 1960 cost of operating the forty Westchester County (suburban New York City) stations alone was $162,500, comprised of $67,500 for cleaning; $36,000 for heating; $24,000 for lighting; and $35,000 for policing, telephone, water, materials, and supplies. Electrical maintenance cost $39,000 and structural repairs $116,000. Snow removal for the 1960–61 winter season was $61,000. Total cost was $378,500 ($3,329,624 in 2020) or an average of $9,500 ($83,570 in 2020) per station, exclusive of staffing, property maintenance, taxes, and insurance.[10]

Because of how they have been viewed by government, railroads have long held the dubious distinction as the only form of transportation, aside from pipelines, that pays local property taxes (in addition to federal taxes). At the nation's airports, hidden subsidies support maintenance and upkeep of terminals and related facilities for the privately owned airlines, and the air traffic control system is underwritten by the federal government. In contrast, maintenance and operation—and taxation—of rail facilities are entirely borne by the privately owned railroads. As airport facilities are an adjunct to municipal services, they are not taxable properties, and fees and lease charges paid by the airlines do not come close to paying for the properties' operations and maintenance.

Each state and community saw a railroad as a captive revenue source, the proverbial "cash cow waiting to be milked," a tax assessor's dream in the days when "tax breaks" had yet to be invented. While taxation policy and rates varied by state and municipality, every railroad-owned property, building, structure, bridge, right-of-way, and track was taxed to some extent. New locomotives and rolling stock were (and still are) taxed upon delivery—frequently delivered to a state with a lower taxation rate before acceptance. As John Gray of the Association of American Railroads explained, "It had been the policy of most local governments to tax rail property at the highest possible rate the market could bear, even if that rate was several times the level of taxation of other businesses within their area of control. What was a railroad going to do—leave

Introduction 5

town?"[11] As for tax breaks, government policy was unsympathetic, almost unyielding (until passage of the Staggers Rail Act in 1980), and was based on the premise that since the railroads were privately held corporations, both federal and state governments could not be seen as helping to support them. Because of this, the railroads alone had to bear the full costs of doing business, even when conducted in the public interest. The obviously different treatment of the bus, airline, and truck competition, particularly in the 1950s, seemed to be a matter that legislators ignored, further frustrating railroad management.

Meanwhile, any improvements or modernization (i.e., betterment) of railroad facilities increased their value and, in turn, their level of property tax. NYC's new Central Terminal in Toledo, Ohio, for example, opened in September 1950 at a cost of $5 million ($54 million in 2020). It did a far better job serving the traveling public than the old station but increased the terminal's annual property tax by $34,866 ($349,180 in 2020).[12] In 1953, NYC's system total state and local tax obligation was $26,028,825 ($253,842,460 in 2020) on $825,348,776 gross revenues ($8.04 billion in 2020). In 1957, it had risen to $39,293,220 ($364,109,714 in 2020) on $741,571,672 gross revenues ($6.86 billion in 2020), of which more than $21 million ($194,596,014 in 2020) was paid to the state of New York and its municipalities.[13]

Property taxes and maintenance were just two reasons why NYC put 406 of its passenger stations across its system up for sale in 1956. Such sales reduced tax, maintenance, and operational burdens and increased proceeds. In one of many instances, the railroad offered the City of Pittsfield, Massachusetts, the opportunity to buy its stately 1914 Beaux Arts station on Depot Street but was rebuffed. The building's tax valuation was $170,000 ($1.63 million in 2020).[14] In 1966, the railroad offered the station and property to the city for $320,000 ($2.56 million in 2020).[15] Having had the station inspected, the city declined saying it wasn't worth that; the railroad responded that this was the city's tax valuation. Nonetheless, the Pittsfield Housing Authority had considered turning it into a transportation center or some other use, but, according to the architectural firm hired by the city to assess the station's condition, it was "well past the point of no return," having been subjected to "gross neglect of routine maintenance."[16] The station was razed in 1968, the property sold to a developer as part of an urban renewal project, and a new "station" opened east of the city—a small waiting room in a yard office.

Subsidization

In a contemporary comparison, Williston, North Dakota, opened a beautiful new airport in 2017. Its cost was $273 million, financed with $106 million from the Federal Aviation Administration, $55 million from the state, and $112 million from bonds supported by airport revenues.[17] Billed as "The Peoples Airport,"[18] in 2020 it was served by one airline offering one flight per day to and from Denver. (Interestingly, until recently, not much has been heard about whether the Essential Air Service Program should continue. It is a federal program that assures air service to small communities that otherwise would not have access to air travel, paying subsidies ranging from $10 to more than $975 per passenger, depending on the destination.)[19]

Few people today understand that when air and bus lines show a profit, it is only because substantial public funding and hidden subsidies let them avoid the full costs of providing their services. There is nothing wrong with this; as a nation we have determined that the social good and economic benefit of these forms of passenger transport is worth the expense. The question is why rail travel, the third leg of the transportation triad, has been—and still is—viewed differently and unworthy of public support?

As Amtrak Chairman Anthony Coscia points out, "Airline tickets, the cost of driving, and commuter train and bus fares would all be prohibitively expensive if users had to fund all costs associated with them. Even our roads and interstates, which road advocates used to love saying were 'user funded,' require billions in subsidies each year, with the feds now providing more than $157 billion in general revenue subsidies for the insolvent Highway Trust Fund since 2008. And, of course, airlines don't build airports, and government at various levels provides substantial subsidies to transit systems."[20]

When it came to passenger service deficits, the increasing costs and other encumbrances placed the railroads in a difficult, often untenable, competitive position. Due to their dominance in transportation, the government's attitude was that the railroads' passenger service was a business for which freight revenues should cover any deficits. This meant that getting to the mid-twentieth-century point where government would provide financial support for railroad passenger service was a tortuous journey. The path to nationalization of this service was strewn with failed attempts of private carriers just to break even financially, let alone earn a modest profit from their operations. Despite best efforts by railroads large and small, the cultural, economic, and political climate after World War II led to a historic decline and collapse of the intercity rail passenger network. This was an abrupt retreat from the prosperous war period when freight and passenger traffic reached new heights and erased the effects of the decade-long Depression. After the war, the railroads' efforts to hold on to their passenger traffic through new equipment and innovative services proved futile. The greatest blow to rail passenger service, and indeed the fatal one, was President Dwight D. Eisenhower's creation of the interstate highway system in 1956. Its construction, with political backing by its support industries, sealed the fate of passenger trains.

The issue of government support for rail passenger service was forced by the 1961 bankruptcy of a major Northeastern railroad, the New Haven, and nine years later that of Penn Central, the primary railroad of the region, which in 1969 was forced to take over the New Haven. Both failures were in large part due to passenger service deficits, mismanagement, and—not to be overlooked—what passed for government policy. As with all monumental failures, there was plenty of blame to pass around: politicians, government policy makers, federal and state regulatory and tax agencies, railroad management, unions, changing markets, social preferences, and a fundamental national transportation philosophy that favored competing modes and viewed railroads as sources of tax revenue rather than as a vital link in the nation's economy.

Cultural Shift

Although the railroads recognized the shift in public preference in favor of highways, they had limited ways to respond, mostly by eliminating trains to cut their way to prosperity—a sure formula for failure, but the national government did not see this as a problem it needed to resolve. For its part, the public widely believed that railroads had abandoned their passengers. There was truth in that, but the opposite was also true. Although people generally liked trains, they had found faster and more convenient ways to travel, leaving the railroads with a huge investment in equipment, personnel, and facilities that consumed more money than it took in.

Another problem was that, when Amtrak was finally created as a solution, it was in the absence of a national transportation policy that, as we shall see, became de facto policy with no room for passenger trains.

"Making the trains worth traveling again" was a noble mission in 1971. Over 50 years, however, that mission has changed with a succession of Amtrak presidents, a few of whom were described as "interim" or "transitional," a symptom of a leadership problem. Amtrak's president is hired by its board of directors, eight out of fifteen of whom are nominated by the US president and subject to Senate confirmation. The secretary of the Department of Transportation has to be one of the members, as must a consumer representative.[21] As political appointees, board members often lacked a rail transportation or hospitality background. Without the guidance of a national transportation policy, each Amtrak board chairman was vulnerable to political pressure while its president was left to establish their own management style and vision for the company's operational mission—with success being measured by compliance with Washington's ever-shifting and politically charged priorities.

As it would be for any company, this is problematic. Politicians generally do not make good managers, especially in areas where they have little knowledge or expertise. Regarding transportation, they often have little understanding of how railroads operate. Except for its first president, it was fortunate that several early Amtrak leaders did come from the passenger rail industry and knew much more about service than the holders of the purse strings who often micromanaged or applied pressure to influence Amtrak operations.

While much has changed in transportation since 1971, travel by automobile still dwarfs that by airline, bus, and rail. Air travel has never been safer and access to it (usually) more affordable, but the special character of moving rapidly while suspended above the earth has faded due to the realities of the age of deregulation. In an early 2019 obituary of Herb Kelleher, cofounder of Southwest Airlines, the *Economist* magazine noted, "And yet somewhere along the line something was lost. Cut-price air travel today is endured rather than enjoyed. It has become a hideous blend of . . . excuses to extort charges for everything from hand baggage that is deemed too big to failing to check in online."[22] (When Southwest was starting in 1971, Kelleher fought tooth and nail with big airlines that did not want competition. Later he fought tooth and nail to block both Amtrak and Texas high-speed trains because he did not want competition.)

Driving long distances is appealing to many but for others is as mundane as a glass of tap water—not to mention scary when congested roads are shared with vehicles driven by less-skilled, frustrated, inconsiderate, or angry drivers. Some commentators have asked why trains could not be replaced by buses—after all, both modes are land-based and run on wheels. What these people miss is that trains and buses—and the experience of traveling on each—are in no way the same: not in comfort, not in amenities, not in convenience, and—when trains are well run—not in the overall travel experience. There is a need for buses, and in fact, they help to extend many Amtrak services, but they are not trains.

The primary purpose of running passenger trains is to provide transportation. There was a time when they earned enough to show a profit or at least minimize losses.

Ralph Budd. *Courtesy BNSF Railway*

They were part of the railroads' business model, and as long as they were not too costly, the railroads strove to maintain attractive and reliable services. Providing that service, though, has always been complicated. In a speech to top railroad officers in September 1948, Ralph Budd remarked, "There is no service on the railroads which compares in complexity and intricacy with the passenger business; I know of no other phase of railroading which requires the cooperation of so many interests and departments. If any one of them fails to please the passenger from the time he thinks about taking a trip until the time he gets home therefrom, his whole trip is spoiled."[23] Budd's comment remains valid today and is a fundamental principle that encompasses all passenger transportation, but Amtrak is particularly vulnerable in this regard.

Alas, comfortable travel in general has surrendered to the mediocrity of expediency; we have redefined the term "first class" so it is measured by a slightly wider seat or by opulence of an intrinsically counterfeit character. Travel styles have changed so much it makes one ask: Is it really necessary to be told that shoes must be worn at all times while moving about on a plane or train, or to ask if your mother would approve of your going out in public dressed like that? Long-distance travel by commercial carrier has become so ordinary that it is no longer considered a special event.

Change is inevitable. As this is written, our nation has been changed by a pandemic virus that, among many other effects, leaves us with no clear vision of the future of our passenger transportation system. For Amtrak, its current leadership must determine what direction rail passenger service will take. Since the rail travel experience is so different from travel by car, bus, or plane, we must ask what level of funding and effort is appropriate in order to provide and enhance that experience. Other modes provide transportation; rail travel is transportation too, but also experiential, focused on the comfort, unique visual vistas, and social interaction only passenger trains can deliver. This distinction is real, and Amtrak has consistently hinted at it and celebrated it in order to attract passengers. The difference lies between what is transportation and what is defined as service.

Introduction Notes

1. According to Robert Gallamore, who was in the US Department of Transportation's policy office at the time, the name for the new entity, "Railpax," came from Assistant Secretary for Policy Paul Cherington, as a hybrid of "railroad" and "pax," an abbreviation for "passenger" in common use in the aviation sector for which Cherington had previously been an analyst; Jeff Davis, "Amtrak at 50: The Rail Passenger Service Act of 1970", Eno, Center for Transportation, October 30, 2020, www.enotrans.org/article/amtrak-at-50-the-rail-passenger-service-act-of-1970/
2. The influence of the rail industry has a long reach. The Railway Labor Act of 1926 also serves as the basis for labor relations in the airline industry.
3. John F. Stover, *The Life and Decline of the American Railroad*, (New York: Oxford University Press, 1970), 114–115.
4. Stover, 115–116.
5. Stover, 117.
6. Stover, 117.
7. Stover, 247.
8. New York Central Railroad 1957 Annual Report, 8.
9. Written correspondence with John Gallagher, n.d.
10. Report by New York Central Legal Department, March 1963.
11. Email correspondence with John Gray, February 13, 2021.
12. Written correspondence of John Gallagher from a report by E. C. Nickerson, April 1, 1958.
13. The annual report noted that this was "an all-time record of taxes paid by any railroad in any state."; New York Central Railroad 1957 Annual Report, 11.
14. "Union Station Up For Sale Along With 405 Other Units," *Berkshire Eagle*, (August 21, 1956), 13.
15. NYC upped its "offer" by $44,000 in 1967, saying the property was simply worth more; "PHA, Mayor Tangle Again on Urban Renewal Issue," *Berkshire Eagle*, (July 13, 1967), 17.
16. "In Brief . . .", *Berkshire Eagle* (September 21, 1967), 18.
17. Ted Reed, "The Newest U.S. Airport Will Open Thursday In A North Dakota Oil Boomtown," October 8, 2019, www.Forbes.com.
18. Joe Petrie, "2020 Airport Business Project of the Year: Williston Basin International Airport,"

June 11, 2020, www.aviationpros.com.
19. "President Trump Wants to Eliminate the Essential Air Service Program," www.onemileatatime.com, accessed September 20, 2020.
20. Anthony Coscia, "Defining Amtrak's True Mission," *Railway Age*, December 2020, 34-35.
21. In 2020 there were only eight members on the board, all but Secretary of Transportation Elaine Chao nominated by President Obama. Four were Democrats and four were Republicans, all of whom had exceeded their terms of office.
22. "The High Priest of Ha Ha," the *Economist* 430, no. 9125 (January 12, 2019), 82.
23. "Top Passenger Officers Talk Over the Market," 46–47.

Railroads are immensely complex, and they seem to
love complexity, just as they love ritual and the past.

E. B. White, "Progress and Change"

This Is What We Had

Monopoly vs. Competition, 1840 to 1945

By about 1840, American railroads had stopped being a curiosity and were an accepted means of transportation. Explosive growth of the system east of the Mississippi in the two decades preceding the Civil War made railroads an essential component of economic life. The Union's railroads helped to defeat the Confederacy, but in the period to century's end, the South also participated vigorously in the expansion of the national network from coast to coast and border to border. It was a time when the railroad both connected and created communities and dominated as an economic and social force. Through efficient transportation of people and goods, the railroad induced economic development, and economic development made railroads ever more necessary. Author Robert Selph Henry noted the pace of change: "From the beginning of American railroad history to the period after the First World War, traffic on the rails consistently doubled every fifteen years, on the average."[1]

It was also a time of minimal regulation of business, and in this climate, the railroads' domination led to abuses. By 1887, they were powerful monopolies led by legendary moguls and financial speculators: Jay Gould, J. P. Morgan, Cornelius and William K. Vanderbilt, and James J. Hill, among others. Their reputation as inflexible and ruthless earned them membership in a sinister pantheon—the "Robber Barons."

Monopoly in the railroad industry should not have been a surprise. It had no competition; no other land transport mode matched its capacity, efficiency, and reliability. So, of course, its masters sought maximum financial benefit, often in conflict with each other. To be honest, the history of the industry would be pretty dull but for fascinating tales of corporate combat, thievery, and skulduggery.

These men are legendary in our nation's history, but their ghosts haunt the railroad industry even today. While there were instances when monopolies actually were beneficial, this did not matter to a government attitude that any monopoly should be broken up for the public good. Not every railroad owner or manager was greedy and corrupt, but the rail monopoly led politicians into a crusade that resulted in increasing regulation of the industry. Farmers in particular, who were a large constituency and had to rely on rail transportation, raised enough protest to spur legislation curbing both real and perceived railroad excesses.

The federal response was the 1887 Interstate Commerce Act, which specifically targeted the railroads. It created the five-member Interstate Commerce Commission (ICC), which began as a regulator but under subsequent laws gained exclusive power to approve or disapprove railroad services and rates.[2] When it was a matter of continuing or discontinuing passenger train service, under its provisions, the Commission relied upon an ill-defined concept of what constituted "public convenience and necessity," and this phrase was often invoked in discontinuance proceedings. How this standard was determined was not always consistent and often involved multiple public hearings in communities served by the service involving rail officials who had to defend their petitions with financial disclosures. Hearings officers' decisions were not always based on the economics of operations.

Commenting on the ICC's governance of the industry, Burlington Route's president Harry Murphy stated in 1963 that train discontinuance procedures for the Burlington were based on trains that actually lost money for the railroad. "That's what's at the heart of the railroad passenger problem," he noted. "I doubt if passenger business nets much for the railroad. Of course, I don't know how much passenger business would be left if the ICC formula were used. As a matter of fact, when we appear before the public commissions for taking trains off, if we used the ICC formula there would be objections and our case would have to be restated. Whenever we take off service, we cost-analyze what it would cost out-of-pocket to continue operations. Until a train actually loses money, we don't attempt to take it off." Murphy pointed out what passenger executives had contended for a long time: "If any other form of business operated under ICC rules such as have been set up for the passenger business, they'd go out of business, fast. But we're obligated to perform. We can't escape it—you have to have due regard for the public."[3]

Over time, ICC governance severely hampered the railroads' ability to earn a profit because their monopolistic grip had been significantly weakened by a new early twentieth-century transportation technology: cars, trucks, and paved highways.

Writing in the middle of World War II, Robert Selph Henry stated the issue: "There was a time when the problem, to some minds at least, was how to keep railroads from making too much money. The problem for the past quarter of a century has been how railroads might make money enough to enable them to finance the improvements they had to have if they were to stay in business as solvent, self-supporting enterprises. That is the real railroad problem of modern times—how railroads can make a living."[4] Henry further noted that war traffic brought new prosperity but also that "the problem" would return and be worse after war's end. Indeed, overregulation would not be seriously addressed until 1980, and since then the regulatory and economic climate for the railroads' freight operations has been vastly improved. Up to that point, highway and even air freight competition, onerous taxation, constraints on ratemaking, loss of mail contracts, and battalions of federal and state regulators had weakened but fortunately did not kill the industry.

There has always been something of a love-hate relationship between the railroads and the public. In the absence of highway and air competition, railroads had to do little to attract passenger traffic. Indeed, other than the introduction of the air brake, all-steel passenger car, and enclosed vestibules, there were few significant innovations in services up to around 1920. Prior to that, passengers were knocking down the doors, with passenger-miles and revenues increasing steadily.[5] There was no incentive to increase patronage since it was so great already. Even the Pullman Company, which operated most of the comfortable, even elegant, sleeping cars on America's railroads, took passengers for granted to a certain degree.

This changed when the country entered the Great Depression following the stock market crash in October 1929. As the economic calamity worsened through the 1930s and ridership declined, the railroads and Pullman had to make greater efforts—such as introducing ice-sourced air conditioning and streamlined trains—to attract passengers.

In the meantime, Henry Ford's innovative method for producing inexpensive automobiles had spread to other firms. By the eve of the Depression, automotive technology had so improved, and the car had been made so useful by the introduction of publicly funded paved roads, that rail passenger traffic had declined by more than a third.[6] People still rode the trains, especially for long-distance travel, but it was becoming apparent that the private auto's effects on the rail passenger network would continue.

In the 1930s, the railroads confronted another challenge: a precipitous decline in freight traffic and revenue—the lifeblood of any railroad. Oddly enough, their passenger trains helped ease the problem. Those trains generated a significantly smaller percentage of railroad revenues than freight trains, but passenger ticket sales provided immediate cash while settlement of freight charges took much longer. Passenger service remained marginally profitable during the 1920s, but by 1930, the traffic decline was accelerating; by 1933, passenger-miles were two-thirds and passenger revenues were three-fourths of what they had been in 1920. Revenue per train-mile was $1.28, less than half of the 1920 figure.[7] Even so, railroads avoided large reductions in service in order to keep passenger cash coming in.

Looming over the railroads was a real danger that alarmed both labor and management—the threat of nationalization. With large segments of the industry in bankruptcy, there was serious discussion of government ownership.

Expression of confidence: New York Central's Great Steel Fleet was lined up at La Salle Street Station on October 23, 1949, specifically for the company's photographer, Ed Nowak. Left to right: the Wolverine, Pacemaker, New England States, Commodore Vanderbilt, and 20th Century Limited. A decade later, that confidence had evaporated.

NYC photo, Geoffrey H. Doughty Collection

Many outside railroading saw it as a viable option, but the railroads wanted to avoid it at all costs. The Burlington's Ralph Budd (1879–1962), one of the industry's most influential leaders at the time, did not mince words, saying that such a move would increase costs, lower productivity, and worsen service. All this had happened during federal government operation of the railroads during World War I but, even so, Depression-era nationalization might actually have evolved if the rails' fortunes did not improve.[8]

Budd also declared that further regulation of the industry would only make matters worse.[9] He cited the Emergency Railroad Transportation Act of 1933, which restricted the railroads' ability to reduce costs by eliminating jobs. Further, a bill limiting freight train length to a maximum of seventy-five cars, "full crew" laws, and another bill providing a six-hour period to calculate a day's pay were proof that government ownership would increase the cost of transportation. Such restrictions would make it impossible for the railroads to compete unless comparable constraints were enacted for their competitors.[10] All the railroads wanted, in the words of actress Greta Garbo, was "to be left alone."

The Great Depression actually was beneficial for railroad passengers because it forced some companies to think differently about that business. In the Northeast, passenger-heavy lines such as the New York Central, the Pennsylvania, and the New Haven, and on some lines running westward from Chicago—the Union Pacific and the Burlington—became aware that their trains would not attract travelers unless the railroads got in touch with the times. Appealing to current aesthetic tastes could make traveling by train popular again. Because of this, beginning in the mid-1930s, the railroads engaged prominent industrial designers such as Henry Dreyfuss, Raymond Loewy, Otto Kuhler, and Walter Dorwin Teague to make their trains appealing through exterior streamlining and innovative interior design.

These efforts, often kicked off by parading the new equipment around the country and allowing public walk-throughs, brought a rewarding blend of good press and increased patronage. The Burlington's 1934 Pioneer Zephyr was one of several such trains and generated many column inches of ink with its dawn-to-dusk dash between Denver and Chicago. More importantly, it proved the viability of all–stainless steel construction, which ensured a long service life and would prove of great benefit to Amtrak.[11]

Even more was to follow. After the bombing of Pearl Harbor and the country's plunge into war, traffic increased exponentially and railroads began earning unprecedented profits, even in their passenger services. The wartime surge seemed to suggest that passengers had come back and would not abandon trains for cars and airplanes after the war. So as early as 1943, the railroads began planning for a postwar traffic surge of both existing and new passengers, especially on long-distance trains, who would flock to new and modern streamlined equipment.

The timing of this optimism was not entirely misplaced. A year or so into the war, the rebounding railroads were flush with cash, and many used these earnings to reduce funded debt.[12] This sound move reduced interest payments and allowed dividend increases to attract investment. Although outcome of the war was still uncertain, the mood changed dramatically with Allied successes, especially defeat of the Germans at Stalingrad in early 1943, the invasion of Sicily in mid-July, Hitler's abandonment of the eastern front, and the fall of Mussolini and Italy's surrender later that year. In 1944, when victory seemed almost in sight, railroads began sending preliminary orders to car builders for new equipment. Management recognized that wartime levels of passenger loadings and revenues would not continue but assumed that current travel habits and innovative new rolling stock would retain a good portion of both. Due to War Production Board restrictions still in effect, few equipment deliveries could be made until 1946. Even so, by early 1945, much of the industry was placing large orders. The New York Central, for example, ordered 721 cars that arrived between 1946 and 1950 and became its third-generation "Great Steel Fleet."[13] The railroads were not doing things by halves.

Transportation Policy: Promotion, Regulation, and Preference

In a country the size of the United States, efficient transportation is crucial to economic development and social well-being. However, there never has been a clear vision of a national transportation policy; what passes for one evolved mainly in response to the urgings of various interests. This was due in part to the nature of the political process but also the belief that free enterprise would determine transportation's course. Unfortunately, the variable character and vision of successive presidential administrations, the changeable composition of Congress, and a lack of comprehensive and identifiable goals made impossible the setting of a coherent policy. The result was a tug-of-war for two centuries over promotion and regulation of various transportation modes.

Merriam-Webster's dictionary defines "policy" in part as "prudence or wisdom in the management of affairs; management or procedure based primarily on material interest; a definite course or method of action selected from among alternatives and in light of given conditions to guide and determine present and future decisions."[14] By any measure, our country, among the most advanced in the world, is sorely lacking a national transportation policy. What passed for one has really been just a series of legislative enactments rather than development of long-term plans.

It was only with passage of the 1887 Interstate Commerce Act and creation of the ICC that regulation of railroads became a guiding principle,[15] but federal involvement in transportation development already had a long history. One major undertaking was construction of the National Road from Cumberland, Maryland, to Vandalia, Illinois, between 1811 and 1834; another was aid to water transportation by improvement of natural waterways such as the Mississippi, Missouri, and Ohio Rivers. Federal involvement in railroad development was primarily through backing construction of the transcontinental Overland Route to California, completed in 1869, and by grants of public land (although in far smaller amounts than is generally perceived) to both encourage and help finance extension of other rail routes, mainly to other parts of the West Coast.

The ICC's original purpose was oversight and regulation of the railroads that eventually led to overregulation to the extent that it was difficult to provide satisfactory service at a profit.[16] Then the early twentieth century brought new competitive pressures from the automobile and motortruck and a not unreasonable demand by citizens for government-funded paved roads. Passage by Congress of the Federal Aid Road Act in 1916 (authorizing $75 million—$717,981,618 in 2020—for construction, matched by state funding) brought the first of a series of massive expenditures of public funds for highway projects, with additional funding voted about every two years. In response, two million automobiles on the road in 1910 became close to ten million by 1920.[17] Further competition appeared in the form of the intercity bus that, together with the auto, cut into the railroads' passenger loadings on their various shorter (nonovernight) routes. Highway vehicles also all but removed the electric interurban railroad from the American landscape by 1940.

Meanwhile, the ICC was having difficulty regulating more than 850 railroads with varying earning abilities. In an attempt to establish a baseline, the ICC initiated a comprehensive study of the transportation problem in 1915.[18] There was talk of the government having to step in to control the railroads, which of course did occur later in World War I, but that was not well received, resulting in agreement that nationalization would result only in "inefficiency, extravagance, and local favoritism."[19]

The 1915 study led to passage of the Transportation Act of 1920, which gave the ICC authority to fix rates so railroads could "earn a fair return upon the value of their properties used for transportation."[20] Based on a principle of private ownership in the interest of the public with regulation by the ICC, rates would be set high enough to pay for operations with a fair return on property; a labor board would be established to stabilize relations with employees; and railway securities would be permitted to earn a return that would attract investment.[21] By passing the 1920 law, Congress attempted to use regulation to strengthen the railroads financially, but it also sought to stabilize their development through consolidation—the idea of combining weaker railroads with stronger ones into large, robust regional systems. A lofty goal, perhaps, but it landed mostly with a thud. Opposition was widespread, and consolidation never went forward—at least, not until the late twentieth century, spurred by economic and competitive factors rather than government edict.

Efforts to help lessen the devastation of the Depression resulted in the Emergency Railroad Transportation Act in 1933. This was part of President Roosevelt's New Deal initiative and promoted mergers and elimination of duplications in service, but its benefits were neutralized by a requirement that any economies not be realized at the expense of labor. The last thing Roosevelt wanted was more unemployment. Furthermore, the 1933 law blessed mergers but only so long as they did not adversely affect competition "as much as possible." The result was a reversal of the positive effects of the Transportation Act of 1920 that allowed for a "fair return upon the value of railroad properties." At the behest of the unions, the 1933 law also repealed the independent labor board meant to settle disputes. These provisions only undercut the railroads' ability to make investments in their properties and attract new capital.

Other regulatory reforms followed. The Railroad Retirement Act of 1935 set up a retirement and unemployment fund for railroad employees; and a 1938 law established an unemployment insurance act to allow payments even when railroaders were on strike. The premise of these and other acts was that "legislation was the best way to cure whatever was amiss."[22]

A balanced transportation policy, however, remained elusive. Development of nonrail transportation modes through subsidies and directives became a standard government tool. Subsidies such as airport construction encouraged growth of an airline network, as did Post Office payments to airlines for carrying mail, a valuable traffic gradually siphoned off from the railroads. By 1925, airlines were delivering fourteen million letters and packages a year over a limited network. Making matters worse was the passage of the Contract Air Mail Act of 1925, called the "Kelly Act" after the bill's sponsor, M. Clyde Kelly of Pennsylvania. It formally authorized the postmaster general to establish air mail contracts with the private sector.[23]

On the passenger side, air travel and public fascination with it made a giant leap forward in May of 1927 when Charles Lindbergh (1902–74), the chief pilot for a company flying contract mail between Chicago and St. Louis, made his celebrated solo nonstop flight from New York to Paris. Lindbergh's feat made him America's first modern celebrity, other than movie stars, and spurred investment in aviation while increasing the popularity of air travel.[24]

Regulatory policy shifted over time from controlling monopoly to controlling competition. The Truman-Wheeler Bill of 1939 not only acknowledged the railroad industry's attempts to earn the cost of capital (interest payments) and pay for its fixed costs but also created the foundation for expanding the ICC's ratemaking jurisdiction—this time to trucking and waterways. The Transportation Act of 1940 that followed sought to normalize carrier competition through regulation. However, this only led to a battle between the public's interest in shipper protection and the private sector's interest in carrier welfare. Its predecessor, the law passed in 1920, had been more in favor of the carriers' interests.[25]

By 1940, of all the problems facing the railroads, subsidized competition emerged as the greatest threat.[26] Commenting on transportation policy, Ralph Budd stated that "a fair and reasonably liberal policy, along the lines of the 1940 National Transportation Policy, administered in the same spirit, should afford an opportunity to earn sufficient revenues to carry out a reasonable program of maintenance and of gradual but constant and steady improvement of railroad properties. On the other hand, hostile legislation, or an unfriendly administration of the laws, particularly if coupled with undue favors to competing agencies of transportation, would retard, and might prevent, improvements in railroad facilities and services which are entirely feasible and will be made if not prevented by harmful legislation or administrative action. It rests with the public to decide what kind of railroad transportation it will have."[27] Budd's comments would be validated in due course.

Postwar Efforts

Following World War II, as a result of a major government reorganization plan adopted in 1950, President Harry S. Truman ordered responsibility for the nation's transport programs to be governed by the Commerce Department under the leadership of an undersecretary of transportation. This gave the country's highest office a pivotal role in the setting of transportation policy, such as it was, through periodic "messages" to Congress on various needs for transportation programs and improvements.[28]

One such message came from President John F. Kennedy and seemed to be a reaction to the "deteriorating railroad situation." The industry's condition was implicitly part of Kennedy's focus in his message (written by special counsel Theodore Sorenson) delivered to Congress on April 4, 1962, where he laid out the objectives of a national transportation policy. In his introduction, Kennedy noted that transportation policy "can and must be achieved primarily by continued reliance on unsubsidized privately owned facilities, operating under the incentives of private profit and checks on competition to the maximum extent possible. The role of public policy should be to provide a consistent and comprehensive framework of equal competitive opportunity that will achieve this objective at the lowest economic and social cost to the nation."[29] Kennedy accurately described the nation's existing transportation policy as "a chaotic patchwork of inconsistent and often obsolete regulation. . . . Such policies must be reshaped in the most fundamental and far-reaching fashion." Furthermore, he stated, "Excessive, cumbersome, and time-consuming regulatory supervision shackles and distorts management initiative. Some parts of the transportation industry are restrained unnecessarily; others are promoted or taxed unevenly and inconsistently. Our system of intercity public transportation—including railroads, trucks, buses, ships and barges, airplanes and pipelines—is seriously weakened today by artificial distortions and inefficiencies inherent in existing federal policies."[30]

In the following twenty-five pages, Kennedy outlined specific targets for Congressional attention—railroads, highways, aviation, and waterways—under the heading of "Even-handed Government promotion of intercity transportation."[31] Although the rail industry was not his principal focus, Kennedy's comprehensive policy message was well timed. The railroads' "deteriorating situation," while involving a wide range of issues for freight railroads, necessarily included the troubles on the passenger side of the business. All passenger-carrying railroads had been negatively impacted by the ever-expanding interstate highway system and steadily increasing auto ownership. An extreme case was the New Haven Railroad that had tumbled into bankruptcy in 1961 and was in desperate straits. Liquidation was a real possibility, and its plight was stark evidence that the industry as a whole was in trouble.[32]

The New Haven's troubles led to the Kennedy administration's convening of the Whitman Commission. The Whitman report was as close as the administration would come to offering specific solutions but still was not a national policy statement. Unfortunately, Kennedy's initiative for policy reform died along with the young president on November 22, 1963. Reforms would come, but at glacial speed, as the rail industry's problems worsened.

Meanwhile, the ICC had become a principal player in the merger cases of the 1960s—the beginning of what had been proposed as "consolidation" back in the 1920s. As other northeastern railroads began to falter, the ill-fated merger of the Pennsylvania and NYC railroads—the Penn Central—was one of the largest, not to mention the least successful. At the same time, mass transit emerged as a priority as highways became clogged with traffic. Urban mobility and high-speed trains began to gain acceptance and federal subsidies to aid implementation followed.[33]

There was some true innovation on the part of the national government, however. The High-Speed Ground Transportation Act of 1965 provided funding

Inherited by Penn Central from the Pennsylvania Railroad in 1968, the Metroliner program introduced high-speed rail passenger service between New York City and Washington, DC. *George H. Drury*

in the Northeast Corridor between Boston, New York, and Washington. With the Pennsylvania Railroad providing about two-thirds of the cost and the federal government the rest, the act helped launch the New York–Washington Metroliner. This truly was something new in North America: self-propelled (that is, nonlocomotive), electrically powered trains capable of higher than usual speeds. It was generally well accepted by passengers but did little in the way of solving the problem of constant deficits. The fact was that new equipment was only part of the answer. Something more had to be done to relieve the railroads of their passenger burden. The answer—ultimately a flawed one—was a dramatic departure from any previous attempt to aid the industry, and it took a crisis to provoke a solution.

A Different Place, 1945 to 1960

Completing the story of what happened to the railroads' passenger services requires a return to the end of the war in 1945. Peacetime seemed to promise the railroads a resurgence of passenger traffic and, for Americans generally, worldwide prosperity and a new era of peace. But the promises quickly faded; there would be neither a railroad renaissance nor prosperous world peace. Following the death of Franklin Roosevelt in April 1945, President Truman faced major postwar challenges: the spread of Soviet totalitarianism, the troubled creation of the State of Israel, and the specter of atomic war once the Soviets had the same weapons as the United States. Early in 1950, Senator Joe McCarthy began his crusade against alleged Communists, and in June, the Korean Peninsula exploded into war. At home, racial tensions surged. In such a disruptive national context, it is not surprising that the troubles of the railroads got little attention.

Running a populist presidential campaign in 1948, Truman claimed the barons of Wall Street, banks, and insurance corporations were partners with Republicans trying to destroy the reforms of the New Deal that had helped so many citizens. Thought to be inept and ill-prepared to be president, Truman had two challengers who split from his party; many believed he would lose the election. Although he had the *Independence*, a Douglas DC-6, at his disposal, he chose to campaign by train. So did his opponent, Thomas Dewey. Truman had the advantage of barnstorming the country in presidential office car US No. 1, *Ferdinand Magellan*. He made a fifteen-day, cross-country tour to California; a six-day visit to the Midwest; and then a ten-day trip to the Northeast and back to Missouri just before the election.[34] Truman loved traveling by train; the railroad business car from which he held up the erroneous *Chicago Tribune* headline about his supposed loss of the election still exists in private ownership.

We were indeed in a different place. The past was not prologue for the passenger train, despite the railroads' optimism at war's end. The conflict imposed significant lifestyle changes on the public, and victory came through broad home front sacrifice—beyond fearing for loved ones in the military—such as a halt in production of new cars and rationing of many consumer goods, gasoline, and rubber for tires. The pleasures of the "Sunday drive" were gone; people walked or took a streetcar or bus to work; they spent more time at home with family and in diversions such as reading, playing cards, going to the movies, or listening to the radio.[35] Civilian auto production did not return until the 1946 model year and offered only warmed-over 1942 designs. With years of thrift and sacrifice at an end, Americans were poised for a new beginning; and although it did not seem so for a while, that promising future did not include the passenger train.

The war's conclusion ended the railroads' business boom and record profits and also brought a rapid rise in costs. The economy jerked from a war footing to a peacetime one, while strikes and material shortages occurred, hampering the railroads' already stressed and faltering quality of service. Passenger traffic dropped precipitously following demobilization, and declines in freight traffic were steeper than anticipated. This plunged many railroads into deep trouble. In the Northeast especially, there were too many railroads competing for shrinking traffic as industry leaders looked to other regions for less militant unions and cheaper labor. In addition, much northeastern freight was shifting to trucks that became ever more efficient as public funding of roads continued. Operating commuter services only worsened railroads' financial losses. Equipment was obsolete, service quality declined, and, as a result, so did public opinion.

Meanwhile, by 1948 railroad car builders were finally delivering new streamlined products that had seemed a wise investment just a few years before. Even in the context of declining traffic, though, the railroads had no choice but to renew their fleets since the war had worn out almost everything on steel wheels. The new cars were the apex of modern rail passenger equipment and rolled through the 1960s, with around 1,200 of them serving as Amtrak's initial fleet. Extremely well built, some stayed in that fleet for almost fifty years.

What appeared to be a new future for rail travel soon turned into more of a death march. Despite new equipment, heavy promotion, and a high level of onboard services, the railroads' share of intercity travel declined over 75 percent between 1946 and 1956 and another 68 percent between 1956 and 1968. Some trains fared better than others, but it was clear that the traveling public had turned its back on steel-wheeled transportation.

Changing Times: Airline and Highway Development

After World War II, there was a dramatic change in how Americans traveled. It was not something new, just an acceleration of trends dating from the 1920s, but it did not augur well for the railroads. The automobile resumed its place in Americans' lives, the embodiment of a move to personal mobility and the conveniences technology could offer. The passenger losses the railroads had experienced in the 1930s inevitably became more pronounced in the 1950s. Furthermore, competition in long-distance travel was no longer among railroads—it was with ever more prosperous airlines that thrived with public investment in air transport infrastructure.

Optimism Personified: The Postwar Car Orders

Railway Age magazine regularly reported on the railroads' postwar plans.[1] On November 1, 1946, America's railroads had 2,598 passenger cars of all types on order. Of these, 192 were to be built in railroad company shops and 2,406 had been ordered from the "Big Three" car builders—American Car & Foundry (ACF), Pullman-Standard (P-S), and the Budd Company. One year later, orders totaled 3,026, with 171 to be built in railroad company shops and 2,855 by the Big Three.

But change came fast. Only 184 additional cars had been ordered by mid-1948, and by year's end only another 14 had been added. At that point, approximately 1,840 cars remained on order,[2] some contracted for as early as 1944. That was still a lot of cars, but the trend was clear: Chesapeake & Ohio (C&O) chairman Robert R. Young projected that the end of the passenger car industry was within sight,[3] a forecast not lost on ACF, P-S, and Budd.

However, they did survive for awhile. ACF shut down early in 1961, having moved to production of transit cars. P-S built its last single-level sleeping car in 1956, its last single-level coach in 1965, and closed out its career with Amtrak's double-level Superliners between 1978 and 1981. Budd's last products for Amtrak were three Viewliner car shells (two sleepers and one diner); the company continued building transit cars until the spring of 1987.[4]

Notes

1. "Passenger-Train Cars on Order," *Railway Age*, vol. 121, no. 20 (November 16, 1946): 797; and vol. 123, no. 20 (November 15, 1947): 188.
2. "Talgo & Train X," *Wall Street Journal* 133, no. 41 (February 18, 1949): 1, 5.
3. Young's singular role in exploring new ways to offer passenger service—and, he figured, at a profit—is discussed at length in Part Two.
4. Telephone interview with Cliff Black, May 28, 2020.

The railroads faced what came to be called, even outside the industry, the "passenger problem." At least nonrailroad business leaders and politicians were beginning to recognize that there indeed was a problem, even if solutions were a long time coming. For the rail industry, those solutions were few and fundamentals were too complex; by midcentury, the rail traffic freefall was well underway. There were occasional upswings during airline strikes and bad weather, but no one—not the railroads, nor regulators and politicians, nor state and local governments—stood up to say that railroad passenger service was a necessary component of the national transportation network.

In fact, it seemed that government in particular sought ways to make things worse. Congress passed the Federal Aid Highway Act of 1956, also called the National Interstate and Defense Highways Act, to connect every major American city. In cooperation with the states, it funded construction of the interstate highway network envisioned by President Eisenhower. The original authorization for construction was $25 billion ($239,327,205,882 in 2020) for a forty-one-thousand-mile system to be built over a period of ten years. The Highway Users Federation, made up of Standard Oil, Phillips Petroleum, Goodyear, Firestone, General Motors, and others, was a proponent and made sure the legislation fulfilled its members' objectives. The resulting interstate system closely paralleled most major railroad main lines and further siphoned off both freight and passenger traffic. Although expanded beyond its original scope, in 2020 the total cost was estimated at more than $530 billion.

Now federal and state governments were subsidizing private highway transportation on a much broader scale than ever, with no thought of the effects on the privately financed rail industry. The Interstate act further invigorated an already well-established highway lobby of contractors, suppliers, and trucking and bus companies, as well as the automotive industry, oil companies, and myriad businesses serving highway travelers. With a much louder political voice, these interests became increasingly influential while the railroads' influence, by this time not particularly strong anyway, collapsed.

Automobile travel by 1956 had far eclipsed rail and air, and, although railroads still carried slightly more passengers than airlines, rail's share of the total was in steady decline.[36] Calling trains outdated, the Highway Users Federation said that the future lay in highways. Furthermore, the railroads were an excellent source of tax revenue, particularly for various states and from a wartime ticket tax that would not be repealed for many years. The military, for whose benefit the interstate system was ostensibly proposed, dutifully turned to highways as a more economical way than rail to transport forces.

For the airlines, the 1958 introduction of the Lockheed Electra turboprop and the Boeing 707 jet about the same time transformed the air travel markets. These innovative planes greatly advanced the reduction in travel times between major long-distance and intermediate cities, furthering the public's obsession with convenience and saving time. Improved comfort was another factor, although this would change in the decades that followed. Ultimately, the

"Well, there she goes—the 5:08 to Los Angeles. Right on time!"
Edward Koren, The New Yorker. Copyright Condé Nast. Used by permission.

passenger train simply could not compete. As NYC President Alfred Perlman remarked, "The supremacy of the jet airplane for long-distance travel lies beyond argument. And when we added the proliferation of limited access highways to the inherent convenience and flexibility of the private automobile, the demise of the long-haul passenger train was certain."[37]

But the airlines also had some serious safety problems. Before sophisticated navigation systems and air traffic control computers, high-profile crashes (often involving celebrities) were common; the 1956 collision of two planes over the Grand Canyon led to the Federal Aviation Act of 1958 and creation of the Federal Aviation Administration as a new regulator of the industry.

On the railroads, "modern" new trains still in many ways were trains of the past and could not compete for the travel dollar, so the future looked increasingly bleak. Passenger fares still brought in much-needed cash but less of it as trains carried fewer and fewer passengers. Rate increases granted by the ICC were often insufficient and lagged behind increasing costs, and the railroads were still treated as monopolies even though their total revenues could not earn the cost of capital. The state and federal governments appeared ambivalent at best as many communities, usually mounting little or no objection, lost passenger service. Still, discontinuance of NYC's famed 20th Century Limited between New York City and Chicago in December 1967 after sixty-five years of continuous operation made national news. Some felt that American culture had lost part of its soul, and, of even more importance, it was one more instance of the passing of civility in travel.

The Golden Age of the Automobile

In 1957, the French philosopher Roland Barthes celebrated automobile design "as the exact equivalent of the great Gothic cathedrals" (apparently confirming that autos had spurred something of a religious fervor among people, especially Americans), a description that forty years before had applied to the country's great railway terminals.[1] Car ownership in the United States went from 45 million in 1949 to 119 million in 1972.[2] By 1955, American auto dealers were selling 7 million cars a year.[3]

In the race to attract car buyers, two- and three-tone combinations of turquoise, yellow, red, green, white, black, and pink had become standard color options. As air travel grew in popularity, car models took an aeronautical theme: Nash's Airflyte series (1949), Oldsmobile's Rocket V-8 (1949), and Hudson's Jet (1953) and Jet-Liner (1954). Plymouth's 1953 novel one-piece windshield, which soon gained wide acceptance, provided what Chrysler called "control tower visibility."[4] By 1958, some Buick models had names that oddly evoked passenger trains (Century, Limited, and Special) but were soon eclipsed with introduction of the Air Born B-58 and the 1962 Electra. In a four-year period between 1956 and 1960, some carmakers offered push-button transmissions for the new push-button age, and by 1957, with a nod to the Space Age, auto brands offered fins that made cars look like rockets on wheels. By 1959, this fad, which proved fatal to some bicycle riders, was out of control, and when vertical fins reached their limits, they became horizontal.

The first Holiday Inn opened in Tennessee in 1956, one of many chains that catered to highway travelers. Families could go to movie night in their cars at hundreds of drive-in theaters, the first of which opened in Camden, New Jersey, in 1933. They also could have lunch or dinner and go to church without leaving the family automobile. By the late 1950s, 90 percent of American families were taking holidays by car, and the American way of life had become equated with the car and the highway.[5] By 1965, there were twenty thousand miles of interstate highways that cost an average of $1,141,000 ($9,426,073 in 2020) per mile, with some segments costing $50 million per mile.[6]

Notes

1. Steven Parissien, *The Life of the Automobile* (New York: St. Martin's Press, 2014), 186.
2. Parissien, 186.
3. Parissien, 187.
4. James M. Flammang, *Cars of the Fabulous '50s* (Lincolnwood, IL: Publications International, 2002), 142.
5. Parissien, 190–191.
6. Parissien, 192.

General Motors and allies Standard Oil of California and Firestone Tire and Rubber Company launched National City Lines to acquire local rail transit systems and replace streetcars with buses. In 1925, it also bought a major stake in Yellow Coach Company, a supplier of Raymond Loewy–styled buses to Greyhound, the nation's largest long-distance bus operator (the famous 1953 Scenicruiser was designed by Loewy). Greyhound competed with long-distance passenger trains,[38] but its traffic base also eroded even after construction of the interstates.

Travel Preferences

Following demobilization in 1945–46, rail's market share of intercity travel declined precipitously while travel by private automobile began its postwar ascent aided by a resurgent auto industry and taxpayer-paid improved roads and highways. Starting around 1950, a marked shift began toward subsidized air travel in the long-distance market from which rail never recovered.

Table 1.1
Intercity travel by mode

Year	Auto (%)	Train (%)	Air (%)	Bus (%)
1946	75.8	15.5	1.7	6.3
1948	82.8	9.5	1.5	5.6
1950	86.8	6.5	1.8	4.5
1954	89.1	4.4	2.7	3.3
1956	89.6	3.8	3.2	2.9
1958	90.1	3.1	3.5	2.7
1960	90.1	2.8	4.0	2.5
1965	88.8	1.9	5.9	2.6
1968	86.7	1.2	8.6	2.4

Source: John B. Rae, *The Road and Car in American Life* (Cambridge, MA: MIT Press, 1971), 92–93.

Political Inaction

In 1951, a Senate subcommittee, under the leadership of Ohio Senator John Bricker, began investigating the railroads' "passenger problem" for a report on national transportation policy. Published in 1952, the 1,500-page document confirmed most of the rail industry's complaints, saying, "The railroads' financial woes are primarily the result of unwise governmental policies rather than the operation of natural economic forces." Furthermore, the railroad industry's predicament was "adversely affected by lavish government subsidies to competing forms of transportation." And, in a swipe at the ICC's turn away from its primary function of safeguarding competition to favoring rails' competitors, the report noted "the absence of fair and impartial regulation."[39]

Despite the conclusions of the report, no action followed until July 1954 when President Eisenhower announced that his administration's commerce secretary, Sinclair Weeks, would chair a committee to study "transport policy and organization." The committee was to determine any changes necessary for fair and consistent treatment of all transport modes. When presented to the president in April 1955, the committee's report was praised by the railroads despite the lack of any mention of help for them.[40] It did, however, make recommendations similar to those enacted twenty-five years later in the Staggers Rail Act of 1980. But only a few months later, Eisenhower unveiled his unprecedented interstate highway initiative. With this, highway construction had become the nation's de facto transportation policy.

Deficit Hearings and Some Action

By January 1958, the passenger deficit situation was so extreme that the Surface Transportation Subcommittee of the US Senate's Interstate and Foreign Commerce Committee began hearings. Congress was finally convinced that the railroads were in real trouble, and passenger services might actually bankrupt many of them. Senator George Smathers of Florida stated at the outset, "Available statistics indicate that the American railroads are heading for serious trouble."[41] What resulted was the Transportation Act of 1958, which allowed greater freedom to eliminate unprofitable trains and abandon branch lines. Prior to this act, the ICC train discontinuance process had been onerous and time-consuming, requiring railroads to present detailed loss accounting at public hearings in numerous affected communities.

However, the ICC was not entirely blind to the railroads' crisis, although it avoided any allusion to its role in the problem. Responding to industry criticism by Young and other rail officials, the Commission had joined with Congress in 1956 to investigate the deficit problem. In its report (Docket No. 31954, May 18, 1959) the ICC stated, "The specific public need and demand for future railroad passenger service cannot be foretold. It is clear, however, that any degree of railroad participation in the travel market on a sound financial basis, requires adjustment of its services and facilities to determined needs."[42] Further,

> The impetus given motor and air travel by Federal, State and local government promotional programs has unquestionably operated to the disadvantage of railroad passenger service. Vast highway, airport and airway modernization programs predicated upon anticipated public needs which are now underway, as well as a policy for continued subsidy to air carriers, offer little solace to an industry which is dependent upon private resources and which has witnessed the gradual erosion of its passenger market. It is not suggested that such programs are not meritorious and desirable in the public interest, but the fact is they do exist; they will, as in the past, have a pronounced impact upon railroad passenger service. Yet, there is little evidence of any comparable governmental effort to promote the public interest in railroad passenger service or to prevent or take into account competitive inequalities that may be induced by such promotional programs.[43]

The report detailed nine recommendations that anticipated several that would come out of the Whitman Commission three years later: elimination of the 10 percent federal excise tax on passenger fares; income tax relief; reduction of the tax burden on railroad property; commuter operational subsidies by state and local communities; a study of "implications of the national transportation policy in connection with the procurement of passenger train services by the Post Office

Department, Department of Defense and other agencies of the Government"; elimination of duplicate trains, terminals, and facilities; experimentation with "new types of coaches, sleeping cars, dining and other facilities"; continuing "efforts to improve the attractiveness of railroad passenger service as a means of stimulating more adequate volume of traffic"; and, finally, that "every possibility of developing additional patronage should be fully and continually explored."[44]

The report called for "an exploration of those public expenditures which operate to the disadvantage of the railroads. We adhere to the principle previously expressed that this country's several forms of transportation should be treated equitably and that no one form should be preferred. We are of the view that the complete elimination of passenger-train [sic] service would not be a solution in the public interest." In conclusion the report stated, "A sense of urgency, therefore, compels us to advocate strongly the adoption of the recommendations outlined herein."[45]

And what was the rail industry's response? In a film produced around 1960, Alfred Perlman spoke for the entire industry about subsidized competition. The NYC marketing department had watched in dismay as new sections of the New York State Thruway diverted freight and passenger traffic in its New York City–to–Buffalo market. Perlman, seated in what appeared to be his business car while the countryside raced past the window behind him, faced the camera to discuss progress made by the rail industry and the challenges it faced due to publicly financed highway and air competition. He closed with his main point: "What we have is a lopsided transportation policy on federal and state levels; a policy that is slowly squeezing the life out of our railroads. What do we ask? Well, that's simple. We ask for an up-to-date fair transportation policy. We ask that all forms of transportation pay their way, as now only the railroads do. Or failing that, we ask the same tax benefits and the same government support under which other forms of transportation operate today."[46]

The Explicit and Hidden Transportation Subsidies

Perlman's arguments remain valid in the third decade of the twenty-first century and warrant a brief examination. While the rail industry's regulatory environment has improved since the Staggers Act (1980), balance in funding appropriation has not. Governments at all levels provide transportation subsidies, but it must be recognized that while some of the support is explicit, much is hidden, and this imbalance skews how transportation systems compete.

This has affected the privately owned railroads since the early twentieth century. When public necessity spurred investment in better roads that drew freight and passengers from the railroads, no thought was given to effects on the rail industry because it was still so dominant and seemingly a monopoly. Between ICC regulation and ever-increasing government support for highways, waterways, and, later, airlines, the tax-paying railroad industry supported itself by profits and privately raised capital. Railroads gradually lost business, and their market share of both freight and passenger traffic declined, even as the economy grew.

The following table of explicit federal government subsidies covers the time period, especially the earlier part when public expenditure imbalance had the greatest impact on the railroads' passenger services.

Table 1.2
Federal modal subsidies 1960–2017 (constant 2017 dollars)

Mode	Total federal explicit subsidies ($)	% of total
Air	510,948,000,000	25.69
Highway	1,155,588,000,000	58.09
Amtrak[a]	54,999,000,000	2.77
Mass Transit	267,416,000,000	13.45
Total	1,988,951,000,000	100.00

Source: Robert Nathan & Associates, "Federal Subsidies for Passenger Transportation 1960–2009," appendix B, 51, 53, 57, 59, as of May 5, 2020, www.bts.gov/explore-topics-and-geography/topics/government-transportation-financial-statistics.

[a] Amtrak subsidies began in 1971; prior to that, the freight railroads paid for their own passenger services.

The second table (below) shows the more recent history of such subsidies and includes state participation, based on federal Bureau of Transportation Statistics data.

Table 1.3
Transportation expenditures, federal and state, 2007–17 (constant 2017 dollars)

Mode	Federal or state	Total explicit subsidies ($)	% of total
Total (all modes)	Federal and state	3,429,328,000,000	100.00
	Federal	959,999,000,000	27.99
	State	2,469,329,000,000	72.01
Air	Federal	216,167,000,000	6.30
	State	210,501,000,000	6.13
Highway	Federal	495,560,000,000	14.45
	State	1,685,964,000,000	49.16
Rail[a]	Federal	27,026,000,000	0.79
	State	0	0
Mass transit	Federal	118,080,000,000	3.44
	State	512,008,000,000	14.93
Water, pipeline, general support	Federal	163,688,000,000	4.77
	State	89,439,000,000	2.61

Source: www.bts.gov/explore-topics-and-geography/topics/government-transportation-financial-statistics, as of May 5, 2020.

[a] Amtrak total for these years, state support was not yet recognized by the DOT Bureau of Transportation Statistics.

The tables exclude hidden subsidies, such as tax-exempt bonds used to fund all forms of transportation, and other debt financing usually issued with tax-exempt status; transportation grants to all modes; government funding of aeronautical research and development; air traffic control; policing costs governed by agency budgets, such as Homeland Security; the effects of removing taxable land for airports, highways, and parking; airline pension funds bailed out by the federal Pension Benefit Guaranty Corporation; environmental costs due to air and other forms of pollution, including oil drilling on federal land; ethanol costs affecting the cost of food and farm subsidies; oil subsidies, including the cost of foreign wars to protect oil supplies; direct airline, Conrail, and Amtrak subsidies and grants (such as direct cash to airlines after the 9/11 attacks) before, during, and after the above period; and transfers from the General Fund (federal) to the Highway Trust Fund (the 2015 Highway Bill transferred $70 billion over five years to the Highway Trust Fund to make up for costs in excess of fuel tax revenues). Receipts from user charges offset some air, highway, and waterway use but are often portrayed as zeroing out some or all of the explicit subsidies while ignoring the hidden subsidies.[47]

The complex weaving of explicit and hidden subsidies at the national and state levels calls for a comprehensive review of how public funds are spent relative to these expenditures' long-term benefit. In his book *Transportation in the U.S.: A Look Back, and Forward*, Gary Toth describes how transportation planners focused on highways without understanding the full implications of the effect on the greater good. He states, "The real point of transportation projects should be building successful communities and fostering economic prosperity."[48] In this context, to suggest only one area of concern to the authors of this book, policymakers may wish to consider the social and other impacts long-distance trains have on the rural communities they serve—and on those they don't serve but perhaps should.

As at the federal level, hidden expenditures occur at the state level too, further skewing transportation policy and hiding the full costs of providing benefits to the railroads' (especially Amtrak's) competitors. In a study done at the Harvard Kennedy School, a working paper entitled *The $64 Billion Massachusetts Vehicle Economy* sheds light on state-level hidden subsidies. The paper's data was through 2019 and identified $35.78 billion of state highway and vehicle costs (55.78 percent) out of a total of $64 billion expended in the Bay State for the study period. The balance, $28.4 billion, was borne by consumers to finance and operate vehicles. Of that $35.78 billion, just a third was covered by user charges. The balance fell on every family at an average rate of $14,000 per year, regardless of whether a family owned a vehicle. Total vehicle and highway costs include congestion, injury, death, the value of land set aside for highways (loss of real estate tax income), and the costs of financing and operating vehicles of pollution.[49]

Amtrak has long been required to disclose profit and loss statements as well as maintain its balance sheet. No other form of transportation is required to show both the explicit and hidden subsidies provided by the federal and state governments. There is no balance sheet or income statement for the interstate highway system. Neither are hidden costs reflected in air fares or highway access costs. This incomplete cost picture, coupled with Amtrak's appearance as an annual budget line item, makes the company a ripe target for those who do not see value in supporting passenger rail services and integrating them with other transportation investments. It has become almost impossible for policymakers, even when motivated, to determine where the public can best be served by various transportation programs, given the skewing caused by unbalanced transportation subsidies, both explicit and hidden. Changes in federal policy—or preference—could foster a sea change in how passenger and freight transportation subsidies are allocated for all modes by making all such subsidies explicit and all costs visible to the voting public.

The Whitman Commission

In the face of such competition, northeastern railroads with large numbers of passengers were especially vulnerable because their freight services incurred higher costs and brought lower revenues than in other regions of the country. Freight profits—unpredictable at best—could not support passenger costs as well as on other railroads. This did not, however, sway government officials. They still theorized that freight revenues should and, worse, could cover passenger losses, thus absolving themselves of any responsibility—until time simply ran out for a major railroad.

The Whitman Commission was a direct result of the second bankruptcy of the New York, New Haven & Hartford Railroad—the New Haven—on July 7, 1961. To industry insiders, the New Haven's problems were widely known. The company earned about 42 percent of its revenue from passenger service and was in a unique and difficult position. The New Haven served close to 10 percent of the nation's population in an area constituting less than 1 percent of its geographic area. It had emerged from bankruptcy in 1946, only to have everything of value, mostly real estate, stripped from it under periods of successive managements. Its large passenger deficits eroded any profits from its freight operations, which were mostly short-haul and vulnerable to motor carrier competition. Yet the New Haven, strategically located along the Northeast coast, was vital to the country's economy and defense.

Beginning in the mid-1950s, with two hurricanes that devastated its main lines and branches, the railroad suffered one financial crisis after another and had survived only because of emergency loans backed by the federal government. Following the departure of President Patrick B. McGinnis for the Boston & Maine in 1956, the New Haven's physical and financial condition steadily worsened. Desperate for help, its new president, George Alpert, took a public stand: the government, with strong support from the Department of Defense,[50] was giving ongoing support to the automobile, bus, trucking, and

"Great Scott! Now what's happened?"
Peter Arno, The New Yorker. *Copyright Condé Nast. Used by permission.*

aviation industries, so it only seemed logical that rail transport be included in order to retain a balanced transportation policy.

Alpert's position was eminently logical but created a dilemma for railroads and governments alike. Giving any kind of ongoing subsidy to a railroad in the 1950s was considered a form of socialism, something not to be tolerated, especially during the Cold War. Indeed, most other railroads were increasingly resistant to the idea of subsidies due to both the strings usually attached and the implied threat of nationalization. Granting subsidies to railroads as a part of government support of transportation would have required a major shift in political philosophy, not likely to occur overnight. But a true crisis, an immediate threat of disaster, can sharpen the mind—and so it was in the case of the New Haven. Its managers did not like the idea of subsidies but needed them to keep the railroad operating.

Fearing the New Haven would simply shut down in a strategic portion of the country, in early March 1962, Commerce Secretary Luther Hodges contacted Frederic B. Whitman, president of the Western Pacific Railroad, for help in addressing the "New Haven Railroad problem."[51] Hodges asked Whitman to form a commission with representatives of seven profitable western railroads and locomotive builder Electro-Motive Division of General Motors to survey, assess, and make recommendations for action to be taken by both the New Haven's trustees and the federal government. This was a new approach: asking the railroad industry what it needed.

The commission's report included correspondence between Whitman and Hodges with this observation: "We are aware that the states involved have their problems with respect to raising sufficient tax monies to support their various governmental activities, but, on the other hand, the importance of the New Haven continuing as a successful private enterprise to serve the states and communities seems to us to outweigh the additional burden which would be placed on other taxpayers to make up the difference from other sources."[52] The "various governmental activities," of course, included the mounting costs of building and maintaining the public highways that put the New Haven in such a predicament. It was clear, however, that the commission expected the states to come up with support for the railroad.

Another problem was management stability, although the report did not suggest a remedy. Beginning in 1948, the New Haven suffered administration changes around every two years. Lack of policy continuity, abrupt shifts in policy, forays into new and costly experimental passenger equipment, and loss of management talent and institutional knowledge all took their toll at a time when stability was needed. This was no way to run a railroad.

The Whitman report was lengthy and detailed and dealt with problems specific to the New Haven: marketing, real estate, operations, management, labor, retirement of employees, and taxation. Most importantly, it was credible and persuasive and cleared the way for states to help the railroad. Although it primarily addressed the New Haven's large commuter service, the report's implication was that there should be a broader application of the principles it articulated, thus setting the tone for future dealings with other troubled railroads needing help.

Regarding the New Haven's commuter burden, the report stated, "If continuation of commuter service is deemed necessary or desirable by the states or local areas benefited, the railroad should not be expected or required to sustain such losses. Funds to make up those losses should be provided in some form or other by the states and local areas served."⁵³ One important point: the report also stated that the federal government should not be expected to cover those costs of operation. It would take much more serious "railroad problems" in later years to bring the national government to the table.

It is important to recognize how the New Haven's impending demise and the value of the services it provided led to a significant change both in government approaches to regulation of rail transportation and in what had been a hands-off attitude toward railroad finances. Soon after the report came out, Connecticut, New York, and Massachusetts entered into agreements with the New Haven to compensate the railroad for commuter service losses. Further, by 1964, New York had passed legislation granting tax relief, and Massachusetts created the Massachusetts Bay Transportation Authority. In 1965 came the Connecticut Department of Transportation. Today, such major metropolitan commuter agencies as Metro North (New York and Connecticut), New Jersey Transit, SEPTA (Pennsylvania), METRA (Chicago), among others, and Amtrak itself can trace their origins to the New Haven's bankruptcy. From its broken eggs, we managed to make some omelets.

Bigger Is Better (?): A Look at Penn Central

In that troubled era for railroads, salvation appeared to be in merger, and "bigger" seemed certain to guarantee success. It had to; there were few favorable options. The combination of historic rivals NYC and Pennsylvania railroads in 1968 was a long time coming and very quickly served as a wake-up call for the government. Arriving at the point of merger took enormous effort on the part of both companies' managements to convince labor, customers, lobbyists, lawyers, regulators, and politicians that merger was necessary for survival. The railroads' passenger problem needed a solution and combining separate services in a regional fashion was one method being explored.⁵⁴

Before the Penn Central (PC) merger could happen, however, connecting and competing railroads, organized labor, the Justice Department, the ICC, and the railroads' customers had to have their doubts and fears mollified. Support from these groups came only through the creation of a tangled and often incomprehensible web of deals.

PC's demise has been well documented; its 1970 bankruptcy was a pivotal event in many ways, but for the passenger train, it brought a true turning point. Struggling with passenger losses of tens of millions a year, in March 1969 (by which time PC was responsible also for all of the New Haven's trains), the company issued a plan to abandon all of its passenger services west of Buffalo and Harrisburg, which then was followed by its filing for abandonment of its remaining thirty-four long-distance trains; this was in addition to fourteen proposed discontinuances already under consideration by the ICC (by this time only 1 percent of the public traveled by rail and 9 percent by air).⁵⁵

With the waning of passenger service on other railroads, Jim McClellan formed a committee at the newly created (1967) Federal Railroad Administration (FRA) embedded within the newly created (1966) Department of Transportation, led by Alan Boyd. Two railroad representatives, C&O/B&O's William Howes (C&O/Baltimore & Ohio played a pivotal role in Amtrak's creation as C&O/B&O and FRA headquarters were near each other; even so, the railroad's chairman, Hays Watkins, did not want any government money) and Illinois Central's Paul Reistrup, were asked to join, the only railroaders on the committee. The realization that passenger service in the country was collapsing (the railroad-owned Railway Express Agency was also failing and the Pullman Company was in the process of ending operations) forced the FRA to conduct a study to find out what was happening, and what the government could or should do.[56]

There was no question that the railroads were hurting, but by how much? The United States Post Office Department was closing down mail sorting aboard Railway Post Office (RPO) cars and shifting first-class mail to the airlines, leaving low-revenue second-class mail on the trains. The reason, at least in part, was that reliability of service and ever-decreasing numbers of available trains made it hard to meet Post Office performance requirements. Another factor was the introduction of the zip code in anticipation of automated mail sorting. To the Post Office, the RPO, with its expensive crews sorting mail by hand in transit, was obsolete.[57] Revenues from RPO services were paying operating costs for many passenger trains and were the only reason they kept running. That did not seem to matter to Postmaster Lawrence O'Brien, and loss of so much of the mail further deepened the passenger train dilemma.

Not-So-Hidden Problems

The threat of Penn Central to stop its trains and the loss of mail contracts had a big impact. While many of the railroads' problems were obvious—declining passenger traffic, overregulation, high taxation, and labor militancy—there were other less visible ones. Like Daphne du Maurier's title character in *Rebecca*, while never seen, these problems were always lurking offstage: passenger fares were not keeping pace with inflation, costs of labor and materials kept rising, and an aging car fleet required ever more maintenance and repair. The railroads were caught in an untenable position, hurtling down a dead-end road from which there seemed no escape.

The cost of labor was a particular problem that consumed more dollars of passenger revenues. This was partly because in negotiation of wages, benefits, and work rules, the railroads frequently made concessions on the freight side to attain labor peace and keep the trains rolling; but this resulted in reduced profits needed to support the passenger side, where similar concessions made running those trains more expensive. A significant part of the rise in labor costs lay in the diabolically complex labor agreements and provisions for conferences, mediation, arbitration, and factfinding buried within the Railway Labor Act of 1926. Presidential emergency boards, arbitration boards, and cooling-off periods were frequently employed to avert strikes and often resulted in more complex rules and "awards" that fostered inefficiency and ultimately made it more expensive to operate trains. This did have a positive effect, for the railroads, anyway, of validating their arguments when petitioning to eliminate trains that did not pay their way, but the ICC did not always grant the desired discontinuances. The railroads also could petition the ICC for passenger fare increases, but this took time and often came too late to address rising labor costs, and fare hikes had the additional effect of discouraging ridership.

Then there was an even more pressing problem on the threshold of the 1970s: the looming prospect of having to invest in new passenger equipment. Although it can be argued that some of the larger railroads were willing to tolerate a certain level of deficits in order to maintain cash flow and retain control of their passenger operations, even for them the prospect of renovating existing or purchasing new passenger equipment was daunting.

In addition to all the problems they faced, various railroads had different views among them about running passenger trains. Some wanted out, while others did not. Curiously, some operating officers believed passenger operations "forced railroads into operating discipline they otherwise would not have. They wanted this," said Bill Howes.[58] On the Seaboard Air Line Railroad, for example (later the Seaboard Coast Line after merger with the Atlantic Coast Line), the passenger problem was not so much a lack of revenues or demand, it was the increasing expenses that all the railroads were enduring. "The traffic was there," said Howes. Other passenger railroads too had decent traffic levels, but for all of them, the economic realities were stark and piling up ever faster, and something had to change.[59]

Killing the Passenger Train?

Trains magazine began publishing in 1940. Railroad enthusiasts have always been part of its reader base, of course, but it has the respect of those in the railroad industry too. In the issue for April 1959, the magazine's longtime editor, the late David P. Morgan, ran a thirty-eight-page study, carefully researched and documented, titled "Who Shot the Passenger Train?" While it was no pro-train puff piece, the article made it clear that its author supported passenger rail and that, if the right steps were taken, there was a future for the passenger train in the United States.

Morgan described the railroads' trains as "a privately financed and tax-paying business providing a public service at less than cost."[60] In analyzing the problem—in probably the best assessment by anyone of the era—he cited much familiar evidence: the reality of passenger deficits and the threat they posed to the rail industry, the unreliability of the "ICC Formula" (discussed later) in assessing the actual deficits, regulatory stranglehold, public subsidy of air and highway travel, and the tax-exempt status of much of the air and highway infrastructure, while railroads had to buy and then build their own and then were taxed for owning it.

Even in the context of the well-documented (and obvious) American love affair with the automobile and the speediness of air travel, Morgan said, a national network of passenger trains could be established on a sound economic basis that would enable continuation of the public service they performed. He proposed several ideas: run passenger trains as a separate business, even a separate national corporation or a collection of regional ones; separate all the commuter services from the corridor and intercity ones; invest in new equipment with lower operating and crewing costs and bidirectional capability; keep carrying the mail but abandon the costly en route sorting of it; and give passenger trains "equal treatment"—if other modes got subsidies, trains should too.

Morgan's article must have been widely read, but from 1959 to 1970, as we have seen, there was no real progress other than relieving the railroads of the commuter burden. Even then, this happened only when it became a crisis, the typical American way of dealing with problems. With the coming of Amtrak, however, Morgan's eleven-year-old proposals began to look like new ideas: a separate corporation to run the trains; new equipment, some modeled after traditional separate-car design, others as bidirectional and high-speed equipment (Metroliner and TurboTrain); and nonsorted mail, which did return to the rails for awhile before being discarded by Amtrak. As for "equal treatment," the annual appropriations that have kept Amtrak going—sometimes better and sometimes worse—are by any measure at least some version of leveling the playing field.

But the American public—and Amtrak—are still hobbled by Morgan's answer to "Who Shot the Passenger Train": it is all of us, and it is the result of perceiving the passenger train as somehow outmoded, part of the past with no place in a prosperous future—except in Europe and Asia. How did this happen? "Not deliberately, not in collusion. . . . There is no one culprit, no group of whom it can be fairly said, 'They did it.' The psychological obsolescence that has overtaken the passenger train stems from a classic failure of all concerned to get the big picture."[61] It would take a great deal of hand-wringing and a lot of hard work to find even the beginning of a solution.

Part One Notes

1. Robert Selph Henry, *This Fascinating Railroad Business* (Indianapolis and New York: Bobbs-Merrill, 1943), 433–434.
2. The ICC expanded its authority to include other modes, including aviation, until the creation of the Civil Aeronautics Board in 1938.
3. "Revenue Firm, Deficit Down," *Railway Age* 154, no. 19 (May 20, 1963): 20.
4. Henry, 435.
5. "Passenger Service Improvement Sets New Record," *Railway Age* 109, no. 20 (November 16, 1940): 705–707.
6. "Passenger Service Improvement Sets New Record," 705–707.
7. "Passenger Service Improvement Sets New Record," 705–707.
8. Ralph Budd 1935 speech before the American Association of Railroad Superintendents, in Richard

C. Overton, *Perkins/Budd: Railway Statesmen of the Burlington* (Westport, CT: Greenwood Press, 1982), 146.
9. Overton, *Perkins/Budd*, 146.
10. Overton, *Perkins/Budd*, 146.
11. Retired in 1960 to Chicago's Museum of Science and Industry, the Pioneer Zephyr can be visited there today, including its restored interior.
12. *Moody's Transportation Manual* (New York: Moody's Investor Service, 1956), a–9.
13. W. David Randall, *Streamliner Cars*, 3 vols., (Godfrey, Illinois: RPC), 1981.
14. *Webster's New World Dictionary of the American Language*, 2nd College Edition (New York: World, 1968), 1102.
15. Byron Nupp, *National Transportation Policy in the United States—An Analysis of the Concept*, University of Denver Law Journal, HeinOnline, pp. 145–146.
16. Overton, *Perkins/Budd*, 124–125.
17. John B. Rae, *The Road and Car in American Life* (Cambridge, MA: MIT Press, 1971), 38.
18. Overton, *Perkins/Budd*, 124–125.
19. Overton, *Perkins/Budd*, 146.
20. Overton, *Perkins/Budd*, 146.
21. Overton, *Perkins/Budd*, 122.
22. Overton, *Perkins/Budd*, 135.
23. Daniel Rust, presentation at the Lexington Group for Transportation History, October 23, 2019.
24. Rust, presentation.
25. Nupp, 150.
26. Richard C. Overton, *Burlington Route* (Lincoln: University of Nebraska Press, 1965), 547.
27. Overton, *Burlington Route*, 547.
28. Nupp, 153.
29. John F. Kennedy, *Special Message to Congress on Transportation* (Boston: Presidential Papers, John F. Kennedy Library), 3.
30. Kennedy, 4.
31. Kennedy, 6.
32. The New York, Ontario & Western, which had survived on government loans before and after the war, was liquidated in 1957, the first major railroad to do so. That same year the Chicago, Aurora & Elgin, a major electric interurban in the Chicago area, exited the passenger business and was liquidated in 1959. In 1961, southern California lost its last commuter rail service, the Pacific Electric, and in 1963, the Chicago, North Shore & Milwaukee was liquidated.
33. Nupp, 157.
34. David McCullough, *Truman* (New York: Simon & Schuster, 1992), 654.
35. Doris Kearns Goodwin, *No Ordinary Time* (New York: Simon & Schuster, 1994), 355–359.
36. Rae, 92–93.
37. Stover, 221.
38. Parissien, 192.
39. Charles O. Morgret, *Brosnan: The Railroads' Messiah*, Volume 1 (Great Barrington, MA: Vantage, 1997), 229.
40. Morgret, 312.
41. 1957 New York Central Railroad Annual Report, 24.
42. Association of American Railroads, *What Can be Done to Solve . . . THE Railroad Passenger Train Problem; Recommendations of the Interstate Commerce Commission*, 1959, 4.
43. Association of American Railroads, *What Can be Done to Solve*, 4, 5.
44. Association of American Railroads, *What Can be Done to Solve*, 9, 10.
45. Association of American Railroads, *What Can be Done to Solve*, 10, 11.
46. YouTube Video, *The Big Train*, MPO Production, accessed August 27, 2020, https://www.youtube.com/watch?v=eT9H44ytagw&ab_channel=DocumentaryClassics.
47. "Federal Subsidies for Passenger Transportation," accessed June 19, 2020, bts.gov/sites//bts.dot.gov
48. "Transportation in the U.S.: A Look Back, and Forward," January 1, 2009, Gary Toth, quoted in *Project for Public Spaces*, accessed November 18, 2020, www.pps.org.
49. "The $64 Billion Massachusetts Vehicle Economy," Harvard Kennedy School, Olsen, Stevie, Berkaw, Charland, Patton, Bilmes 2019. www.hks.harvard.edu/publications/64-Billion-Massachusetts-Vehicle-Economy.
50. The military has often played a vital role in transportation. Railroads were used extensively in times of war. The airline industry was a beneficiary as well. Passenger aircraft owe their origins to the government's postal service and the military; jet aircraft development also was due to the military.
51. US Department of Commerce, *Report of the Railroad Professional Survey Group*, 1962, v.
52. US Department of Commerce, *Report*, 21.
53. US Department of Commerce, *Report*, 31.

54. Combining passenger services was not a new idea. The consulting firm of Robert Heller & Associates had conducted studies in the early 1950s that found considerable synergy in a combined New York Central, Pennsylvania, and Baltimore & Ohio passenger operation, but the proposal was never followed through.
55. Rae, 92–93.
56. Personal interview with William F. Howes, February 12–13, 2019.
57. Telephone interview with William F. Howes, June 9, 2020.
58. Howes, February 12–13, 2019.
59. Howes, February 12–13, 2019.
60. David P. Morgan, "Who Shot the Passenger Train?" *Trains*, (April 1959): 14–51.
61. Morgan, 14–51.

Amtrak was born in a country
that didn't have a transportation policy.

William F. Howes

Creating a New National Network 2

Trial and Error—or the Impossible Dream

In the post–World War II years, the nation's railroads can fairly be credited with earnestly trying to introduce high-quality, well-run new passenger services to the traveling public, even absent understanding what changes were taking place in the intercity market. As well built and attractive as all the new trains were, however, they were based on designs and technologies developed in the 1930s and in many ways did not actually introduce new approaches to the "passenger problem." Some equipment innovations helped, at least for a time. The Budd Company's stainless steel self-propelled Rail Diesel Car, (the "RDC" or "Budd Car"), for example, enabled preservation of many passenger routes at less cost than a locomotive-powered train but was unsuitable for long distances. There also was the introduction of inexpensive sleeping cars ("Slumbercoach," among other similar names), which gave travelers private accommodations—with private toilet facilities—for coach fare plus a modest room charge.

Unfortunately, these "pluses" were offset by "minuses" such as reductions in or elimination of traditional onboard amenities—dining, lounge, and parlor car services—and reduction of train frequencies on major routes, not to mention the problems arising from some deferred maintenance of rolling stock that still was steam heated.

Even with these challenges, some railroads made concerted efforts to make passenger services work—if not profitably, at least at a smaller annual loss. One in particular was C&O/B&O. The Chesapeake & Ohio Railway had gained control of the Baltimore & Ohio Railroad in 1963, but both still operated as separate companies. In the mid-1960s, led by Paul Reistrup, B&O's passenger department offered several innovations and a cheerful marketing campaign in an effort to attract passengers. As evidence: the public timetable of April 25, 1965, printed on coated stock in bright colors, declared that "Trains Are Fun!"

and offered "Red Circle" incentive fares to encourage travel on traditionally slow days and in slow months. (An extensive explanation of the fares featured a well-hatted couple—pillbox on the wife, fedora on the husband, pipe in mouth, Junior with a lollipop. Dad is saying "You mean—this is all it costs?"). A round-trip for two between Washington, DC and Chicago in a private room for two (with private toilet annex), if travel was on the Red Circle days of Monday through Wednesday, was around $124 ($1,024 in 2020, $512 per person, covering both round-trip transportation and two nights' accommodations). On board the trains, depending on the route, a traveler could find "Glass Topped Stratadome Cars" with searchlights to illuminate nighttime Appalachian scenery, free "current release movies-on-the-train," and full lunches and dinners for as little as $1.95 ($16.50 in 2020). Other railroads tried hard too, but nothing seemed to help as ridership continued to decline and deficits rose inexorably.

Meals typically were quite affordable; quality mattered too. This advertisement was in the October 1966 Pennsylvania Railroad timetable and contrasted an in-flight meal and one that offered a decidedly more refined experience. *Jeffrey Darbee Collection*

Could Innovation Save the Day? Robert R. Young and the Modern Train

While some quipped that the railroads were 100 years of tradition unencumbered by progress, there were a few in the industry who tried to prove otherwise. Attempts to solve the "passenger problem" began well before the mid-1960s, and much came from the mercurial mind of one man.

There likely has not been a more colorful, controversial, and complex player in the rail industry than Robert Ralph Young, an intelligent, gifted, clever, ambitious, savvy, flamboyant, energetic, impetuous, hyperbolic, and resourceful financier. Beginning as a financial advisor at General Motors in 1922, through a Wall Street brokerage Young amassed a stock market fortune by the onset of the Depression. In 1936, he and two associates bought the railroad assets of the Alleghany Corporation, the holding company of the late and eccentric Van Sweringen brothers, two real estate entrepreneurs in Cleveland. This gave Young control of the Erie, Chicago & Eastern Illinois, Hocking Valley, Pere Marquette, Missouri Pacific, and Wheeling and Lake Erie—a railroad empire that came to be viewed as the fourth Eastern system after the Pennsylvania, NYC, and B&O. Young's crown jewel, however, was a block of two-million-plus shares of the Chesapeake & Ohio (C&O) Railway. By 1940 he had become a modern-day railroad mogul.

Young earned a solid reputation for reinvigorating financially strapped railroads. In the course of his career he not only managed to attract the public's attention to the postwar plight of the railroads but simultaneously divided the industry over his motives and ideas. His failure to achieve lasting influence or results did not, however, make him irrelevant. His lonely quest was not quixotic: he was trying to show the industry a new way forward that could have made a substantial difference in the fate of the passenger train. For that reason alone his complex story is worth recounting.

Seeing the railroads as overregulated and controlled by banking and insurance interests, Young sought to reform the rail industry to enable it to make more money for its owners, particularly small investors holding fewer than 500 shares of stock. He decried investment banks' controlling the capital the railroads needed and argued against inequities in federal transportation policies, subsidies to the competition, and destructive federal and state taxation and regulation.

While some saw Young as visionary, he seemed more like a threat to the rail industry establishment. Having alienated that constituency, he found support in America's most potent interest group: the voting public. He promoted a cause he believed affected them on the broadest scale: how they traveled. Passenger service would be the means of achieving his goals, and he burst onto the national stage as the self-anointed champion of the American railroad passenger. Better train service was critical to his populist mission, and he proposed achieving it through control of the Pullman Company or, failing that, of the New York Central. Failing both at first, he focused on creating "new trains."

Robert R. Young, 1897–1958. *C&O photo. Geoffrey H. Doughty Collection*

Combating the Deficits

Running passenger trains is complex and expensive. Labor is the highest cost center, followed by infrastructure and facility maintenance, locomotive and car maintenance, and materials and supplies. Taxation remains a burden. Young went further, arguing that the accounting methods used to determine passenger losses were from the period when railroads were transportation monopolies, which they no longer were.

Accounting was based on the ICC "formula" for allocating costs between passenger and freight services. Under it, many passenger trains met their own costs and some earned a small profit, but when costs of supporting human and facility infrastructure were added, passenger services lost money overall. Young

The Infamous ICC Formula

At about the turn of the twentieth century, the ICC needed a method of identifying the costs of a railroad's operations to aid in regulating freight and passenger rates and determining a company's profit or loss. The method employed a complex accounting process—the "formula"—that broke down, or allocated, time spent, material and maintenance expenses, wages and benefits, and other expenses incurred by departments and employees engaged in generating revenues.

In the case of a railroad whose only function was to transport freight, it was a straightforward exercise to apportion the time and expense of management, superintendence, operations, engineering, mechanical, and clerical functions. It became much more complicated when a railroad transported both freight and passengers and needed to determine the contribution of each kind of traffic to profits or losses. Many railroads used only "out-of-pocket" costs to identify expenses of a particular service and thereby define for their own purposes any profits or losses, down to the calculations for each individual train. Today these are also called "above-the-rail" costs. The costs of property maintenance, superintendence, equipment, and so on, remained, but above-the-rail costs associated only with a particular train became a measure of that train's contribution to or burden upon revenues.

---

claimed that railroads wanting to eliminate trains often took advantage of the formula's complex nature by inappropriately assigning to the passenger side of operations the costs of superintendence, maintenance, accounting, and so on, to inflate losses and justify train discontinuances.

As essayist E. B. White once observed, "The book-keeping of railroads is as mysterious as the backing-up of a train in the night."[1] The ICC formula was indeed mysterious but was the only official accounting method the railroads could adopt. Unfortunately, by using the formula, about the only way a railroad could demonstrate that its costs declined often was when a train or a service, such as a sleeping car or diner, was eliminated. This had the effect of driving many railroads to using out-of-pocket costs to better identify losses. Even fifty years after the founding of Amtrak, eliminating some passenger services in order to reduce losses produces limited results because all the other overhead costs are spread over fewer revenue-generating services.

The Battle for Pullman

Robert R. Young was at the forefront in raising these and other issues. It appeared that he was trying to save the passenger train, but his real aim was to make its operation profitable—what would prove to be an impossible dream. His battle to change the industry began with his attempt to control the Pullman Company, which owned and operated the vast majority of the sleeping and parlor cars on American railroads, a fleet critical to intercity trains offering first-class services. Young needed the influence of Pullman to craft the reforms he envisioned. He believed that to attract passengers the railroads had to replace the entire existing car fleet with new luxurious equipment, thereby creating the zenith of comfortable and pleasurable travel.[2] Hurry, he said, or the airlines would dominate the market. Time would prove him right about the airlines and wrong about trains. To him, the passenger train was a staple of the American economy and culture and would endure, but the culture was already in transition.

Transcontinental Passenger Service

Despite Young's flamboyant efforts, Pullman was sold to a group of railroads in December 1945, so he took his battle in a different direction. Using the C&O's in-house publications and the national press as a megaphone, Young continued his crusade. It was aimed first at the public's disdain for big business, but he needed a more tangible issue and found it, or rather created it, by running full-page ads noting the railroads' lack of transcontinental passenger service. True coast-to-coast rail travel, he claimed, was impossible because a passenger had to change trains at Chicago, St. Louis, or New Orleans, something air travelers did not have to do; and this enhanced the popularity of the airlines to the detriment of the railroads.

Young assumed there actually was a market for transcontinental rail travel and undertook an extensive letter campaign berating the railroads for not offering it. He challenged the Eastern carriers by advertising in national publications that the C&O and the Nickel Plate would initiate such a service. The most famous ad featured a hog riding a boxcar, holding a cigar, while a hapless family watched from trackside; the copy noted that a hog could travel coast-to-coast without changing trains but people could not. The "hog ad" first appeared on March 4, 1946, and an overwhelming public reaction took everyone, including Young, by surprise. He took credit when the NYC, Pennsylvania, and Baltimore & Ohio were pushed into working with Western carriers to provide "coast-to-coast" service.[3] But Young was not done yet. There was more to do if travelers were to be drawn back to the rails.

The Chessie

With the C&O's treasury flush with wartime profits, Young forged ahead. In July 1945, in the heat of the Pullman court battles, he sought to validate his belief that luxury trains would attract and keep passengers. This had worked well, although briefly as it turned out, when service in the C&O-controlled Pere Marquette Railway's Detroit–Grand Rapids corridor was upgraded with two handsome sets of passenger coaches and diners. Taking that as a green light to proceed, Young persuaded the C&O board to approve buying 46 cars to outfit three stunning 14-car Budd-built stainless steel trains for a daylight Washington, DC–Cincinnati streamliner called Chessie (named for the

Geoffrey H. Doughty Collection

company's widely loved advertising kitten). The cost was set at $4 million but was revised within a year to $5.1 million. Unfortunately for Young, it took until October 1948, and a budget increase to $6.1 million ($65.9 million in 2020), to complete all the Chessie equipment, including cars for connecting trains, before the new train could go on tour. Three specially designed locomotives for the train were another $1.6 million ($17.3 million in 2020).[4]

Then it all abruptly vanished from view. Unlike its namesake, Chessie was stillborn.

What happened? The cost was the main problem. A downturn in the economy and a coal strike in mid-1948 placed the railroad in a financial bind, and to this was added the stark realization that there was no passenger market in the Washington–Cincinnati corridor that would support such a luxurious train. It is hard to believe that a seasoned railroad's board of directors would have overlooked something like this; Young must have been an astoundingly good salesman. The Pere Marquette service, which began with great promise, had suffered major traffic declines and added further discouragement. A few of Chessie's cars stayed in the C&O fleet while the rest were sold to other railroads, but by then Young had already moved on.

Train X and New York Central

Characteristically, failure did not stop Young; he just turned to another approach. He declared that airlines had the advantage over trains for long-distance travel, so the passenger train should focus on the short- to medium-distance market of 200 to 400 miles. Such service could offer savings in time and cost when compared to the automobile. Young further stated that the current design of passenger equipment was obsolete and largely to blame for ridership declines, so new trains had to be developed, and he looked to the airlines for innovation. There was the future! For help in his crusade he hired an American Airlines executive, Thomas Deegan, as an advisor and as communications director at C&O.

Deegan recognized that the profile of the passenger was in transition and convinced Young that a new passenger market with differing travel values was emerging. To attract business, airlines of the period were innovative, offering at-seat meals, free alcoholic beverages, and comfortable seats. Their astute advertising made air travel appear sophisticated, relaxed, and enjoyable while saving travelers a lot of time—although flying in this period was risky. All of this would change late in the century, but in the 1950s, air travel's positive attributes brought the airlines ever-increasing traffic.

Young asserted that what airline-competitive rail corridors needed was new lightweight trains with a low center of gravity to enable operation at high speeds over existing tracks. They would cost less than conventional equipment to build and operate but most importantly would attract passengers who desired lower-cost, faster travel times between city centers rather than to outlying airports. Young initially called this new conveyance Train X. (Corny as this might seem today, at the time, the dawning of the Space Age, "X" connoted innovation, experimentation, modernity, and what would come to be called high tech.)

During development of a test car while he was still at C&O, Young returned to a familiar crusade: his second attempt at a takeover of NYC. Pullman had been denied to him in part due to the influence of the NYC. Young believed he would have more influence promoting Train X and reform of the rail industry as the head of NYC than if he stayed with the C&O. After a long and bitter contest for control, Young prevailed in 1954 and the Train X project took off in 1956 with Young proudly claiming it would rescue Central's faltering passenger service.

Car builders at ACF, P-S, and Budd each introduced versions of the new prototype, but within a year all of them fell short of their goals. Production was rushed, the equipment lacked proper testing, and it required sophisticated maintenance unfamiliar to railroad shop forces.[5] Plagued also by a rough ride on their single axles, the "trains of the future" failed to attract and keep passengers as Young had hoped.[6]

The fact was that by 1956 the automobile was the people's choice for both short- and long-distance trips, the same year President Eisenhower unveiled his interstate highway

RIGHT To generate public enthusiasm for the concept of completely new trains, Robert R. Young promoted Train X with a naming contest in a flyer distributed at the 1948–1949 Chicago Railroad Fair.

Geoffrey H. Doughty Collection

BELOW Young went to some length to explain his ideas. It is not certain how many people actually took the flyer, read it, and sent in proposed names. Even author Jeffrey Darbee's father, a rail supporter, did not fill out and submit the mail-in card.

Jeffrey Darbee Collection

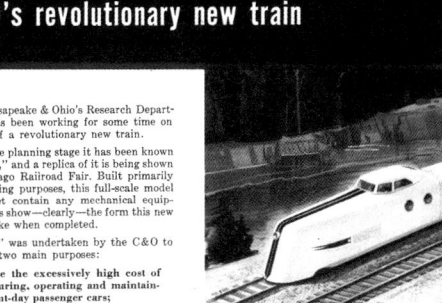

Creating a New National Network   51

initiative, and the situation seriously undermined Young's efforts. Taking a more practical step, Young created a research team at NYC to analyze the prevailing regulatory environment, labor restrictions, operations, rate structures, traffic patterns, and costs. The team undertook yeoman's work identifying several areas that had to be addressed if restructuring of the Central's passenger service was to be successful. In the areas of cost accounting, facility management, and regulation, Young mounted a frontal attack. He and other rail executives went to Washington to demand a change in policies and regulations that had seriously limited the railroads' ability to earn a profit and a respectable return on investment. The NYC, like the rail industry as a whole, was in a period of transition as 1956 dawned, beset by debilitating passenger losses that had increased yearly since the end of the war. What seemed unthinkable, merger with NYC's arch-rival, the Pennsylvania, was next on Young's agenda.

End of the Line

The odds against success in Young's long passenger service crusade were overwhelming. He is mostly remembered for the failures of Chessie and Train X, which showed his inability to read the markets, let alone deal with the larger issues of governmental regulation, taxation policies, and resolution of huge labor cost issues. Despite this, the ideas behind the new trains and the policy changes he championed succeeded in laying a foundation for both regulatory reform and resolution of the passenger problem that would emerge more than 20 years later. Sadly, Young did not live to see this, as he took his own life in January 1958. His ideas were just a generation too soon. Although controversial, to his credit he had championed railroads at a time when the industry needed a champion, and with his passing began the final chapter in the tale of the privately operated American passenger train.

The Growing Crisis

By the time of Robert R. Young's suicide, operating passenger trains was threatening the viability of even the healthiest railroads. Government transportation priorities clearly favored highways and airlines, and these modes had spawned a network of support industries with significant economic impact and therefore political influence. The same was true of the railroads—they generated business for various suppliers and services—but on a much smaller scale and with less impact and influence. The railroads still were somehow perceived as different, their passenger services less important to the national economy and thus less deserving, if at all, of public support. In addition, in the case of the airlines in particular, no one seemed to care that public money helped them make profits that did not go back into the public till.

By the mid-1960s the crisis facing commuter rail services in the Northeast Corridor (NEC)—especially in the New York City metropolitan region—had validated the concept of government support for those services that had come from the Whitman Commission. There had been only two options: government funding or no trains. The floundering PC and the very real prospect of cessation of all of the Corridor's many commuter routes had the salubrious effect of energizing the debate and the search for solutions—the beginning of the era of state and regional transportation authorities. Over time and to this day, in the NEC and in other parts of the country, these entities have built up, maintained, and continue to expand both commuter and regional rail services that have proven essential to the nation's economic and social well being. Several examples are discussed in appendix 1.

However, no such support was forthcoming for intercity train services. As time passed, service standards slipped on this dwindling fleet, sending even some loyal customers to other modes. The loss of passengers varied from railroad to railroad: some trains remained well patronized and maintained high standards, while others were reduced to a locomotive and an amenity-free coach perpetuated by ICC or state utility commission edict because of "public convenience and necessity." Few, however, covered their operating costs out of ticket revenues. Additional problems were the need to maintain and staff expensive and heavily taxed passenger depots to accommodate what passengers there were. And there was that annoying 10 percent federal ticket tax that—irony of ironies—was intended to discourage travel on overburdened World War II trains. It was not repealed until November 1962, implementing another recommendation by the Whitman Commission.

Overall the system was unraveling in a vicious downward spiral: as ridership declined, service declined further in the number of trains available, the routes served, and the amenities offered on board—all of which further discouraged ridership. By 1968, the railroads were capturing only a meager portion of the travel market, and gigantic passenger losses made their lives ever more difficult. With many other life-threatening issues facing them (loss of traffic to trucks, overbuilt networks, industrial decline of the Rust Belt, unprofitable short hauls) the passenger-carrying northeastern lines in particular became the poster children for the problem, with the hapless PC the largest child on that poster.

Pre–World War II problems of overregulation and heavy taxation continued at the same time the railroads were losing passenger traffic and were beset by rising labor costs, expensive benefits packages, and arcane work rules.[7] These were consuming more of each revenue dollar, especially on the passenger side of the business, and contributed to the railroads' arguments for eliminating trains. Petitioning the ICC for rate increases took time and often came too late to catch up with rising costs. There just was no way for railroads to make passenger service productive enough to reverse the deficit trend, and abolishing passenger trains seemed to be the only solution.

Some who worked on the passenger side in this period observed that several healthy railroads were willing to bear the costs of passenger train operation simply to remain in control and as long as the ICC would allow the discontinuance of trains that lost significant money. Some felt their trains had public relations value as potential investors in their stock and managers of many of their freight customers still used trains for business travel. These were valid reasons. The Santa Fe had earned much of its reputation by the superlative operation of its famed Chief and Super Chief, and the company's president, John Reed, was determined to sustain the high standards of those premier trains, some of which likely covered their above-the-rail costs. The Burlington (Burlington Northern after 1970), Union Pacific, and Seaboard Coast Line felt the same way, but for many others it was operating costs and the prospect of having to finance upgrading and, more likely, replacement of fast-aging car and locomotive fleets that became the critical issue and the incentive to find a way out.[8] Finally, the loss of Post Office mail contracts was decisive. The railroads saw no solution to their dilemma other than eliminating their trains altogether.

So the long-distance crisis was as real as it had been in the commuter services: losing the entire intercity passenger rail network was a distinct possibility. The ICC and state commissions were inundated with blizzards of train-off petitions, requests by railroads to discontinue specific trains. These involved protracted and sometimes repetitive hearings; not every petition was successful, but most were. From about 1965 on, railroad after railroad dropped passenger trains entirely or reduced frequencies to, at most, one or two trains a day on a given route. In some cases of intrastate trains, which sometimes had been previously interstate trains until cut back with ICC approval, state commissions also said no. But "no" was not a solution to the problem.

The answer really was simple, if controversial: if American railroads were required by regulation, or by Congressional preference, or by public demand to provide passenger trains, paying for them would have to come from some source other than the railroads. Assuming the country really needed and wanted passenger trains, nationalization of the whole rail system appeared to be the only remedy, but the country had looked at this before and had come away aghast. Despite pretty much every other rail-served nation in the world having gone that route, the USA was uncertain at best that it should too.

How Bad Was It?

It warrants mention here that, despite the fact that the American passenger train was in extremis in this period, travel by train was not always an exercise in misery. The general perception was that the railroad companies were so hostile to their trains that they did all they could to discourage travel by cutting services, eliminating amenities, ignoring rude crew behavior, allowing maintenance to lapse, and so on. Actual experiences, however (including those of the authors), proved that this was not typically the case, especially on a few railroads that really kept on trying. Trip notes from those years include notations about friendly crews, good and affordable food, comfortable rides,

"This is a hell of a way to run a railroad! You call that a dry Martini?"
Peter Arno, The New Yorker. Copyright Condé Nast. Used by permission.

and consistent on-time performance. The reality was that the people who ran the trains—the engineers, conductors, trainmen, dining and lounge personnel, as well as dispatchers, station agents, and tower operators—were professionals, typically of long experience, who had a job to do and intended to do it the best they could in the circumstances.

It certainly was true that passengers could encounter failed heating or air-conditioning, or a snack bar coach on a train that only recently had a full dining car. Sometimes crew members could be grumpy (they were human, after all, and facing either unemployment or reassignment to freight service). Undoubtedly

Dinner Aboard the Super Chief

CHICO RECOMMENDS...

Our Super Chief Champagne Dinner

SUPER CHIEF SPECIAL - $3.40
GENUINE CALF'S LIVER SAUTE WITH
BACON OR FRENCH FRIED ONION RINGS
Dinner Rolls
Dobosh Torte or Vanilla Ice Cream
Beverage

De Luxe Sandwich Dinners

$2.85
Consomme (Hot or Jellied)
OPEN FACED CHICKEN SALAD SANDWICH
ON TOAST
Sliced Tomato, Hard Boiled Egg and Capers
Apple Pie or Fruit Gelatin with Cream
Beverage

$3.60
Chicken Gumbo Soup
OPEN FACED HOT TENDERLOIN OF BEEF
SANDWICH ON TOAST
Onion and Tomato Slice - Dill Pickle
French Fried Potatoes
Dobosh Torte or Vanilla Ice Cream
Beverage

Salad Dinner

$2.65
A Combination of Crisp Lettuce, Romaine, Chicory,
Escarole, Wedges of Tomato, Julienne of Ham
and Cheese, Hard Boiled Egg, Choice of Lorenzo,
1000 Island or Garlic Dressing.
Plain or Cheese Rolls
Layer Cake or Apple Pie
Beverage

NOTE: When desired your steward will arrange special diet, or will quote a la carte prices for individual items listed on this menu.

Table d'Hote Dinner
Holders of "One Price Ticket" Please Present When Ordering

Pascal Celery   Queen Olives
Choice of Appetizer
*CHARCOAL BROILED SALMON STEAK,
ANCHOVY BUTTER 4.40
*OMELETTE WITH STEWED FRESH BLUEBERRIES,
CONFITURE 3.95
*SPRING CHICKEN SAUTE, MARENGO 4.80
LONDON MIXED GRILL 5.70
CHARCOAL BROILED SIRLOIN STEAK 6.95

Mashed Potatoes   Fresh String Beans with Almonds
Lyonnaise Potatoes   Cauliflower Polonaise
Chiffonade Salad
Dinner Rolls
Choice of Dessert and Beverage

CHILDREN'S MENU
(SERVED ONLY TO CHILDREN UNDER 12 YRS. OF AGE)

#1 - $1.50
Children's portion Selected from
Entrees Marked with Asterisk
Potatoes   Vegetable
Roll and Butter   Ice Cream
Hot Chocolate or Milk

#2 - $1.35
Cup of Soup
Peanut Butter and Jelly Sandwich
or
Hamburger on Toasted Bun
Potato Chips   Pickle
Melba Sundae
Hot Chocolate or Milk

WAITERS ARE INSTRUCTED NEITHER TO TAKE NOR TO SERVE ORDERS GIVEN ORALLY.
PLEASE PAY ONLY ON PRESENTATION OF MEAL CHECK ON WHICH YOU HAVE WRITTEN YOUR ORDER.

A la Carte Suggestions

Appetizers
Fresh Shrimp Cocktail 1.30
(On Table d'Hote Dinner - 50c. extra)
Queen Olives 45
Marinated Herring in Sour Cream 75
Pascal Celery 50
Chilled Tomato Juice 45
Chicken Gumbo Soup, Cup 45; Tureen 65
Consomme en Tasse, Hot or Jellied, Cup 45

Salads
Lettuce, Peach and Cottage Cheese,
Chatelaine Dressing 85
Combination 80
Lettuce with Roquefort Dressing 65
Chiffonade .70

Desserts
Vanilla Ice Cream 45; with Cookies 55
Chocolate or Wild Blackberry Sundae 60
Apple Pie 45
Fruit Gelatin with Cream 40
Choice of Melon 65
Blueberry Pie 50
Dobosh Torte 50
Layer Cake .35
Roquefort Cheese 50

Beverages
Coffee, Pot .40
Tea, Pot 40
Milk or Buttermilk 25
Demi Tasse .40
Sanka Coffee, Pot 40
Hot Chocolate, Pot 40

An extra charge of fifty cents will be made for
each meal served outside of Dining Car.
Prices shown on this menu are subject to various state,
occupation expense, school and sales taxes.

6-1-68 ♦ 3803

Chico invites you to enjoy a **"Wake-up Cup"**

Just tell us the time you want your morning coffee between 6:30 a.m. and 12 noon and we will bring a cup right to your door compliments of the Santa Fe Super Chief

Time I want my
"Wake-up cup"_____AM
(Train Time)
Number of cups wanted_____
Room_____ Car_____.

(Please fill in and hand to Dining Car Steward)

ABOVE The Santa Fe (Atchison, Topeka & Santa Fe Railway) used themes derived from Western Native American art and imagery to tie together its promotional publications, timetables, passenger car decor, dining service china, and, as seen here, dining car menus.

TOP Inside the menu was a broad array of dinner offerings for Super Chief passengers. Dated June 1, 1968, this was evidence of the Santa Fe's commitment to high service standards right up to the start of Amtrak.

LEFT This card was clipped inside the Super Chief's dinner menu. A small gesture, perhaps, but a little extra consideration shown to Santa Fe passengers—albeit with stereotyped imagery unlikely to be used today.

All, Jeffrey Darbee Collection

there were instances of efforts to drive passengers away,[9] but these were the exception, not the rule; problems such as failed heating or worn-out cars had more to do with budget realities than conspiracies to scare off patrons. On a few railroads, it was made clear by top management that every aspect of service quality was to be maintained to the end, and this directive was followed by railroad personnel. It is important that this be understood: quality of service had everything to do with the passenger experience in the early days of Amtrak, because, at least at first, the same people would be running and staffing the trains under the aegis of the new company. And in its early years, Amtrak was determined to maintain as many of these traditions and amenities as it could in striving toward its goal of attracting passengers.

Finding a Solution

During this time of angst, what about the passengers themselves? What about the people who still traveled on trains, saw them as necessary, but seemed largely to be left out of the discussion? In May of 1967, as the passenger dilemma was reaching its crescendo, the National Association of Railroad Passengers (NARP, still active today as the Rail Passengers Association [RPA]) came into being. Its founder, Anthony Haswell, is an attorney with railroad experience who remains a thorn in the side of antirail and rail-ignorant political figures. NARP/RPA was not then and is not today a group of rail enthusiasts nostalgic for a glorious past. It is serious, professional, and dedicated to achieving a balanced national transportation system that includes commuter, corridor, and long-distance passenger rail. The organization deserves significant credit for the fact that Amtrak has survived as long as it has and operates as well as it does.

Not to be overlooked, too, was the 1968 launch of *Passenger Train Journal* (which still publishes quarterly). Its founder, Kevin McKinney, was a student at Michigan State University at the time and would later play a role in establishing Amtrak's routes and several of the new trains added as the system expanded in its early years. His purpose in starting the magazine was to initiate "a dialogue on how to save the passenger train."[10] Other periodicals around the same time kept a close eye on both good and bad aspects of what was happening in the rail passenger world (*Railway Age* and *Modern Railroads* covered the topic; another was *Rail Travel News*, inexpensively produced, not at all slick, but full of information). *Trains* magazine, as noted, had been around since 1940 and was definitely pro-passenger. Few Americans spent any time thinking about passenger trains, but many others did think about them, and these people often had loud voices.

As a result, by the late 1960s there was significant pressure on Congress from NARP, the railroads, state and local politicians, private citizens, and others with a stake in the issue. This finally forced the government to address the intercity "passenger problem," ignored and unsolved for so many years. It

"I just never imagined they wouldn't finally come up with <u>some</u> form of government aid."
James Stevenson, The New Yorker. *Copyright Condé Nast. Used by permission.*

did not seem too much to ask of our political leaders: if commuter rail services were important and deserved government support, what about long-distance trains and corridors outside the Northeast? Were they not part of the national transportation network too?

When in March of 1969 PC management petitioned to "kill everything west of Buffalo and Harrisburg," it was a tipping point—PC was making its position clear and was prepared to act. In response, if quite belatedly, the ICC conducted a comprehensive cost survey on ten railroads to determine avoidable costs—the deficit that could be eliminated if passenger trains were gone. Results: C&O/B&O: $12 million a year; Atchison, Topeka & Santa Fe $22 million, and so on. It was seen as a lot, close to $300 million ($2,095,863,760 in 2020) altogether, with $63 million of it on PC alone.[11]

Regulators and the rest of the industry were stunned: push had come to shove. PC was on the threshold of bankruptcy, and the ICC—to that point, at least—had been a major roadblock when it came to discontinuing passenger trains, which was the only solution so far offered to the suffering railroads. And getting rid of all of them was not a realistic or palatable solution, anyway. Following the PC bankruptcy petition, John P. Fullam, the judge overseeing the case, along with Jervis Langdon Jr., the lead trustee of PC, forced the ICC's hand: if the ICC refused to allow the discontinuances before it, Fullam would ignore the ICC and shut down all PC passenger trains. The consequences were frightening. Not only essential service in the NEC would be gutted; too many other railroads' trains outside the Corridor connected with and depended on PC trains. Losing them would paralyze rail service in much of nation's northeast quadrant. As Bill Howes noted, "Then they started talking turkey."[12] The government had to act.[13]

What further worried legislators and others was that PC was not alone; even healthy railroads elsewhere in the country were enduring crippling passenger deficits. The Whitman Commission report had expressed as much, and things had only gotten worse in the intervening years.[14] It would require a radically different approach to transportation policy: something had to be done at the federal level—government had to overcome its reluctance to take any responsibility for the industry's dilemma. Like it or not, if the nation wanted trains, the government had to be involved and subsidies of some sort would have to be provided to the railroads.

Desperation Breeds Legislation

As PC was unraveling early in 1969, work on addressing the passenger problem finally got under way. We have seen why, contrary to logic, the railroad industry in some cases was willing to tolerate a certain level of deficits and keep running at least some passenger trains—advertising value, customer and employee convenience, and cash flow. Even more importantly, though, they sought to keep control of railroad operations and avoid the much-feared ogre of nationalization—of passenger services, at least—should railroad bankruptcies continue. In addition, there was a natural reluctance to walk away from the huge amounts of capital already invested in the railroads' passenger infrastructure. This included not only locomotives and cars but also a great deal of real estate, structures, and buildings. However, not losing so much money every year, they felt, could encourage needed investment.

Reacting to constituent complaints and sensing a transportation calamity, some members of Congress began to search for a way to keep passenger trains a fact of life while relieving the railroads of some or all of the associated costs. From early 1969 into the fall of 1970, there was a lot of sausage-making, complicated by a Nixon administration opposed to subsidies and not much interested in rail passenger services anyway. This roughly 18-month hashing of ideas—whether and how the government should subsidize passenger trains or find another way to keep them operating—only aggravated the problem, and train discontinuances proceeded apace.[15]

There were plenty of ideas: pay subsidies directly to the railroads to keep the trains running, create a government-owned passenger car pool, form a public corporation including the government and the rail industry. Players included the Association of American Railroads (AAR), the ICC, the US Senate, and the US Department of Transportation (DOT)—not to mention industry and other private advocates. Indiana Senator Vance Hartke, a strong promoter of passenger rail who had garnered both rail industry and AAR support, put forth a subsidy proposal, actual legislation, providing that if a railroad wanted to discontinue a train, and the ICC refused, the government would have to subsidize it. But the legislation stayed away from anything resembling government control. Some railroads avoided the idea of accepting subsidies until they thought about the need to replace their passenger equipment; this miraculously made subsidies more palatable.

The Hartke legislation might actually have become law had it not been for the election of Richard Nixon in November 1968. That changed everything. With Nixon's election, a new FRA head was appointed. This was Reginald Whitman, who assigned his deputy, James MacAnanny, formerly of the B&O, to work with FRA's Jim McClellan and John Robinson, an FRA lawyer, to examine options and draft legislation that would create a national passenger train operating entity.[16] Early in 1970, the DOT introduced a plan for Railpax, a public-private entity that would receive significant start-up funding. It took the Nixon administration all of one day to shoot down this idea. Because the administration was adamantly opposed to subsidies,[17] the draft proposal had to be modified to the point that the new corporation was to be perceived as a profit-making undertaking.[18]

Years later, McClellan recalled, "Most (including a number of us on the planning team) were dubious of the 'for profit' claim, but the reality was that neither the White House nor the more conservative members of Congress were going to sign off on an entity that was set up to be a perpetual ward of the state."[19] Profitability, while unrealistic, would prove to be acceptable to the White House—but both the impression and the expectation it left would haunt Amtrak for decades; even today, unknowing business and political types still think passenger trains should be profitable. "The first and still a big strike [against Amtrak] is that it was sold to the Nixon administration as a money-maker," says former Norfolk Southern chairman and Amtrak interim president Wick Moorman. "Conservatives' ire is raised with every mention of 'losses' and 'deficit' of Amtrak."[20]

At a White House meeting, "The arguments went back and forth with a lot of focus on the numbers, and I weighed in as appropriate," wrote McClellan. "When one key staffer cited a Stanford University study that showed that passenger trains lost a lot of money, I dismissed the results as biased because the study was funded by the anti-passenger Southern Pacific. The Stanford study was actually pretty good, but the goal was to win the argument, not to discover the truth."[21]

The solution, however, appeared to be a necessary evil; many believed that isolating the acute contagion of declining passenger patronage would achieve its primary goal of granting relief to the railroads.[22] As commentator Fritz Plous has observed, "This short-range defensive tactic worked: the federal government's assumption of passenger trains and their deficits gave the nation's privately owned freight railroads the oxygen they needed to survive for a decade until deregulation allowed the industry to sit up, breathe on its own, dangle its legs over the edge of the bed and start eating solids."[23] It would, however, take many months of Sturm und Drang to get there.

Throughout 1970, some members of Congress and most of the Nixon administration—even though faced with a true crisis in the railroad industry—displayed no interest, skill, or patience regarding creation of a national rail passenger entity. Supporters of the idea such as Senator Hartke and Transportation Secretary John Volpe faced fierce opposition from federal budgeteers and the White House. The result was various proposed solutions that received either no administration response or a flat rejection. The turning point came when much to the White House's surprise,[24] the Senate's Commerce Committee unilaterally approved a bill that would provide a $435 million ($2.8 billion in 2020) cash *loan* and also put the government into the passenger car purchase and repair business.

To the administration this would not do, but it was afraid the Senate committee's bill might actually pass both houses and end up on the president's desk. With a determined judge staring at them and with pressure coming from many other quarters, Nixon and congressional opponents both blinked, and the House and Senate came up with revised legislation, the Rail Passenger Service Act of 1970. It established the National Railroad Passenger Corporation,[25] a quasi-public entity funded by taxpayer dollars and charged with the duty to operate a nationwide intercity passenger service. Thus, Amtrak (a name adopted in 1971, proposed by marketing agency Lippincott & Margulies) was born thanks in large part to the by then bankrupt PC. As Jim McClellan observed, "Our overriding concern was to find a solution that removed the passenger burden from the back of the PC and the other freight railroads. The collapse of passenger railroading was acceptable; the collapse of freight railroading was not."[26] PC, a sterling example of "a hell of a way to run a railroad," ran 35 percent of the nation's passenger service and 64 percent of the Northeast's,[27] so the stakes were very high indeed. Nixon signed—three days before the midterm elections—and the bill became law on October 30, 1970.

Congress authorized $40 million ($257 million in 2020) to pay for Amtrak's start, far less than what had been proposed. As Rush Loving pointed out, this "provided only enough to incorporate and organize the company," while the White House refused to request any more.[28] Meanwhile, the railroads paid Amtrak $197 million ($1.3 billion in 2020) to take over their trains, money that quickly went back to many of them to pay crews and fees for operating over their tracks.[29] Writing about those payments in 2017, Jim McClellan noted, "In essence, the same government that had forced them through regulation to stay in the business was now going to make them pay to leave. When the Mafia does a shakedown like that, someone goes to jail."[30] Unfortunately, Amtrak was left without any working capital for maintenance and other expenses.[31] David

Gunn opined, "It was a classic Washington solution—solve one problem and create another."[32]

To be clear: as welcome as it was to supporters, Amtrak was the façade of what appeared to be a solution to a problem. While the railroads agreed they could not make money operating passenger trains, they also did not want somebody else's trains running on their tracks. The industry's preference was to keep operating its own trains and, as outlined in the Whitman Commission report, have governments that wanted those trains pay for them—and then leave them alone.[33] They did not get this, of course, but they certainly got something: Amtrak was created less to preserve rail passenger transportation and more to ensure the viability of freight railroads on a destructive path to bankruptcy due to passenger service losses. In addition, it meant that the railroads would be dealing with a single rather than the other possible option, a series of state and regional entities/authorities with varying goals and demands for passenger rail services.

Unfortunately, Amtrak was given leadership by a presidential administration whose intent seems to have been to undermine it and ensure failure. According to Bob VanderClute, Roger Lewis, the company's first president, "went around saying that Amtrak was experimental and after three years, if it wasn't profitable, it would simply shut down and go away," and Lewis did what he could to make sure that happened.[34] Few saw Amtrak as a testing ground for what could be done, and no strategic plan was developed.[35]

We Have to Have This Ready by *When*?

Passing a law and implementing it are two different things. Considering all that had to be done, as well as the roadblocks of political, legal, and logistical issues, it is nothing less than miraculous that Amtrak became operational and ran as well as it did on Day One and beyond. Its many midwives deserve huge credit for what they achieved in a very short time. In a sense, some of it was easy, at least for the host railroads' operating personnel: Amtrak trains would largely run on routes where railroaders were accustomed to operating passenger trains, so not much had changed in that regard. They knew how to get trains from point A to point B and how to take care of passengers. But to any strategic planner worth his salt, much of the effort to get to Day One, to make sure there were trains ready to run on May 1, 1971 must have looked like a dog's breakfast.

Complicating it all were "back of the house" matters such as setting up the corporation, acquiring legal and technical counsel, and cultivating relationships with the freight carriers to establish market-oriented schedules and negotiate contracts with both the railroads and labor. For the most part, the administrative structure of Amtrak had to be created from scratch. There was little guidance from the DOT about starting it up; Jim McClellan was on his own. The reason was that DOT was still young, ("chaotic" by one description), had suffered rapid turnover of leaders with personal agendas, and had a bevy of young hires, a few from the ICC but most from the Federal Aviation Administration and with little knowledge of railroads.[36] Time was running short; they had six months to sort it out.

Creating a Route Structure

As difficult as it was just to get legislation in place, the work of creating a whole new passenger carrier was just beginning. There was considerable argument between and within both Congress and the Nixon administration over where the new company's trains would actually go. Secretary of Transportation John Volpe was tasked with designating the endpoints of the system—destinations such as Boston, New York, Washington DC, Florida points, Chicago, Kansas City, Houston, Seattle, San Francisco, Los Angeles, and so on. Actual routing of trains between these points was up to Amtrak planners. The idea, at least, was to choose routes with the strongest chance of attracting and keeping passengers.

Jim McClellan was still with the FRA and was involved in initial route planning at Amtrak. Reputedly, he sat at a bar one day and sketched out the basic route structure on a napkin. Imagine his surprise when publisher Kevin McKinney ran a map in an issue of *Passenger Train Journal.* He had come up with this on his own, but it matched almost perfectly the system McClellan was developing but was not ready to publicize. Certain that McKinney had somehow learned this closely held information, McClellan called McKinney, talked it over, and by the time of McKinney's graduation from MSU he had the offer of a job at FRA and later moved to Amtrak.[37]

On November 30, 1970, a month after Nixon signed the Railpax/Amtrak bill, Volpe announced the proposed route network. At first it was pretty skeletal, especially compared to what was running on American rails at that time. Amtrak's initial routes were to be New York to Boston, Washington, DC, Buffalo, Chicago, Miami, and New Orleans; Washington to St. Louis; and Chicago to Detroit, Cincinnati, St. Louis, Miami, New Orleans, Houston, Seattle, San Francisco, and Los Angeles. Under pressure, Volpe two months later added New Orleans–Los Angeles, Seattle–San Diego, New York–Kansas City, Washington–Chicago, and Norfolk/Newport News Cincinnati. After another two months, final routings were announced—how the trains would get between the cities they were to serve.

There also was the matter—a big one—of the equipment that would make up the trains on the selected routes. Obviously the passenger-carrying railroads would provide them. Between January and May 1971, a number of two-person teams roamed the nation's coach yards and engine terminals, selecting almost 300 locomotives and 1,200 passenger cars that looked as though they could do the job without failing too soon. These teams were consultants but all had relevant experience.[38] The mechanical department also had to figure out what shops to use for locomotive and car maintenance once the contractual arrangements with the individual railroads ended. The best in the country were Topeka and Emerson (Rocky Mount, North Carolina), with some capabilities on Burlington Northern and elsewhere, including Hamburg Industries' shop near Augusta, Georgia, which had contracted with the Seaboard Coast Line to operate and repair its extensive sleeper operation following the demise of the Pullman Company. The most important negotiations, though, were between the railroads that owned the equipment and the consultant teams helping Amtrak acquire the equipment it needed.[39]

Not every passenger-carrying railroad chose to join Amtrak; participation was not mandatory, but those choosing not to join had to keep running existing trains. The Denver & Rio Grande Western, the Southern, the Chicago, Rock Island & Pacific, and the Georgia Railroad chose not to become Amtrak participants. The Rio Grande's Denver–Ogden route was later taken over by Amtrak as part of the Chicago–San Francisco service. The Southern Railway's Southern Crescent between Washington, DC and New Orleans continued to run and was later taken over as an Amtrak train (the Southern had some other trains that were dropped at that time). The Rock Island had trains from Chicago to Peoria and Rock Island, Illinois, that eventually stopped running as the railroad plummeted into bankruptcy and dismemberment. The Georgia Railroad ran a single mixed passenger/freight train between Atlanta and Augusta, as well as similar service on three branch lines, all of which were eventually discontinued.

The nonjoiners' motivation seemed mostly due to reluctance to submit to Amtrak decisions and/or pride in their passenger services as well as the cost of maintaining a skeletal service compared to the cost of joining Amtrak.[40] The Rock Island could not afford to buy Amtrak stock, the mechanism by which a railroad "joined," and had discussions for state subsidy of its services. The Chicago, South Shore & South Bend, which ran electrified trains between Chicago and South Bend, Indiana, was among ten determined to be commuter railroads or ones that had some commuter operations. They were exempt from having to join Amtrak (despite several having routes in the 75- to 125-mile range) but also were not allowed to discontinue trains (the South Shore continues today as a well-upgraded and busy commuter route and is considered the nation's last electric interurban). In all, 20 railroads joined Amtrak.

As the May 1 start-up day approached, not everyone—including supporters—was happy, and well into April there were various federal lawsuits and Congressional moves. Some in Congress wanted a delay, apparently to have time for further planning (or perhaps to defend favorite but threatened trains); unions wanted the status quo of working rules and were unhappy with proposed compensation to members who would lose their jobs; NARP wanted time to unlock more funding from Congress and add more routes. In the event, a federal judge and then a federal appeals court ruled against the various suits on April 30, clearing the way for Day One the next day.

May 1, 1971

With the last barrier to Amtrak's start-up gone, American rail travel entered a new era both filled with promise and fraught with peril: promise because, at long last, the federal government appeared to have accepted its responsibility for supporting the country's passenger rail system; peril because, in order to get political support, the company had to turn a profit. Seasoned transportation people knew this was absurd. Passenger trains had not been profitable for decades, so why would they suddenly become profitable now? Here was the demon that has bedeviled Amtrak all its life.

On Day One, however, promise prevailed. After all, passenger trains were still running, just under a new company that wanted to operate them; and although Amtrak had established a modest initial network, the company could expand its routes if states came through with funding. So what was it like to be aboard a passenger train in the early Amtrak years? It operated about a third of the trains the railroads were running by 1970 on the tracks of 13 carriers, and those trains often had the same locomotives, cars, crews, even much the same schedules

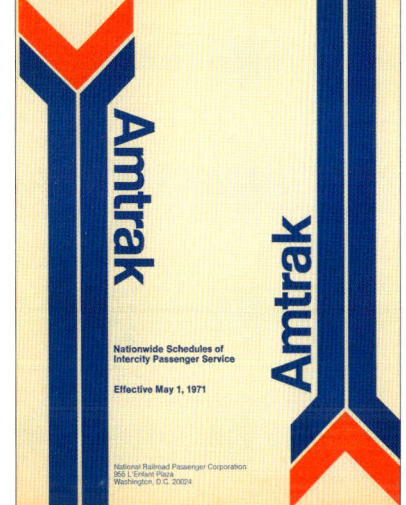

RIGHT Amtrak's first system timetable could not have been simpler and featured the company's original "pointless arrow" logo in red and blue ink on ivory-colored paper.

BELOW Amtrak's initial route structure focused on the services deemed most likely to have the strongest customer base between the government-mandated endpoints.

Both, Eugene Harmon Collection

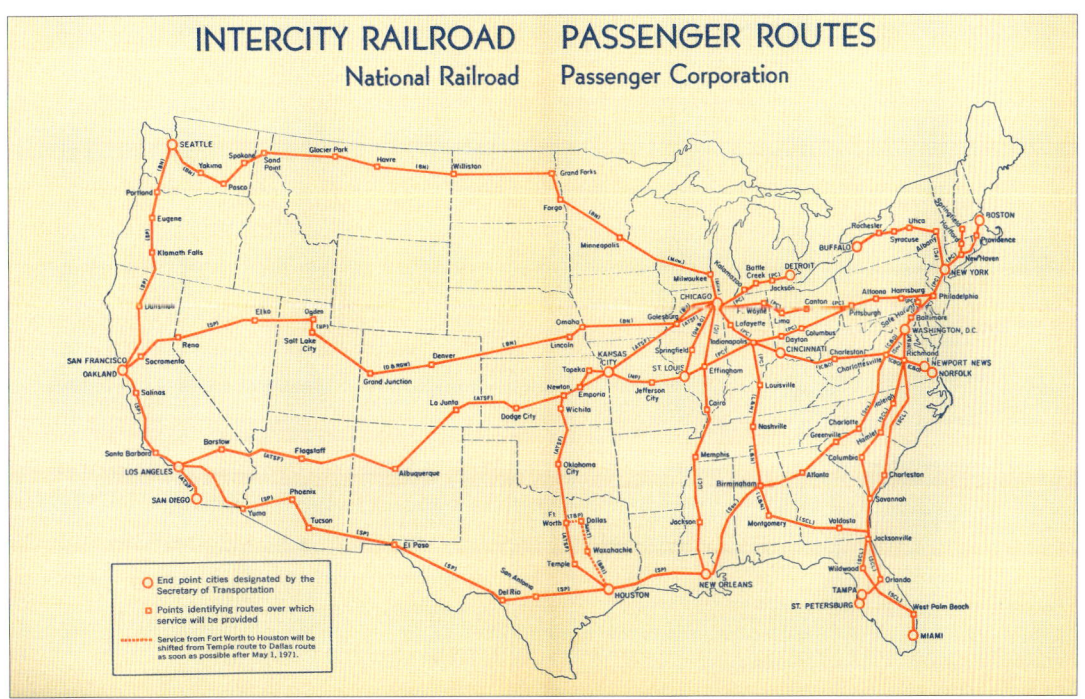

NATIONAL RAILROAD PASSENGER CORPORATION

955 L'ENFANT PLAZA NORTH, S.W. • ROOM 8060 • WASHINGTON, D.C. 20024 • Tel (202) 554-5700

DIRECTORS:
DAVID W. KENDALL, Chairman
FRANK S. BESSON, JR., Vice Chairman
CATHERINE MAY BEDELL
DAVID E. BRADSHAW
JOHN J. GILHOOLEY
ARTHUR D. LEWIS
CHARLES LUNA
JOHN P. OLSSON

Dear American Traveler:

This publication is the first systemwide schedule of intercity passenger trains to be operated by the National Railroad Passenger Corporation. The trains, services and stations listed herein comprise what the Directors of Amtrak believe is a large step toward an integrated national system of rail passenger service.

We feel that this network of trains -- which has been developed through months of intensive analysis -- provides a solid base upon which to build and expand the scope and quality of intercity passenger service. This new system can and will succeed because it unifies for the first time the operation and promotion of the nation's rail passenger service. Now, a single management can devote its energy exclusively to serving the passenger. Refurbishing of terminals and equipment and innovative improvements of ticketing, reservation, and food services can be attained on a systemwide basis.

We know these changes which are vital to upgrading rail service cannot be accomplished overnight. We are optimistic, however, that continuing improvements will attract hundreds of thousands of people who have not recently -- or ever -- relied on railroad transportation. We think the Amtrak system will become increasingly attractive to those who travel for business and pleasure, young people and older people, families and travel groups.

The Board of Directors of Amtrak asks the support of the traveling public as this schedule is introduced and service improvements are implemented. We ask also the enthusiastic response of every rail passenger employee who shares with us the task of providing the best in intercity travel service to our riders. On our part, we pledge our best efforts to providing the American people a modern, attractive rail service as rapidly as possible.

Sincerely,

David W. Kendall
Chairman of the Board

Expressing great hope for the future, Amtrak's first board chairman welcomed passengers with this letter in the company's first timetable.
Eugene Harmon Collection

as before. This could not, however, be static, just a continuation of what had existed: Amtrak's job, at least to those who believed in it, was to revitalize the passenger train and attract passengers. It was restructuring the national passenger rail system, moving beyond what it had been. "Restructuring" in later years became Orwellian code, usually used by media and political opponents, for cutting funding, reducing routes, canceling trains, and degrading onboard services. In the early years, however, restructuring meant adding new routes, increasing the number of trains on a route, improving onboard services and amenities. It was a period of optimism that Amtrak was the last best hope for the passenger train and could give it a new place in the nation's passenger transport infrastructure.

The Seventies (Lewis, Reistrup, and Boyd Administrations)

With state support under Section 403(b) of the 1970 law, within a few days of May 1 Amtrak began "added" services: first the Lake Shore (Lake Shore Limited today), New York City–Chicago; then the "Inland Route" Boston–New York City via Springfield, Massachusetts; and the Illinois Zephyr Chicago–Quincy, Illinois. "Experimental" services included the North Coast Hiawatha triweekly Chicago–Seattle via Butte, Montana, and the West Virginian Washington, DC–Parkersburg, West Virginia, dubbed "Harley's Hornet" for Harley Staggers, the West Virginia congressman who got it started. All were in a spirit of trying new things to attract passengers. If some people—with a wink and a nod—saw Amtrak as a short-term phenomenon, the people making it work did not. As Kevin McKinney said in a 2011 interview, "Eventually, we thought, we would look back at this moment and say as painful as it was [to lose so many trains that were running pre-Amtrak], it was a new beginning for rail passenger service in America."[41]

There were problems aplenty. "Rainbow Era" cars in the various railroads' colors typically had steam heat, steam ejector air-conditioning, deferred maintenance, and incompatible electrical systems. Paul Reistrup recalled, "The cars didn't like each other." Bad track on some host railroads, PC in particular, reduced train speeds. Possibly exaggerating, Reistrup said, "I was afraid to walk on the track, never mind ride on it."[42] This would not be fixed until the early 1980s, after Conrail took over PC and other northeastern bankrupts and mounted major track rehabilitation. Despite problems, however, people were traveling by train, and Amtrak even resurrected some past services. These would disappear with new equipment, but for a time many trains offered parlor cars with individual seats, some with food and beverage service (similar to business class today); observation cars at the rear end, often with lounge service; or a unique experience such as the "Turquoise Room" on the former Santa Fe route Chicago–Los Angeles: private dining with a dedicated waiter. Unfortunately, such niceties were not well promoted, and few in the company were even aware of them.[43]

Indeed, good marketing proved essential. The railroads had done it well in the postwar period but, with few exceptions, reduced their efforts as ridership declined in the 1960s. Amtrak knew it needed effective marketing and,

The first Amtrak system timetable included a guide to the various routes and the railroads operating Amtrak's trains.

Eugene Harmon Collection

ironically, turned to the airlines, which were admired for their marketing skills. The company hired Hal Graham, head of marketing at Pan American Airways, who brought others from American, Trans World, Aer Lingus, and British Airways to work on sales, onboard services, and reservations.[44] He aggressively courted tour companies and travel groups[45] and produced growth of about 15 percent a year.[46] Some of this resulted from catchy slogans—"Making the Trains Worth Traveling Again," "America's Getting into Training," "You Take Our Trains; We Take Your Credit Cards." Some came from attractive pricing: a $9.90 fare ($63.61 in 2020) between New York City and Boston brought a surge of customers.[47]

Jim McClellan, though, worried that a hearty response would place the company in an awkward position.[48] The marketing people assumed the company's equipment was equal to the task, but it was not, due to a shortage of serviceable cars. Bruce Heard said, "We were selling space on cars but we never knew if there would be equipment to provide the space."[49]

Maintenance suffered. Roger Lewis not only avoided asking Capitol Hill for money; when Congress wanted to fund Amtrak more generously in its second year, Lewis said he had more than he needed and refused the increase.[50] Under normal conditions, equipment was on a four-year maintenance cycle, but under Lewis cars were unpredictably held up for repairs.[51] There was no established maintenance cycle, and renovation was slow in coming due to reticence by Amtrak mechanical management still getting used to the fleet.[52]

This inadvertently fit well into the Nixon plan to allow Amtrak to fail.[53] A secret memo between advisors H. R. Haldeman and John Ehrlichman outlined a scheme that only breakdowns were to be repaired.[54] At one point, "approximately 1,000 cars out of Amtrak's 1,600 were waiting for heavy maintenance, and that year [1973] only about 650 of them would receive it."[55] Lewis spent what money he had on redecorating car interiors in garish colors typical of the 1970s while the toilets and air conditioning failed.[56] Locomotive breakdowns caused delays, and malfunctioning cars brought complaints. A reputation was in the making, and it was not good.

The 1973 energy crisis brought on by oil-rich Middle Eastern countries in response to the Yom Kippur War pushed Amtrak to act. People returned to trains in greater numbers, forcing the company to send teams to rail yards for coaches and sleepers bypassed during initial fleet selection.[57] Truly, the crisis saved Amtrak,[58] but team member Bob VanderClute said that shop crews were in such a hurry that many cars were renumbered and had red, white, and blue adhesive window striping applied on only one side before being rushed back into service. When they returned to the 8th Street Yard in Los Angeles for maintenance, the other side was done to match. "This must have caused some confusion for the yardmasters because [until then] the cars had two numbers!"[59]

Rising ridership was heartening, but improving service was critical and sometimes took a wrong direction. Trying to appear hip and progressive, management took steps that had little value. Bill Howes remembered, it was

Amtrak's first new locomotives were delivered in 1973. Built by the Electro-Motive Division of General Motors, the SDP40F incorporated a steam generator to heat Amtrak's inherited passenger cars. These locomotives fell from favor after a series of derailments and were replaced by the smaller but equally powerful F40PH. *George H. Drury*

"obsessed with uniforms. It became a fashion show."[60] Less than helpful too was the red, white, and blue Amtrak logo, an arrow minus an arrowhead. Given the company's always uncertain future, this "pointless arrow" sent the wrong message. It is long gone, but its negative image persisted. On the plus side, Amtrak benefited from its national reservation system, national timetable (unfortunately abandoned in 2016), a stable and uniform rate structure, and coordinated national marketing—things the railroads never were able to achieve.

Another upside was diversity in railroad employment. Historically, with the exception of clerical forces, railroad employment was male dominated, structured by class and race in a command and control environment. In general, crew and service personnel such as conductors, brakemen, trainmen, locomotive engineers, and dining car stewards were Caucasian while dining car cooks and waiters were African American. Some dining and lounge personnel were of Asian heritage. Women served as hostesses or stewardess/nurses on some trains. Pullman porters were largely African American. With the advent of Amtrak, as veterans of Pullman and other railroad services retired, the path was opened for both men and women of different races and ethnicities to come aboard and advance their careers on the trains and elsewhere.

To the marketing department, service improvement required contrasting rail travel and its competitors. Traveler comfort mattered, and passenger trains had enjoyed a good reputation, however tarnished it was on some railroads in the run-up to Amtrak. Meeting expectations of passengers and keeping faith with marketing promises posed a real challenge, between dealing with variable comfort levels of the heritage equipment and at the same time trying to bring maintenance costs under control. Cuts driven by inadequate federal funding detracted from the overall passenger experience. Those cuts unfortunately meant downgrading some of the well-appointed and artfully designed interiors of cars that made pre-Amtrak trains so attractive. Dining service also suffered cuts in quality.[61] Dinner in the diner had always been an attraction for passengers, but Amtrak had to streamline and standardize menu options and in 1972 held a massive sale of its inherited china and silverware. It purchased new china, but dining car china authority Chuck Kratz opines that it was not clear whether "Amtrak's blue pattern represented anything in particular. The original blue china was utilitarian just like a plain white plate could be. Blandness may very well be the identity

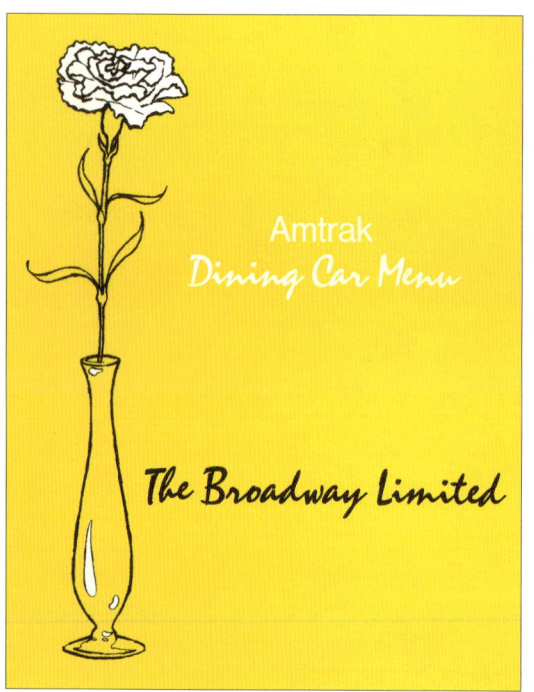

Three years after the refurbished Broadway Limited was introduced, Amtrak was still offering high-quality service. This breakfast menu, printed for this one train, is dated September 1975. The Broadway's breakfast offerings were quite generous. In this period, the "Special Golden Brown French Toast" was a favorite of regular passengers.

Both, Jeffrey Darbee Collection

At the time of the refurbished Broadway Limited's unveiling in 1972, Amtrak had introduced new employee uniforms but was still using dining car china acquired from its member railroads. The table setting in this Amtrak publicity photo is Santa Fe's celebrated Mimbreño pattern, with designs inspired by Southwestern Native American imagery.

Amtrak; George H. Drury Collection

direction because plain blue china could appease bean-counting bureaucrats who are a design audience when government subsidies are at issue."[62]

Now marketing efforts were even more important, and managers and staff had broad authority from the board to focus on the mission: *attract passengers*.[63] So on Amtrak's first birthday it rolled out a refurbished Broadway Limited New York City/Washington–Chicago. It had heavy patronage and typically ran with 12 to 14 cars, boasting full dining service and offering traditional and Slumbercoach sleepers and a square-end observation car. Soon the company's first international train, the Pacific International, started running between Seattle and Vancouver, B.C. Other pluses included new electric locomotives to replace the Pennsylvania Railroad GG1s of the 1930s and 1940s; an initial order for 57 Budd Company Amfleet cars (based on the Metroliner car body), followed by 435 more; acquisition of the former NYC Beech Grove, Indiana, car shops; an order for the first bilevel Superliner cars from Pullman-Standard; and orders for 25 diesel locomotives from General Electric and 30 F40PH General Motors locomotives, which would prove to be among the best Amtrak ever had. That new power replaced the derailment-prone SDP40F units ordered in 1972.

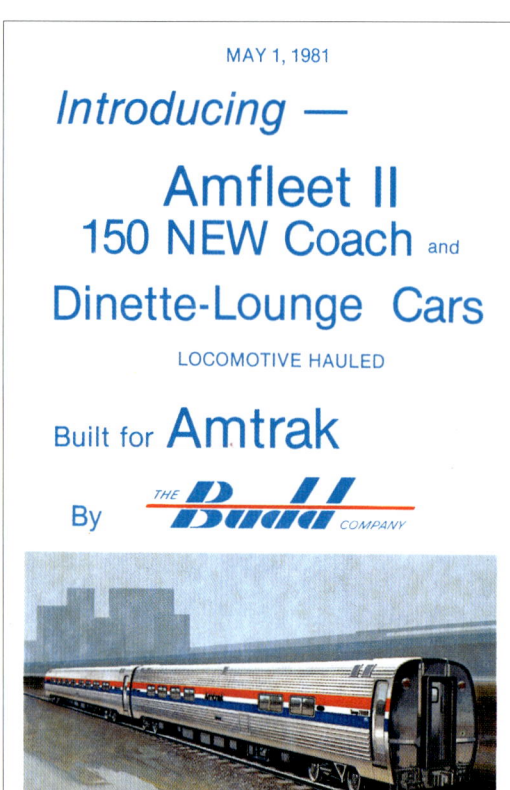

Deliveries of Amtrak's original Amfleet cars began in 1975, followed by Amfleet II cars in the early 1980s. The locomotive-hauled Amfleet cars were derived from the Metroliner design. *Kevin J. Holland Collection*

In its stations Amtrak faced the same problem the passenger railroads had—costly facilities too large for the traffic. Late in 1972 its first new station opened in Cincinnati. This and many that followed replaced some grand architectural gems—in this case Cincinnati Union Terminal—but doing so was essential. Most of the replacements were strictly utilitarian one-story buildings of not very inspiring design. Some other stops received boxy glass enclosures quickly dubbed "Amshacks." (Amtrak later returned to Cincinnati Union Terminal in the summer of 1991, using a small portion of what had become the Cincinnati Museum Center.)

Other new trains during the 1970s included the Inter-American Fort Worth–Laredo, Texas (later extended to St. Louis); the Illini Chicago–Champaign, Illinois; the Black Hawk Chicago–Dubuque, Iowa; the San Joaquin Oakland–Bakersfield, California; the Adirondack New York City–Montreal, P.Q.; the Blue Water Chicago–Port Huron, Michigan; the Mountaineer Norfolk, Virginia–Chicago; and the Arrowhead Minneapolis–Duluth/Superior, Minnesota. Not all would survive; some still run today as state-supported trains (see appendix 1). One of Amtrak's biggest steps was the April 1976 acquisition of the entire NEC as Conrail started up; now the company had its own railroad to run. The Corridor had about a billion dollars' worth of deferred maintenance, but at least Amtrak could call all the shots, subject, of course, to the whims of presidents, governors, and legislators who often did not quite understand the complexity of operating passenger trains.

Case in point: September 1979 brought major "restructuring" after an evaluation by Congress and USDOT that looked at ridership and revenues. Six trains were discontinued, leaving, for example, the New York–Pittsburgh–Indianapolis–Kansas City route and the North Coast Hiawatha route, among others, without rail service. This retrenchment was known as both the "Amtrak Bloodbath" and the "Carter Cutbacks." It was not just Republicans who had their knives out.

There were several other developments on the bright side: USDOT issued a favorable report on emerging corridors that could have higher speeds and more service frequencies than the longer once-daily routes. Based on the success of the Amfleet cars, Amtrak ordered 150 Amfleet II cars; the NEC fleet of the sturdy and reliable AEM7 electric locomotive reached 55 units; and the 1970s closed with the Pennsylvanian beginning New York City–Pittsburgh service.

On the electrified Northeast Corridor in the mid 1970s, bidirectional E60C locomotives from General Electric gave a fresh face to Amtrak trains previously hauled by former Pennsylvania Railroad GG1 locomotives dating to the 1930s and 1940s. *George H. Drury*

Closure of the grand Buffalo Central Terminal in favor of a modest station in Depew, New York, was unfortunate but necessary, with the new station located near the city's airport but far from the downtown area. BWI Airport station on the NEC also opened in this period, enabling air passengers to connect easily to many rail-served stations. In November 1980, the transcontinental sleeper that had run from the East Coast to the West Coast via New Orleans was dropped.

The close of Amtrak's first decade found the company with a blend of successes, failures, and ongoing challenges but also with continuing—if almost always inadequate—federal funding. Indeed, this would remain true all through the decades to come. As author Frank Wilner observed, "Congress has rejected all efforts to kill off Amtrak. But Congress has provided Amtrak mostly with a subsistence diet while those same lawmakers frequently demand of Amtrak world-class service and an Amtrak route through their states and districts."[64] This has been an ongoing struggle for Amtrak's leadership.

The Eighties (Boyd and Claytor Administrations)

In this decade, Amtrak was still headed by railroaders and a management staff who understood passenger trains and services. Consequently, most of the themes/trends of the seventies continued into the eighties: a solid intention to give the passenger train a future, new services to places that wanted them, efforts at making rail travel a unique and memorable experience, and trying to find the right quality level in food and beverage services. But there also were

Amtrak's first Superliners were delivered by Pullman-Standard in 1978. Their two-level design was inspired by Santa Fe's Hi-Level fleet, built by Budd in the mid-1950s. *George H. Drury Collection*

issues such as reroutings due to bad track, service reductions when experiments did not work out well, and, as always, funding issues.

There was much to celebrate. The Superliners, which served mainly Western trains but showed up in the East as well, hit full strength with delivery of the last car in July 1981. In addition, by March 1982, Amtrak's entire car fleet was all-electric, fed by head-end power (HEP) from locomotives or overhead wires in the NEC. The Silver Star on the Florida route was the last train to run with steam-heated equipment. Unfortunately, the change to HEP also enabled diner crews to microwave meals rather than continuing to use traditional stoves and ranges. It was a small step in the scheme of things but a sign of ongoing uncertainty over food and beverage services—and their cost—that persists to this day.

A prototype for what would become the Viewliners—single-level sleepers and diners with more generous ceiling heights than in the Amfleet cars—went into testing in July 1985; the first Viewliner arrived in September 1987. The boxy Horizon cars for corridor service and shorter routes, 104 in all, were first ordered in June 1988. General Electric received an order for 52 locomotives for NEC service. In January 1983, Amtrak made its first direct hires of crews; contracting with the railroads was gradually phased out. Early that same year the company began offering package express service, an echo—but still revenue-producing—of what once had been a huge nationwide business for the railroads.

All through the eighties there were additions to and extensions of train service to cities such as Detroit, Peoria, Indianapolis, Atlantic City, and Philadelphia's airport; revival of seasonal service to Cape Cod; and additional service Birmingham–Mobile, Alabama, and Chicago–Milwaukee. The San Joaquin service in California received a third round-trip, and the California Zephyr was permanently rerouted on the Rio Grande Railroad's scenic Denver–Salt Lake City line, today still a major attraction for passengers. In late 1983, Amtrak revived the Auto Train, which remains highly popular. The Carolinian began service in October 1984 and was discontinued in September 1985, and then was returned permanently in 1990. January 1989 saw a special celebration of the 20th anniversary of the Metroliner.

Station improvements continued apace as well. In June 1986, a new facility in Providence, Rhode Island, opened (the historic station has been preserved in a new use). In January 1988, Amtrak unfortunately (but again necessarily) moved out of the former Michigan Central station in Detroit, but at this writing it is marked for renovation by the Ford Motor Company. In September 1988, a fully restored Washington, DC, Union Station reopened. Other improvements during the eighties included real china, glassware, and flatware (described as "enhanced dining" in the timetable) on the Empire Builder and Southwest Chief; and the Air-Rail Travel Plan in cooperation with United Airlines, offering joint ticketing to travel one way by air and the other by rail.

However, political and budget/financial realities began to intrude in a major way. Early on, Amtrak was a mere rounding error in the federal budget (many today would argue that it remains so, or is even less than that), but its increasing funding needs due to inflation, catching up on deferred maintenance, service expansions, and the cost of new equipment brought more scrutiny. Budget constraints forced discontinuance of some trains at the end of September 1981; service to Duluth, Minnesota, ended in April 1985; and other discontinuances came in January 1986.

Even after Amtrak bowed to these realities, it still faced an existential threat born of the persistent fantasy that passenger trains somehow were not really transportation, something the airline and highway systems never had to face. Most troubling was the nonsensical idea—still circulating today—that Amtrak should be privatized, manifested in an on-again, off-again privatization movement. Frank Wilner wrote that this was "a regular feature in President Reagan's budget proposals during the 1980s. In 1987, Reagan proposed selling the NEC to the highest bidder, separating it from Amtrak's national intercity rail passenger network."[65] If this sounds familiar, it is because the same idea has been trotted out regularly over the decades and is enjoying currency as this is written. There is in fact some thinking that a stand-alone NEC could be self-sustaining but only in covering its above-the-rail costs. Public ownership (and responsibility for maintenance and capital costs) of the physical plant (track, roadbed, power supply, stations, and so on) would be necessary, and it is doubtful whether politicians and the federal government are ready for that.

Introduced in 1976, the F40PH was the workhorse of Amtrak's diesel locomotive fleet for almost two decades. *George H. Drury*

As for the rest of the network, the idea in 1987 was to farm out long-distance and other routes to private operators who would, it was assumed, flock to compete for such an opportunity. Those proposing this apparently had forgotten that "a failing privatized passenger rail network was the reason Amtrak was created in the first place,"[66] or, possibly, knew it was a plan for failure that would justify ending all but NEC services.

There was even a Commission on Privatization, established in 1988, that made a similar recommendation—essentially to keep the NEC and forget all the rest.[67] This of course showed disregard for the various states that by then had done extensive work to establish and support passenger rail corridors and had formed essential connections with various Amtrak services. The idea has gone nowhere so far, but it could resurface again.

The Nineties (Claytor, Downs, and Warrington Administrations)

Through most of the nineties, Amtrak had the benefit of railroaders of broad experience still leading the company, bringing to it a deep understanding of the realities of making passenger trains work. They understood the freight business as well, an important matter because Amtrak had to have an amicable and sustainable relationship with its freight-only host railroads. Thomas Downs, the company's fifth president, succeeded W. Graham Claytor in December

1993 (Claytor would pass away the following May at age 82) to continue the series of railroad-experienced chief executives that followed the company's first president, nonrailroader Roger Lewis. Downs left in December 1997, and George Warrington, head of Amtrak's NEC Business Unit, moved up to the top job. He had railroad experience in commuter rail as well but not in intercity services, a much different operation.

In an atmosphere of still striving to get all its many parts working smoothly and consistently, Amtrak celebrated its 20th anniversary on May 1, 1991. During the company's third decade, acquisition of new locomotives and cars continued, along with service improvements. Locomotive orders included 20 units from General Electric in November 1991 and introduction of the GE Genesis model in mid-1993—still the mainstay of much of the locomotive fleet. Car orders were even more significant. An order for 50 Viewliner sleeping cars went out in December 1992, and the company ordered 140 Superliner II long-distance bilevel cars early in 1991. Delivery began in August 1993, and an order for 55 more followed that December.

Amtrak experimented beginning in 1993 with European trainsets—the Swedish X2000 and the German ICE (intercity express) in the NEC as the company contemplated reequipping the Corridor services. Spanish-built Talgo equipment began a six-month demonstration service in April 1994 between Portland, Oregon, and Seattle. The Talgo did go into regular service, but the other foreign-built equipment did not—though it did provide data and experience useful in developing high-speed equipment.

In one of its most significant initiatives, Amtrak introduced Acela (a blend of "acceleration" and "excellence") in the NEC in December 2000.[68] This turned out to be premature, and technical problems resulted in service suspensions and bad press, but as with all such issues, they were eventually worked out. Track

Beginning in 1993, General Electric's Genesis models replaced the F40PH in Amtrak's diesel locomotive fleet.   *Kevin J. Holland*

conditions have not permitted the highest speeds of which Acela is capable, but by any measure it has been a success anyway. At the end of January 2000, the new electrified territory between New Haven, Connecticut, and Boston was complete, making diesel power almost entirely unnecessary in the NEC. Amtrak introduced initial Acela service of two daily round-trips, but it has grown to become the Corridor's hallmark. Corridor ridership would quickly surge by 45 percent and revenues by 77 percent.

May 1993 saw the first (partial) smoking ban on Amtrak trains; today the company remains entirely smoke-free, with crews announcing stops where passengers can detrain and have time to light up.

New or expanded services in the nineties included a weekend-only sleeping car on the Niagara Rainbow New York City–Toronto, the first new sleeper service of the Amtrak era between those cities. The state of California did its part too. Its Capitol Corridor, service began at the end of 1991, and shortly after that the state ordered 88 bilevel California Cars, for both Amtrak and commuter services. The Pioneer, a Chicago–Seattle train, had been running as part of the California Zephyr, from which it split at Salt Lake City. In mid-June 1991, the Pioneer switched to a new route through Wyoming (which had no rail service) after splitting from the Zephyr at Denver; the train was discontinued in 1997. In April 1994, the triweekly Sunset Limited, which had been operating New Orleans–Los Angeles, was extended to Miami, creating a single-train transcontinental route. It was cut back to Orlando in 1996 and to New Orleans in 2005 after Hurricane Katrina. The Kentucky Cardinal began running in December 1999 between Chicago and Jeffersonville, Indiana, on an overnight schedule offering sleeper service; it was later extended to Louisville, Kentucky. The train made its last run in July 2006.

On April 6, 1991, Amtrak left the historic Grand Central Terminal in New York City and consolidated all its intercity services at the widely unloved Penn Station, a 1960s concoction that had replaced the magnificent 1910 station; but the move there made sense since it stood astride the tracks of the NEC and several intercity routes. A track connection on the west side of Manhattan enabled access to the former NYC route to Albany and points west that had been served from Grand Central. That restored landmark still thrives as a commuter rail terminal.

In June 1993, Philadelphia's Thirtieth Street Station, a 60-year-old former Pennsylvania Railroad (PRR) facility, reopened with appropriate ceremony after a thorough renovation. Serving both NEC and intercity trains as well as regional and commuter services, Thirtieth Street became a modern transportation center while preserving all its historic design character as well as markers of its PRR heritage. Sharp-eyed viewers will recognize it as the setting of some television commercials (so too for Los Angeles Union Station, which advertisers seem to love).

The nineties also saw a number of discontinuances due to financial issues—the monkey that seemed always to be on the company's back, especially at federal budget time. It got out of the commuter business, which it probably should not have been doing anyway, when the last Calumet ran from Chicago to Valparaiso, Indiana. Other losses and reductions were more significant: the end of Atlantic City service from Philadelphia in October 1991; re-routing of the Cardinal in the summer of 1993, resulting in slower timing between Chicago and Indianapolis; and in April 1995 the Vermonter, a daytime train Washington, DC-St. Albans, Vermont, replaced the overnight Montrealer, ending service to the Canadian city via that route.

In October 1993 the Texas Eagle south of St. Louis, the Pioneer west of Denver, and the Desert Wind went to tri-weekly schedules, and the Empire Builder was cut to four times a week. December 1994 found Amtrak facing a $193 million ($339 million in 2020) revenue shortfall, resulting in a plan to cut 21 percent of its service starting in February 1995; and 212 employees at the Beech Grove shops in Indianapolis lost their jobs. 1995 indeed proved to be disastrous, with service cuts including discontinuance of the Palmetto and the Gulf Breeze Birmingham-Mobile, Alabama, and dining service cuts on the Silver Star resulted in only café service and tray meals offered to passengers, including those in the sleepers. Probably most distressing of the 1995 cuts was termination of the Broadway Limited in September. It once was the company's premier train.

In July 2000 Amtrak retired its original "pointless arrow" logo in favor of a design that (to the authors, at least) suggests a rising (rail)road leading to new places and adventures.

This book has not discussed accidents on the Amtrak system, an unfortunate reality for any transportation mode, because they are outside its focus; many, and some of the most distressing, were not Amtrak's fault. "Safety First" has long been a railroad industry watchword, but circumstances sometimes lead to terrible results despite everyone's best efforts.

The Aughts (Warrington, Gunn, Kummant, Crosbie, and Boardman Administrations)

The first decade of the new century found Amtrak up and running well (late in 2001 it reported that close to a million passengers had patronized Acela in its first year), but observers sensed a change. The company worked every day at achieving its mission, but there seemed to be more downgrades of service than upgrades—triggered by rising financial issues and political pressures, harbingers of things to come.

On the upside, there were ongoing improvements in train service. In late December 2001, what proved to be a highly successful regional service began: the Downeaster Boston–Portland, Maine, later extended to Brunswick. In 2003, the Hoosier State returned on the Chicago–Indianapolis route in July, operating on days Cardinal did not run, and in October, the Cardinal extended its route to New York City. In November 2004, the Pennsylvanian service

Pittsburgh–New York City was discontinued, but it returned in April 2005 when state funding came through and has continued since. In March 2005, the Three Rivers, a replacement of the New York City–Chicago Broadway Limited, restored that service but on a different route west of Pittsburgh, Pennsylvania, through Akron, Ohio. In October 2004, the last of the pre-Amtrak "heritage" sleeping cars ceased running.

In late 2008, the Passenger Rail Investment and Improvement Act (PRIIA) became law.[69] It authorized $8 billion for intercity rail for 2009–13 (most of this funding was eliminated by Congress in 2011) and required action on Amtrak's accounting methods, repair of NEC infrastructure, financial and budget plans, establishment of service metrics (mainly concerning the host railroads' obligation to run Amtrak trains on time), and safety; board membership also was reduced to nine members, seven of which were to be chosen by the president. Paradoxically, given Congressional unpredictability in funding commitments, the law also endorsed a national rail passenger system, including long-distance services; promoted development of high-speed services; and set up a program in which freight railroads could establish passenger routes (again defying logic, since the railroads had paid heavily in 1971 to get out of such services). The law provided a matching grant program to encourage state-supported services. And, finally, it contained a statement that bears on current debates about Amtrak's future: that many communities had been left without air and bus service and that Amtrak could provide "the only feasible common carrier transportation option for a growing number of areas."[70] The bill looked great on paper, although it became overly bureaucratic and there were lapses in follow through.[71]

By 2009 "farebox recovery"—the portion of operating costs covered by revenues—hit 71 percent; and, in a bit of unexpected favorable press the next year, *Time* magazine named the Heartland Flyer between Fort Worth, Texas, and Oklahoma City one of the 50 Best Inventions of 2010.

Station improvements included a new Albany–Rensselaer, New York, station in September 2002, and in December, Kansas City, Missouri, dedicated its restored Union Station, which had a small adjacent Amtrak facility. In December 2003, the restored Main Street Station in Richmond, Virginia, reopened, and in December 2004, work began on a new temporary station in St. Louis to replace a 30-year-old temporary station that had enabled a move out of the nearby historic Union Station. A permanent Intermodal Transportation Center (trains, buses, light rail) would later be built. The Milwaukee airport station opened in January 2005, and in 2007, Amtrak started its Great American Stations initiative to work with communities on station renovation and construction.

Cutbacks in the decade included the 2004 termination of mail and express due to limited revenues and negative effects on passenger operations and the April 2004 cutting of Chicago–Toronto service back to Port Huron, Michigan, where it has remained since. Onboard service cutbacks included the May 2002 replacement of regional menus with a standard national menu; the April 2004 introduction of dinette tray meals on the Cardinal; and, that same month, the replacement of the Silver Palm and its full services with the Palmetto, offering only coach and dinette service. This left Florida's west coast with no sleeper service.

Two additional bright spots in this decade: in May 2002, David Gunn became Amtrak's seventh president, bringing long rail passenger experience to the job (see Parts Three and Four regarding Gunn and his relatively brief term), and in January 2009, the newly elected President and Vice-President, Barack Obama and Joseph Biden, traveled by train from Wilmington, Delaware, to Washington, DC for their inaugurations.

The Teens (Boardman, Moorman, Anderson, and Flynn Administrations)

Amtrak's fifth decade began inauspiciously with yet another privatization plan. Republican congressmen John Mica of Florida and Bud Shuster of Pennsylvania introduced the Competition for Intercity Passenger Rail in America Act in June 2011. It called for auctioning the NEC to private investors supposedly anxious to run high-speed rail service. All long-distance and non-Corridor trains, presumably, would just stop running or be left to the states to support. Democratic Congressman Jerry Nadler of New York observed, "This bill throws the entire passenger rail system off a cliff and hopes a safety net will suddenly appear."[72] No private sector proposals were forthcoming, and the legislation soon breathed its last.

Amtrak has long had a difficult relationship with Congress despite efforts to court its good will. This proved impossible with Mica, who continued a one-man crusade. As chairman of the House Transportation Infrastructure Committee, he held several hearings to complain about Amtrak as a waste of taxpayer dollars, in August 2012 criticizing money "wasted" providing food and beverage service aboard trains. He claimed the company lost $84.5 million in 2011, with $1.70 spent for every dollar of food and beverage revenue. Amtrak countered that food and beverage offerings are essential to providing service and to retaining passengers, which should not have been a hard thing to comprehend. In a subsequent hearing, called "Examining 41 years of Taxpayer Subsidies," Mica claimed that "taxpayers have been footing the bill for Amtrak's gravy train for over 40 years, and all they've gotten in return for their $40 billion investment is an inefficient, costly, soviet-style passenger system." Amtrak responded by reporting record ridership, with 85 percent recovery of its operating costs through ticket sales and other revenues and a reduction in federal operating grants by nearly 50 percent since 2004.[73]

In the meantime, the trains kept running and Americans kept traveling on them. One sad note during this period: in February 2014, Milton Williams Jones, one of the last Pullman porters, died at age 98. His 37-year career began in 1942; he went to the Santa Fe in 1968 and to Amtrak in 1971 and retired in 1979. Top-quality service to passengers was the Pullman credo.[74]

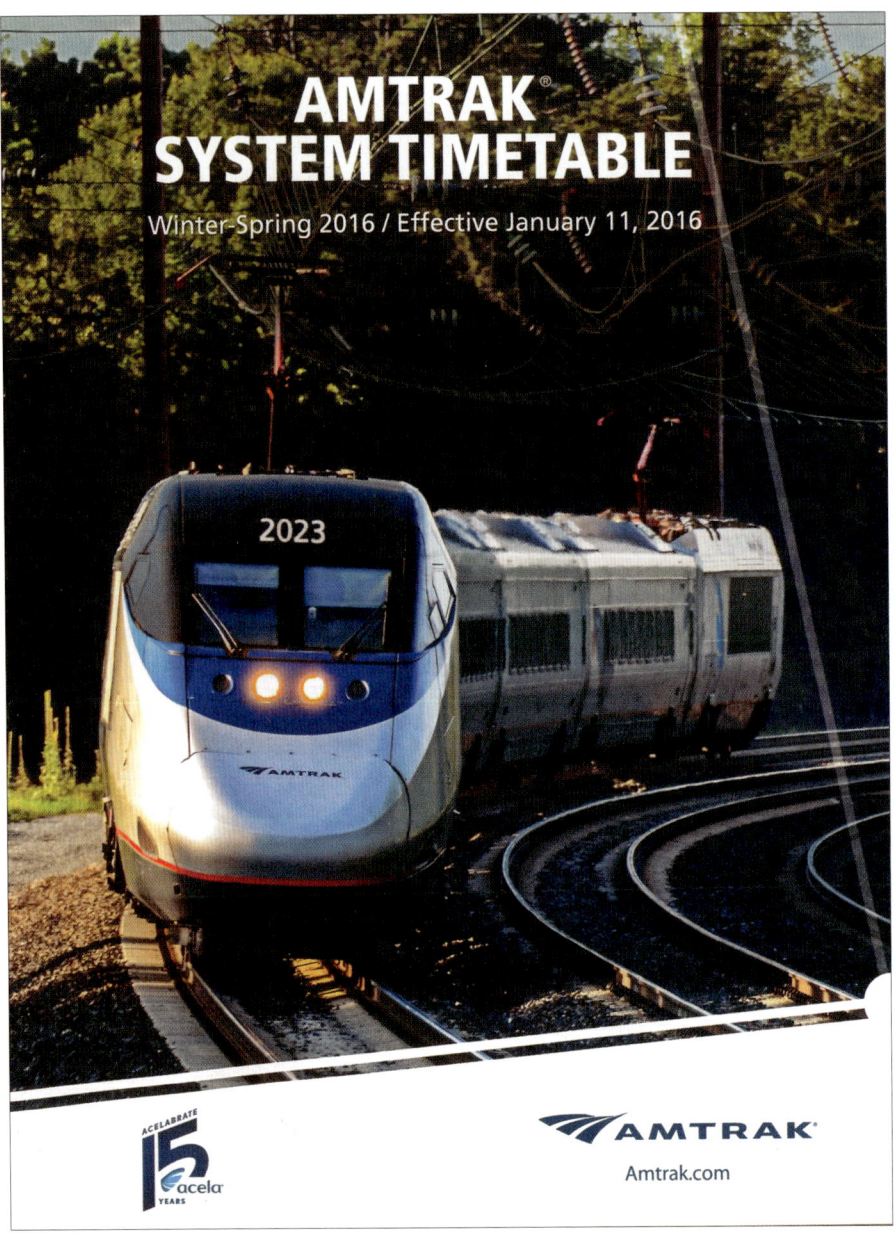

Among more recent cutbacks was elimination of the system timetable, which has made it much more difficult for the traveling public to plan trips or even find out whether Amtrak serves a given destination. Note, however, the increase in design quality when compared to the first timetable in 1971. *Jeffrey Darbee Collection*

Improvements in train and onboard services in this decade included the October 2011 return to service of the prototype Viewliner diner. Twenty-five more were to come from the Beech Grove shops. In 2012 Amtrak introduced "Healthy and Humane Dining," which included a menu notation that the company's suppliers produced eggs humanely.

In March 2015 came introduction of Viewliner baggage cars. Keeping suitcases happy was not the priority; of the Viewliner order these probably were the easiest to build and get out the factory door. (Amtrak introduced the Viewliner II sleepers in September of 2019, but they would not enter service for some time.) In June 2016, the last of the AEM-7 electric locomotives was retired; their design was Swedish in origin, and they provided long and reliable service in the NEC. In December 2017, the first refurbished Amfleet Business Class car rolled out of the shop under the "Amfleet Refreshment Program" to redo the 40-year-old cars.

Station improvements continued apace as well. Lawrence, Kansas, dedicated its renovated station in December 2011; in July 2012, Amtrak introduced a plan to remake Washington, DC Union Station into a larger facility for high-speed and commuter rail, transit, and buses. St. Paul, Minnesota, Union Depot reopened in December 2012 after renovation as a transportation hub; Amtrak returned to it in May 2014. In February 2014, it returned to the renovated Denver, Colorado, Union Station. During 2017 and 2018, new or redone stations opened in Alton, Illinois; Rochester, New York; Joliet, Illinois; and Springfield, Massachusetts. The bad news among all this was that in April 2018, Amtrak eliminated ticket agents at 15 stations on seven long-distance routes, reducing in-person assistance to travelers. Perhaps the most ambitious undertaking was the renovation of New York City's cavernous Penn Station and simultaneous renovation of the Farley Post Office complex across 8th Avenue from Madison Square Garden and the opening in early January 2021 of the Moynihan Train Hall. Serving Amtrak and Long Island Rail Road passengers, the renovations were designed to relieve the mass of human congestion at Penn Station, America's busiest rail terminal.

Financial constraints forced cutbacks in onboard services, especially toward the end of the decade. In August 2013, Amtrak, citing an annual savings of $500,000, eliminated free pillows for coach passengers, instead offering a passenger comfort kit (inflatable pillow, blanket, earplugs, sleep mask) for eight dollars. During this period, the company phased out the chief of Product Development Department, Brian Rosenwald, who had initiated the West Coast's Pacific Parlour Car service that was terminated in 2018. Amtrak had refurbished the cars, reintroduced them, and then in 2018 eliminated them. This move was ominous for the future of amenities that made train travel special. Karl Zimmermann, long-time observer of the rail passenger scene, said the department's philosophy had been "improve it and they will ride. I wonder what he [Brian Rosenwald] would make of the current situation."[75]

In the spring of 2014, Amtrak sought to "increase revenue" on the Auto Train by eliminating complimentary wine from the sleeper section's diner; the "Welcome Aboard" wine and cheese party for first-class passengers; the separate first-class lounge car; and by offering a single dining car menu for both coach and first class. Amtrak did not explain how it would increase revenue by offering less. In 2019 it announced that "food trucks" also would be available for Auto Train passengers in Lorton, Virginia, and in Sanford, Florida.

Over time, real-world economic forces and constant budget issues drove downgrades of other services. These included the mid-2015 elimination of the Silver Star dining car in favor of a smaller "dinette" and, in 2018, introduction of cold boxed meals on the Lake Shore Limited and Capitol Limited offered in the dining car or delivered to sleeping car rooms. In addition to the discontinuance of the five Pacific Parlour Cars in February 2019, Amtrak initiated its "flexible dining service," a slight upgrade from boxed meals. Bowing to the inevitable, Amtrak said that "our continued success depends on customer satisfaction while becoming more efficient."[76] This was a difficult balance to strike in an effort to comply with wording in the Amtrak reauthorization legislation mandating elimination of losses in food and beverage service. Cuts affected travel quality, making it difficult to keep onboard services of a high-enough quality to avoid losing patronage, but they were deemed essential. The past was a different place. It was time to move on.

Also affecting Amtrak's customers was the ongoing and growing problem of poor on-time performance of many long-distance services, a complex problem with no easy solution. It is driven by the realities of railroad technology. Unlike other transportation modes, the "fixed guideway" (that is, track) on which passenger and freight trains operate is inflexible. Aircraft can fly anywhere to avoid congestion, and highway traffic can take detours. To avoid congestion or blockages trains sometimes can run on alternate routes, but usually not. So the issue on a rail route between two points is track capacity. Some freight trains can weigh 15,000 tons or more, so the laws of physics demand pretty wide physical separation between trains—usually several miles. In earlier times, some railroads had separate passenger and freight main lines; others did not but generally gave passenger trains priority so they could stay on schedule.

By the time Amtrak began, however, the nation's railroad picture had changed dramatically. Several important freight railroads were failing and were in fact on the verge of nationalization in the Northeast. Freight traffic was down, which meant that there was considerable excess capacity on many main lines that could easily absorb the remaining Amtrak passenger trains in then-current rail operations. Part of the problem was that many railroads removed some second and third (or more) main tracks in order to cut operating, maintenance, and tax expenses and to "right-size" their physical plant for current traffic loads—which reduced capacity. As traffic has grown since the "railroad renaissance" following deregulation in 1980, Amtrak does not pay market rates for slots on railroad lines used today. For example, a coal train or United Parcel Service intermodal train pays far more to the host railroad than does Amtrak (for a passenger train). Although this is no excuse for poor handling of passenger trains by host railroads, the context is important to understand that the railroads are not, by and large, discriminating against Amtrak as they often struggle to move freight for their own customers with limited capacity.

To understand how much track capacity is required by Amtrak versus freight trains, Amtrak trains often run at speeds from 79 to 90 miles per hour over many main lines, while freight trains run from 50 or 55 to 70. This removes a good deal of capacity to have faster Amtrak trains on the same tracks. Adding station stops takes even more capacity away from the freight railroads, especially on single track .

In March 2015, the US Supreme Court decided that Amtrak is a government agency with the legal authority to set metrics for minimum performance and service quality, including timekeeping, and in June 2019, the Court indicated that it favors establishment of on-time standards by leaving in place a lower court ruling that the host railroads had to run Amtrak trains on time. There is no real villain here, and it may be that the only solution is providing the host railroads with capacity expansion at critical points.

What Have We Learned Over Fifty Years?

Running a national rail passenger system obviously is no easy task. When Joseph Boardman retired in 2016, Jim McClellan said, "You need a guy with a lot of strong operating experience. Someone who is in his fifties. Somebody older than that won't have the energy. I wonder if Jesus Christ could run it! It requires, you know, a perfect person. Amtrak doesn't have a strategic plan. They kind of wander around. You've got to have a vision. I haven't heard them articulate that vision."[77] This may have been somewhat harsh, but it is true that the fate of Amtrak rests largely with the quality of its leadership, an issue addressed in detail in Part Three. But it is important to remember too that, for no good reason at all, Amtrak has always been something of a political football, with its masters in Congress running unpredictably hot and cold, at various times showering funding on the company and then taking it back again later. The fact is that, until the coronavirus pandemic upended everything in American life, Amtrak had shown progress—admittedly with some fits and starts—in its primary goal of attracting passengers, more than 32 million in 2019. A reasonable observer should conclude that a fact such as this is evidence that Americans want to be able to travel by train. And the perennial talk of severing the NEC from the rest of the Amtrak network seems to be over. Former Amtrak president David Gunn long ago stated the political reality regarding this idea: politicians from states with long-distance service support funding the NEC as long as NEC politicians support funding long-distance services. If the long-distance trains are killed, so are those in the Corridor; if we kill the spirit of the national system the original Amtrak legislation called for, the Corridor will have a much harder time surviving.[78]

Although critics have charged that Amtrak's leadership has made deliberate decisions to dismantle the long-distance network of service, a statement by board chairman Anthony Coscia appears to be in contrast: "We recognize the critical role that long-distance routes already play in communities across

America. These trains provide essential transportation and contribute to both economic opportunity and quality of life in places that have long ago been abandoned by the airlines and bus carriers." He goes further, arguing that creating new corridors connecting with long-distance services will make long-distance trains more viable and the national network more essential. In his remarks, Coscia also addressed employee furloughs, train frequency reductions, and plunging ticket revenue due to the pandemic. Further, he took the question of "profitability" head-on: "Profitability is not Amtrak's mission. Our mission, as defined by Congress, is 'to provide efficient and effective intercity passenger rail mobility consisting of high-quality service that is trip-time competitive with other intercity travel options.' As our governing statute has recognized since the 1970s, Amtrak will never generate enough revenue to be profitable from an accounting perspective, i.e., to fully fund its operating and capital needs. Mobility is not a moneymaker if you have to pay for 100 percent of the cost of getting from point A to point B. No mode of passenger transportation fully pays for itself."[79]

In testimony before the House Transportation and Infrastructure Subcommittee on Railroads, Pipelines and Hazardous Materials on September 9, 2020, James Mathews, president and CEO of the RPA, read into the record a statement to Congress on May 25, 2020 by then-president of Amtrak, William Flynn: "[Amtrak] understands how important [its] service is to the nation and, particularly small communities across the nation where we play a unique role in connecting these communities to the rest of America. How can a single daily train to a small town . . . be accurately described as 'essential' to the people it serves? To understand, you have to look at the dearth of transportation options faced by rural and small-town Americans. Over 62 million people live in so-called 'Flyover Country,' a quarter of whom are veterans, another quarter are senior citizens over the age [of] 65. Intercity rail plays an outsized role in these communities, with almost one-fifth of Amtrak's passengers traveling to or from a rural station with no access to air service. Make no mistake: these trains are essential to the communities they serve. Congress didn't let the Federal Highway Administration close highways four days out of seven when gas tax revenues flatlined, and it shouldn't stand by now and allow Amtrak to introduce [triweekly] service to hundreds of communities across the US (a reference to Amtrak's reductions of daily long-distance services on October 1, 2020)."[80] A single station may serve multiple communities within a radius of a hundred miles.

With luck, good management that has committed to keeping the national rail passenger network intact, and—one would hope—a Congress that really wants the company to be a success, Amtrak should be able to emerge intact from the difficulties of the pandemic and fulfill the responsibilities given to it in its original legislation.

Every so often, proposals to "reform" or "restructure" Amtrak surface and then submerge again. In fact, any well-run organization is always being reformed as its managers seek constant improvements in efficiency and in the quality of its product. Amtrak is and should be no different, but it and its funders must be guided by two simple realities: (1) you cannot cut your way to prosperity, and (2) Americans want to be able to travel by rail. However, a difficult political climate persists. As Frank Wilner says in his book, "The poverty into which Amtrak was born continues to this day, with Congress providing just enough funds to keep the trains running, but not enough to keep them running as well as a large segment of the public continues to demand."[81]

Fifty years after its creation, Amtrak is not your grandfather's passenger service, but it has survived somehow. A lot of credit for this belongs to people who wanted to see that it endured and were in a position to make it happen. But, there were others who had different points of view as to what form it would take.

Part Two Notes

1. White, "The Railroad," 264.
2. Young grandiosely pledged $500 million (that he did not have) to replace Pullman's fleet.
3. Offering through trains was not a new idea; the Pennsylvania and the Santa Fe had studied providing such a service as early as 1937, but the war put an end to discussions. Broader studies resumed, however, in early 1944, with proposals between the Pennsylvania and major railroads coming in September 1945. Despite Young's pressure, through trains never got going, but there was a brief period when some individual sleeping cars ran coast-to-coast—even in the Amtrak era.
4. Herbert H. Harwood, "This Was The Train That Was (But Never Was)." *Trains* magazine, July 1968, 46.
5. One issue with NYC's Xplorer was the locomotive's German Maybach engine that required use of metric tools. Shop forces at Collinwood Yard (Cleveland) did not use metric tools and had to go to a nearby Volkswagen dealership to fulfill their needs.
6. Ironically, at the same time these trains were being unveiled, the Budd Company was delivering Santa Fe's high-level stainless steel all-coach El Capitan and Burlington Route's popular and profitable second-generation Denver Zephyr. Both were designed to attract passengers, which they did, and patronage of these trains stayed high for a long time.
7. Fortunately, once Amtrak was under way, organized labor gave the corporation its support and was willing to negotiate labor contracts that would save jobs but also help Amtrak control costs.
8. Howes interview, February 12–13, 2019.
9. One trick was to break a given route—between St. Louis and Cleveland, for example—into two parts. This required a through passenger to make a connection between trains, which the railroad scheduled so it was not possible to make that connection, forcing a wait of several hours or even overnight. Another was to run a train in one direction between two cities but not in the opposite direction. Yes, the railroads could be clever in this period of stress, but given the desperate situation they faced, it is not surprising that things like this happened.
10. Telephone interview with Kevin McKinney, February 24, 2020.
11. Howes interview, February 12–13, 2019.
12. Howes, February 12–13, 2019.
13. Loving, *The Men Who Loved Trains*, 123.
14. US Department of Commerce, *Report of the Railroad Professional Survey Group*, 1962, 27.
15. Much of this narrative about the birth and 50-year history of Amtrak is drawn from a detailed account in Harold A. Edmonson, *Journey to Amtrak* (Milwaukee: Kalmbach, 1972), 11–12. Additional information came from George Fletcher and Mike Schafer, "The Amtrak 40th Anniversary Time Line" Parts One and Two, *Passenger Train Journal* 34, no. 2 (2011–2), 20–33 and no. 3 (2011–3), 14–22, and other issues of *Passenger Train Journal*; and from www.history.amtrak.com/amtraks-history/historictimeline. Not every significant event in Amtrak's history is recounted here; the purpose is to communicate an overall sense of the company's direction over time.
16. Telephone interviews with Britten Richards and William F. Howes, October 15–16, 2019.
17. Aviation and highway subsidization has always been deemed an "investment." Amtrak, by contrast, has been viewed by its critics as an "expense" and a waste of taxpayers' dollars.
18. Public Law 91-518, section 301, Creation of the Corporation: "There is authorized to be created

a National Railroad Passenger Corporation. The Corporation shall be a for profit corporation, the purpose of which shall be to provide intercity rail passenger service, employing innovative operating and marketing concepts so as to fully develop the potential of modern rail service in meeting the Nation's intercity passenger transportation requirements." The original draft bill made no reference to the corporation being "for profit."
19. Jim McClellan, *My Life With Trains*, (Bloomington: Indiana University Press, 2017), 189
20. Personal interview with Charles "Wick" Moorman, August 7, 2019.
21. McClellan, 191.
22. Anthony Perl, *New Departures* (Lexington, University Press of Kentucky, 2002), 102.
23. Frederick K. Plous, "The Amtrak Era is Over, It's Time For a Replacement," *Railway Age*, 219, no. 10, (October 4, 2018), 10.
24. The Railpax proposal was never formally transmitted to Congress—somebody leaked it. Jeff Davis, "Amtrak at 50: The Rail Passenger Service Act of 1970," Eno Center for Transportation, October 30, 2020, www.enotrans.org/article/amtrak-at-50-the-rail-passenger-service-act-of-1970/
25. Originally the National Railroad Passenger Service Corporation; the word "service" was dropped in the final bill.
26. McClellan, 186.
27. 1969 Penn Central Transportation Company Annual Report, 2.
28. Loving, *Men*, 129.
29. Loving, *Men*, 129.
30. McClellan, 189.
31. Loving, Men, 129.
32. David Gunn. "Amtrak's Place in a Rational Transportation System," Policy paper of the Free Congress Foundation in *Amtrak–Past, Present, Future* by Frank Wilner, (Omaha: Simmons-Boardman, 2012), 65.
33. Safety was the primary consideration for this approach. Operating rules of each railroad had to be taught, followed, and enforced. Operation by any entity other than each railroad could not guarantee obedience to the rules and would jeopardize lives and increase liability. When Amtrak and later when state-supported commuter agencies first began operations, train and engine crews were employed by the host railroads. They developed agreements over time as the railroads were happy to get rid of commuter operations.
34. The appointment of Roger Lewis, a man without any railroad experience (at one time he had been Assistant Secretary of the Air Force, executive vice president of Pan Am, and chairman of General Dynamics Corporation, a major government contractor), as Amtrak's first president was a clear indication that the Nixon administration expected him to preside over Amtrak's demise. At its May 1, 1971, inauguration, Lewis referred to Amtrak as "Ampax." For more on Lewis, see "Stewardship" in Part Three.; Telephone interview with Robert VanderClute, May 28, 2020.
35. Howes interview, February 12–13, 2019.
36. Telephone interviews with David DeBoer, May 18, 2020, and William F. Howes, May 20, 2020.
37. McKinney interview, February 24, 2020.
38. Email correspondence with Michael Weinman, June 6, 2020.
39. Weinman, June 6, 2020.
40. The commitment by the Southern to keep its passenger trains running was driven by W. Graham Claytor, who at the time was a Southern vice president and would later serve a long term as Amtrak's president. He had been given the job of cutting the Southern's passenger losses; as an admitted "railroad buff," Claytor found it painful to do so but by 1971 had reduced the company's trains by 80 percent, to five round trips. The Southern Crescent was the flagship. Even though its operation alone cost the Southern some $20 million between 1971 and when Amtrak took over the route in 1979, Claytor felt it was justified for reasons of public goodwill but also because company personnel could avoid travel costs by traveling it at no charge on their many trips between Washington and Atlanta.; Morgret, 351–355.
41. Fletcher and Schafer, "The Amtrak 40th Anniversary Time Line, Part 1," 16.
42. Personal interview with Paul Reistrup, July 16, 2019.
43. Weinman, June 6, 2020.
44. Telephone interview with Bruce Heard, June 27, 2020.
45. Heard, June 27, 2020.
46. Loving, Men, 130.
47. Telephone interview with Kevin McKinney, April 28, 2020.
48. Loving, 132.
49. Heard, June 27, 2020.
50. Weinman, June 6, 2020.
51. Loving, 130.
52. Weinman, June 6, 2020.
53. Telephone interview with Rush Loving, June 4, 2020.

54. Rush Loving, *The Well-Dressed Hobo* (Bloomington: Indiana University Press, 2016) 189–190.
55. Loving, *Hobo*, 190.
56. Loving, *Hobo*, 190.
57. VanderClute, May 30, 2020.
58. Telephone interview with Cliff Black, May 29, 2020.
59. VanderClute, May 30, 2020.
60. Howes interview, February 12–13, 2019.
61. Loving, *Men*, 132.
62. Email correspondence with Chuck Kratz, January 12, 2019.
63. McKinney, April 28, 2020.
64. Frank N. Wilner, *Amtrak–Past, Present, Future* (Omaha, NE: Simmons-Boardman, 2012), 64.
65. Wilner, 107.
66. Wilner, 107.
67. Wilner, 107.
68. Wilner, 83, 85–86.
69. The Senate was taking its time passing the bill until a horrific crash of a commuter train in Chatsworth, California; that got its attention and the bill was passed with broad bipartisan support.
70. Wilner, 28, 58, 87–88, 115, 119–120, 131,140.
71. Telephone interview with Joe McHugh, January 4, 2021.
72. Wilner, 113.
73. *Passenger Train Journal* 35, No. 4, (2012-4), Issue no. 253, 10–12.
74. *Passenger Train Journal* 37, No. 2 (2014-2), Issue no. 259, 5.
75. Karl Zimmermann, "Where Have All the Flowers Gone?" *Passenger Train Journal* 37, No. 2 (2014-2), Issue no. 259, 14, 44.
76. Kevin McKinney, "The Journal," *Passenger Train Journal* 41 (2018-3), Issue no. 263, 5.
77. C. B. Hall, "Who's Next at the Throttle?" *Passenger Train Journal* 40, No. 2 (2016-2), Issue 267, 19.
78. Telephone interview with David Gunn, September 27, 2020.
79. Anthony Coscia, "Defining Amtrak's True Mission," *Railway Age* website, November 23, 2020, https://www.railwayage.com/passenger/intercity/defining-amtraks-true-mission/.
80. James Mathews, testimony before the Transportation Committee, US House of Representatives, September 9, 2020. Rail Passengers Association website, https://railpassengers.org/happening-now/news/blog/testimony-of-jim-mathews-september-9th-2020/.
81. Wilner, 65.

Railroads are not airlines.

William C. Vantuono, from an interview with the authors

Where Do We Go from Here?

3

After World War II, Edward Budd, founder and president of the Budd Manufacturing Company, commented that travel was one commodity that had no saturation point. He believed that a postwar demand for travel would provide a natural market for each of the principal means of travel—railroads, airlines, bus lines, and the automobile. "If each of these means of transport adequately develops its own facilities and services, there need not be ruinous competition between any. Railroads are essentially the wholesalers of passenger traffic. Airlines may be regarded as specialists, providing high speed at a price; the bus and the private automobile should largely function as feeders to the railroads and the airplanes. While these fields may overlap, they need not eclipse each other."[1] To reach this goal, however, would require a balanced approach to supporting transportation at the federal level. That balance was not achieved—a fact that nearly resulted in elimination of railroad passenger service.

In his 1959 *Trains* magazine article "Who Shot the Passenger Train?" the late David P. Morgan contended that there was not a single assassin, but a firing squad—multiple actors public and private. The train was not killed but instead was wounded by a combination of people, events, and circumstances. "Passenger operations were the only thing going for the railroads," as former Amtrak president Tom Downs put it.[2] Governmental intravenous feeding has improved its health since 1971, and the people who make Amtrak run have labored for half a century to save it. But the passenger train remains imperiled—by perceptions that it is a transportation afterthought; that it ought to turn a profit (or the corollary, that it shouldn't receive a subsidy); that it does not deserve an equal place at the table with other modes. This has left it subject to the caprice, biases, and hostility of a succession of presidential administrations, politicians, and more recently its own board of directors.

Public funding for transportation is a long tradition. In the mid-1830s when Abraham Lincoln was running for the Illinois legislature, he advocated for an

In the 1940s, the Motor Bus Lines of America promoted this rosy view of the future of highway travel. *Geoffrey H. Doughty Collection*

expansion of government investment in roads, railroads, and waterways. As historian Doris Kearns Goodwin points out, this was the apex of the internal improvements era: the public would be the ultimate beneficiary of such investments, he said.³ Not all were successful, but the concept in general was confirmed. Highways, air services, and waterways have since become permanent fixtures in the country's transport infrastructure, and federal funds allocated to these modes are presented to the public as "investments." By contrast, Amtrak is presented as an expense rather than a national asset. Over time, the focus of Amtrak management shifted from operating a national network to that of cutting expenses—recently to the extent of basing top management bonuses on the percentage of cuts they could achieve.[4] Innovation was discouraged because it added expense. Amtrak also ceased gauging passenger satisfaction through periodic surveys. Tom Downs observed, "You cannot measure success in this business without a metric that tells you how well you are doing your job."[5]

Opponents perceive train travel as outdated and long-distance service amenities as an extravagance, part of a bygone era, archaic in the age of airplanes, cars, and buses. Those who travel by rail are derided as "train lovers" who do not want to fly, take a bus, or drive. This could not be further from the truth, but getting past this perceptual roadblock is perhaps the biggest challenge.

It should be noted that the federal government, working primarily with local communities, has long provided funding—even enthusiastically so—for rail transit projects in cities and metro areas that vary greatly in population. This has, of course, required substantial local funding as well—but the communities that have stepped up see the great benefits of such undertakings by state programs (see appendix 1). Among many state and local units of government, this enlightened attitude has evolved: they also put substantial funds into commuter and corridor rail passenger services they see as essential to commerce and economic development.

Those who say Amtrak ought to be self-supporting can only be unaware that no common carrier passenger transport mode is, so there is no logical reason to expect it of Amtrak. Some argue that Amtrak's long-distance trains inappropriately soak up funds from NEC services; others say NEC costs have been inappropriately charged to long-distance services (could it be a case of figures lying or liars figuring?). It can be demonstrated that the NEC's revenues "above the rail" meet its operating costs, but when infrastructure maintenance, depreciation, and capital costs are factored in, the Corridor costs more than it brings in. But it does not really matter.

Why not? Because Amtrak provides a national network of rail travel services that cannot and should not be expected to break even, much less turn a profit. Government services are not intended to make money, so they cannot "lose" it. What is spent on them is simply the cost of providing the service. Of course, any such service should be provided in a businesslike manner to minimize costs and maximize revenues but only in ways consistent with providing a level of excellent service.

"Providing consistent service has always been a problem," says Tom Downs. "Different trains, different crews, different routes, the condition of a host railroad's track, condition of equipment—so many variables—it's tough to get it all right." And yet, "People are still voting for Amtrak with their feet and money."[6]

The issue of funding is complex and needlessly political. Worse still, regular bouts of uncertainty about funding cause disruption in continuity of planning and capital investment. One often-suggested solution is to establish a trust fund

Thomas Downs, Amtrak president, 1993–1998. *Courtesy Bob Johnston*

similar to that underpinning the highway system. In the words of Anthony Perl, a professor of urban studies, "Trust funds now represent the gold standard in terms of America's fiscal policy in transportation, and only Amtrak and the intercity passenger train remain outside the loop where the vast majority of these funds are raised and appropriated."[7]

Perl continues, saying, "Initially, no trust fund was proposed for Amtrak because the corporation was designed to be for-profit and thus fully self-supporting in the tradition of modern American railroads." Besides, "Skeptics assumed that passenger trains would not be around long enough to require extended public support."[8] And when it came to vying for federal funds, other transport modes, including transit, didn't like the competition and offered considerable resistance that Amtrak was unable to overcome. This led to Amtrak's further institutional isolation within America's transportation investment framework.[9]

The effects of insecure funding are deep rooted. The institutional dysfunction and pervasive uncertainty of Amtrak's future affects employee morale and level of service, not just maintenance and investment in equipment. Amtrak remains a prisoner of the belief that it must become profitable or be shut down. According to Perl, the passage of the Amtrak Improvement Act of 1978 "came closest to discarding this market test by modifying the corporate mandate to read that Amtrak was to be 'operated and managed as' a for-profit company,"[10] but the passage of the Amtrak Reform and Accountability Act in 1997 reversed this by reinstating a return to a for-profit "litmus test for Amtrak's future."[11]

Governance versus Leadership

Since its first day of operation, one of Amtrak's biggest problems, more extreme in recent years, have been board chairmen, top management, and presidential administrations, along with many members of Congress and media pundits, who believe it should not exist. This is in the face of abundant evidence that the public desires just the opposite. The sad fact is that this public service with broad civic support has been almost entirely politicized to its own detriment and to that of the nation it serves.

Politics in transportation, or any other public service such as the Postal Service, is nothing new.[12] Before Amtrak was created, the rail industry had been relatively "left alone." With the creation of Amtrak, rail passenger service instantly became sullied by partisan politics. Downs observed, "The politics bedeviled Alan Boyd. David Gunn called them 'byzantine.'"[13] "Starting at the top," David Gunn commented, "a secretary of transportation should know correct governance and have vision. Board members should be technically competent and have some knowledge of the [railroad] industry."[14] Several of Amtrak's early leaders—Reistrup, Boyd, Claytor, Downs, Gunn—knew and loved the industry's history. As journalist Rush Loving points out in his story about the creation of Penn Central and Conrail, "Men who love their industry make better managers than those who simply fill the role of president or chairman."[15]

Its chairman must be an advocate of Amtrak and all its services, devoid of personal/political agendas. Several people familiar with today's inner Amtrak's workings have described it as a "snake pit." In this environment, what Amtrak needs is superb stewards.

Stewardship

The only job to have on a railroad is president.
The author's Uncle Bob to his nephew.

Stewardship involves accepting as a duty the responsibility of caring for people, a property, or an institution, and doing so faithfully and to the best of one's ability, even—or especially—in the face of problems and difficulties. In the world of freight railroading, success is typically due to superlative leadership—top management accepting the task of stewardship and then acting in positive ways. Stewardship and leadership are not the same but are inextricably linked, as has been borne out in the success of the privately owned freight railroads, now widely acknowledged as essential freight transportation providers. On the passenger side of railroading, however, the "orphan" nature of Amtrak has made it difficult to lead the organization effectively.

When Amtrak has worked well, it has been due to a strong sense of stewardship on the part of its leaders, an acceptance of the responsibility to care for its employees, and operating a high-quality service efficiently, one that attracts passengers and meets the country's passenger transport needs. While the company's chairmen and presidents have varied by degree in quality of leadership and generally have met the obligation to carry out its service agenda, they also have unfortunately had to spend a lot of time explaining and defending it. Gaining outsiders' belief and trust in their vision for Amtrak has been an ongoing challenge and often marred by intense partisan pressure. Both Democrats and Republicans have lined up for and against it. "They still perceive Amtrak as creeping socialism," said Tom Downs.[16]

Amtrak serves the national interest far beyond operating trains; it connects people and places. To provide the appropriate quality of service its employees have to know what to expect and what is expected of them; there has to be a sense of shared trust, direction, and purpose in any such organization. Over Amtrak's half-century of life, as succeeding US presidential administrations have shown indifference or hostility toward Amtrak, something of a systemic institutional dysfunction has become entrenched due to continued uncertainty about the future and, more recently, the limited vision of its recent short-term leadership. Stewards of Amtrak are guardians of its future, but not all of Amtrak's stewards have been its guardians. "A president's job is to grow the business, not shut it down," says Downs.[17]

Amtrak got off to a bad start with the appointment of Roger Lewis as its first president and has not yet fully recovered. Some viewed his leadership as a placeholder, the first of several. He served four years at the helm of a new company that employed older seasoned onboard service professionals, many of whom were heading toward retirement, but also younger enthusiastic employees who wanted the company to succeed.

Lewis was the consummate outsider, an aviation industry executive when he came to Washington in March 1953 as assistant secretary of the Air Force for procurement. He held that post for two years before resigning to become the executive vice president of Pan American World Airways. In 1962, he joined the General Dynamics Corporation, becoming president, board chairman, and chief executive officer of the giant defense contracting concern. He worked on company financial recovery programs and helped guide work on such programs as the F111 aircraft and Polaris missile submarines.[18] After being fired when he became embroiled in a personal dispute with the corporation's largest stockholder on the board, he was chosen by President Richard Nixon to lead Amtrak.[19]

Lewis was bereft of any railroad or hospitality experience appointed by a president who was uninterested in rail passenger service. He lacked interest in or knowledge of the industry's past and showed no professional concern or regret if the new corporation failed. But his views and those of the administration (among them, Nixon henchmen H. R. Haldeman and John Ehrlichman) and members of the board (Louis Menk of Burlington Northern) were at odds with employees who wanted to see Amtrak thrive.[20]

Perhaps it is inconceivable that a company could function with these two opposing viewpoints. Since he had no idea how to run a railroad, Lewis had passionate and dedicated employees who did know and let them take care of its operations.[21]

Making matters worse, Amtrak was not immune to problems of a personal nature. Early corporate leadership was plagued by stories of alcohol abuse and marital infidelity that exacerbated management problems and cost the company respect. These were serious matters in any corporate leadership, but Amtrak was just getting underway and had enough difficulties without these additional burdens.

During those early years, the public's attention was occupied by the end of the Vietnam War, Watergate, high inflation, and—even more significant—the "shortage" and high cost of gasoline and having to wait in line for it. Add to this Nixon's resignation in August 1974. Few paid attention to the toddler years of Amtrak, but following some blistering negative press reports, Senate politicians and select members of the Amtrak board maneuvered to remove Lewis. Paul Reistrup, a seasoned railroader, replaced him. After leaving Amtrak, Lewis went to New York and became a senior vice president and director of a brokerage firm. He died in Washington, DC in November 1987.

According to Tom Downs, leadership takes a mix of diplomacy, style, skill, and credibility and "it takes tenure to effect change in any organization. Constant turnover does not provide continuity of policy."[22] In the end, though, the years the railroad ran the best were the years when railroaders were at the top.

What are the qualities that make a good, great, or superb, leader? Certainly competency, honesty, and empathy are important qualities, as are personal and communication skills, but so are institutional knowledge (history) and leadership that deeply cares about the organizational mission and employees' welfare. As an Amtrak executive with access to top management, Cliff Black, long-term company spokesman, was in a position to reflect on the attributes possessed by the presidents he believed served the company's best interests.

1. Total integrity and the ability to set a high moral tone that filters down through management and to the front-line worker. Seeking and telling the truth. These qualities help make a leader gain the confidence of his or her employees and the many other constituencies he/she must serve, including customers, competitors, suppliers, business partners, politicians, and the general public. The end result is trust and respect, which are difficult to obtain and virtually impossible to recover when lost.

2. A person who tours the ranks of employees and does not sequester himself/herself among an exclusive high-level cadre of executives and politicians. This helps gauge morale among the rank and file—and boosts it. This is a tightrope, but it must be walked. Simply befriending low-level employees and having no vision for the company or courage to push through with decisions and commitments has little value. Both qualities are necessary.

3. An effective leader must be publicly accessible, through the news media, other modern media, and in dealings with his/her constituencies. Leaders who adopt an inaccessible persona come across as latter-day Wizards of Oz, who are afraid the world will discover how little they actually know and how little

leadership they actually possess. Similarly, imperial-style intimidation never works and ultimately fails.

    4. Thorough knowledge of the product he/she is producing or service he/she is selling. The leader can have prior experience with related products and services but must also be willing and able to learn from experienced staffers with first-hand knowledge of the product.

    5. Strong fiduciary responsibility to shareholders, including taxpayers, as well as employees in order to protect their pay and benefits. The duty to employees applies, of course, to valued and necessary employees. (See also item 6)

    6. A manager's skill in right-sizing the employee pool. Too many or too few employees, or poor deployment of the right number of employees, are deleterious to the functioning of a company. The leader must be able to recognize highly skilled and experienced human resources managers, hire them, and stay in constant contact with the VP of HR. An adjunct to this is an effective VP of labor relations. HR and LR have a huge impact on the success of a company. Of course, hiring qualified employees is part of that, and it is an increasingly difficult challenge.

    7. A great leader must have an abiding interest and belief in the service or product the company is producing and selling.

"Interim presidents are sometimes necessary and unavoidable, but they can have a negative effect on employee morale, since their temporary nature is topmost in the minds of employees, a situation that engenders a sense that whatever comes down from the top is temporary and can be safely ignored."[23]

    What Amtrak presidents think about the corporation and its mission is of vital importance. Each brings a different vision for the company. In the following interviews, four former Amtrak presidents offered their visions for the company, its problems, and its future. In places there are opinions, contrasts, and also agreements. These are important to spell out as each had his own reasons for taking on the job and wanting to focus on what they believed had to be done to make Amtrak function efficiently.

Experienced Leadership: Paul Reistrup (July 16, 2019 interview)

Don't let yourself get stuck in the Passenger Department.
Paul Reistrup to Bill Howes at C&O/B&O.

By the time Paul Reistrup was hired, Amtrak had managed to survive four years of management that was ambivalent about its success. Only through the intervention of senators and journalists who saw the fledgling company's leadership as a byproduct of the Nixon administration did the ranks of those who wanted to see it succeed prevail. Company morale had "plummeted under

Paul Reistrup, Amtrak president, 1974–1978. *Courtesy Amtrak*

[Roger] Lewis," according to retired Amtrak marketing manager Bruce Heard. A few days before he took over, "Reistrup took the train to Florida and back overnight, talked with every employee he could, and walked into the office the next day. Employee morale shot upward from that point on."[24]

The hiring of Reistrup, a seasoned railroader who knew and understood passenger service, finally gave Amtrak a vision of what the company could be. Amtrak was ready to move forward, but before Reistrup could get going he had to repair the damage done by Lewis.

Paul Reistrup, born on May 24, 1932, grew up in Sioux City, Iowa, and as with many railroad presidents, he discovered his love of railroads at an early age. He was three years old when he took his first ride on an Illinois Central locomotive in Sioux City. He never forgot it. Following his graduation at Central High School, he was appointed by an Iowa congressman to West Point. In the Army he was in artillery and was a paratroop jumpmaster. "I took off more times than I landed in an airplane."

Preparation

Along with others who assumed the top leadership role of a railroad, the combined experiences gained from a variety of positions assisted Reistrup in his railroad career advancement. The practical experience of managing operations figured prominently, as did managing people. He also credited his leadership training in the Army. His abilities were recognized early by other managers who made his advancement possible.

After leaving the Army, he was hired by the Baltimore & Ohio Railroad, entering its two-year training program in 1957. He was moved into Engineering and Operations, becoming general yardmaster at Painesville, Ohio, and by 1964 had advanced rapidly in Transportation holding a variety of positions, including that of general superintendent of car utilization and distribution. It was here that he was offered a special assignment by Jervis Langdon, who was president of what had become C&O/B&O. His assignment: reorganize and lead the Passenger Department in an effort to determine whether any portion of the service could become self-sustaining.

With ridership decreasing steadily on most American railroads and especially at C&O/B&O (which Reistrup described as a "takeover" by C&O of B&O and not an "affiliation"), the Passenger Department was considered a dead end. Concerned that his career would suffer, he was assured by Langdon that he need only stay on the passenger assignment for two years. In early 1965, during Reistrup's tenure, C&O's rail and marine passenger services (the latter on the Lake Michigan carferries) came under his jurisdiction. He consolidated passenger marketing, mail, baggage and express, dining car, and operating functions into a single profit center reporting directly to Langdon. As it turned out, he served as director of Passenger Service for C&O/B&O until early 1967.

Reistrup brought in new talent, including David Watts, who would later succeed him, and introduced many marketing innovations such as movies on the train, "Red Circle Day" demand-sensitive pricing, and Chessie's "Take-Your-Auto Service," among others. But, it was to no avail; the overnight sleeping car services remained unprofitable.

After serving briefly in the Executive Department of C&O/B&O, Reistrup accepted the position of vice president Passenger Service on the Illinois Central in 1967. Once again he was faced with mounting deficits and was tasked with cutting IC's long-distance trains by half. Given 18 months to do it, he simultaneously was told to strengthen what remained of IC's intercity services and upgrade the road's aged electric commuter operation. In 1969, he became vice president Intermodal and in 1970 he was appointed senior vice president Traffic and elected to the road's board of directors.

Repeatedly offered the head job at Amtrak, Reistrup recalled Langdon's promise that he would not be stuck long-term in the Passenger Department and turned down the Amtrak offer five times. In May 1975 he relented, becoming the company's second president/CEO; he was also on the board of directors but never was chairman. He stayed three years and observed that railroading was "very military" and Amtrak was too—along with the airlines—with up to 20 percent of employees being former military people. Under his leadership he and his staff "tried to keep it a railroad," and not turn it into a federal agency.

Motivations

Why did Reistrup accept the job at Amtrak after refusing it five times? Although just the thought of acceptance was enough to give one pause, he instead was confident, drawing on his experience. "I knew I could help them. It was a disaster and couldn't get much worse." A call had come from Charlie Luna (head of the United Transportation Union) and from the National Association of Railroad Passengers (NARP, which Reistrup called the "National Association for the Prevention of Cruelty to Passengers"). In addition, he was courted by four-star army general Frank Besson, who had been one of Amtrak's incorporators. Reistrup finally succumbed to the intense pressure and took the job.

Expectations

"Many believed the new corporation might not survive, and perhaps had been planned to fail. It had been founded as a two-year experiment and was on life support."[25] But, he had accepted the position and wanted it to work, so he set out to visit every train station and become familiar with it. Did he know what he was in for? "I really did." At the time, Amtrak was functioning with old worn-out equipment, a hodge-podge of passenger cars equipped with steam heat and different electrical systems (32-volt, 64-volt, 110-volt, both AC and DC). "The cars didn't like each other." There also was the poor financial condition and bad track of some of the host railroads. "What scared me were the track and locomotives. I was afraid to walk on the track, never mind ride on it, and why have steam heat on a locomotive with all that electricity in it? It didn't make sense. The Chicago & North Western was running commuter cars with head-end power (HEP) and, as the technology was available, it was time to turn it around." The Night Owl operating between Boston and Washington became the first train to have HEP coaches and sleepers.

As for the trouble-plagued SDP40F locomotives that had earned a reputation for derailing, he remarked that he hadn't ordered them, "but I got rid of them. They were terrible. Crews called them the 'Ruby-Breasted Rail Breaker.'" As far as the replacement F40s were concerned, "I was proud of them."

Once in office and as he got to see what the operation was like, nothing surprised him. "I knew it all going in. That's why I turned it down [initially]." Dealing with "the Hill" was daunting too. "A Kansas congressman, for example, said that if he was to support 'your' Northeast Corridor, he wanted a train through Kansas too." He wasn't alone. There were others who applied pressure to have trains through their home towns. "Indiana Senators (Birch) Bayh and (Vance) Hartke were known as 'Buy and Bought.'"

Missions

"Roger Lewis was scared to death. It was a terrible thing to do to ask him to be Amtrak's first president. He used to hide when riding a train to avoid having to talk to passengers about Amtrak." This may have been the result of a CBS Television *60 Minutes* program segment that in Reistrup's view was "mean"; it targeted Lewis and the James Whitcomb Riley Chicago–Indianapolis route and focused on the poor track and timekeeping due to PC's woes.

Under Lewis, the politically appointed board of directors (which included consumer representatives) had its own mission: "Just to hang on." Reistrup's mission was fairly clear: "To try to save it." By the time a new board hired him, the philosophical missions coincided and the board's makeup seemed to work well, but trouble lay ahead: greatly increased ridership due to the energy crisis, with its long lines and expensive gasoline. Although he had "feelings" about whether Amtrak should serve the whole country, the NEC—Boston–New York–Washington, and possibly on to Richmond—"was critical." He founded the "Emerging Corridors Initiative," looking at "spider webs" of services centered in Chicago, St. Louis, and Milwaukee.

His first concern was to keep the trains on the track. With reliable motive power, trains could use just one locomotive, not the three or four of which one or more could be expected to fail en route. "The equipment was awful." Still, the equipment seemed like the easy part compared to the much more difficult track. It wasn't Amtrak's, and the new corporation had no ability to improve its condition.

In addition to keeping the trains on the tracks, Reistrup's mission included a commitment to "serve the rail passenger needs of intercity riders," in regional corridors but not commuter services. More to the point, though, he had priorities: "Keep the passengers (a) alive, and (b) assuming they're alive, comfortable. I'm not so worried about French toast." Most trains provided adequate meal service, but there was a need to trim costs, so Reistrup experimented with a food bar coach similar to what the Baltimore & Ohio, New York Central, Pennsylvania, and PC had initiated. He saw no need for "a big dining car," observing that passengers walked in the door but immediately went away. "They were not used to that kind of dining. They were put off by the formality and tablecloths. We were taking care of the coach passenger." Indeed, the profile of the rail passenger was in transition from that of ten or more years before. Times had changed, and so had passengers' expectations.

Reistrup recognized that he had to confront several issues simultaneously. Passenger comfort was related to the equipment, and passengers wanted to count on being delivered safely and on time to their destinations. Providing good service is essential: provide heat, air-conditioning, and a comfortable ride. "Amtrak's cars and equipment have to be maintained."

Service

So equipment came first, then working with the Class I railroads. "It was their track." He called John Reed, CEO of the Santa Fe, and other railroad CEOs and "met with every single one." He made a point of going to them in their offices, not requiring them to journey to Washington to see him. "Some were very pro-passenger."

Amtrak's equipment was tired but its useful life had not yet expired. The cars had maintenance problems, but they also came from railroads in different parts of the country with differing weather conditions. Not all heating and air conditioning systems were alike. "That equipment . . . we're hauling human beings. We froze them in the winter and cooked them in the summer. You leave Boston in a snowstorm and go to Florida where it is 100 degrees. You're asking a lot of a sleeping car." Equipment problems were endless.

Reistrup recounted how he once used a plastic coat hanger to close a relay in a car that had electrical problems. "The passengers didn't know I was the president." He once chased a mouse in a car. The car attendant told Reistrup the mouse "checked out each passenger at the station stops to see what they had for food." The attendant said, "That mouse knew what he was doing!"

Amtrak needed to look at new coaches and, eventually, new sleeping cars. It was under Reistrup's administration that the new Amfleet coaches began arriving, and he thought they had both good and bad attributes. The cars possessed a "great carbody inherited from the Metroliners, but which rode like a farm truck." A great and sturdy car with a poor ride was a problem. "Later modifications improved the ride," but on rough track no car rode really well. On the Corridor, "Well, that was scary at 110 mph. They [Penn Central] didn't want to do slow orders. There [were] still coal trains on the Corridor. It was all caused by the problems of the railroads—Penn Central, New Haven, Milwaukee Road—all had track that was getting bad; Erie Lackawanna too. It was spreading like a cancer. It came to a head with the Rock Island. It was the earth-shaker."

Providing good service comes at a cost. Reistrup knew first-hand the economics of onboard services: "You can't force passengers into high-cost diners." But should Amtrak be expected to earn a profit on food and beverage service, as mandated by Amtrak's reauthorization legislation? "No. You have to feed them if you haul them that far." Provide "enough to keep them from being hungry; three meals a day; continental breakfast is OK. You need a McDonald's or an Arby's on wheels. Expectations of passengers have changed; tastes have changed. Amtrak shouldn't be so rigid."

In Reistrup's view, Amtrak in general needed more flexibility. "Amtrak became bureaucratic. It was talking instead of doing. Management needs to get out on the railroad and see for itself what travel is like on a train," which he did.

Support

"The DOT simply gave the railroads pats on the back, but essentially they were ignored. They wanted Amtrak to fail." There was no interaction or support from the Federal Railroad Administration, which had been established in 1967. At the time, however, he did receive tremendous support from individual members of Congress, from both sides of the aisle. But "Amtrak needed two people—a chairman to handle Congress and a CEO to run the railroad. Only Graham Claytor could do both; he was there 11 years." Still, "We got a good start. We took care of the equipment but couldn't fix everyone's track." Amtrak needed equipment that could be easily cared for by any shop. "Working together with the railroads' shops was difficult."

Funding

Absent a major change, Amtrak will always face funding issues. Its nationalized passenger service was sold to everyone on the false premise that it would earn a profit, and that expectation has continued. "Amtrak is different from a profit-based airline and bus service. Railroads and Amtrak have always been viewed differently by politicians when it came to subsidies. I think it's the politicians—it's their toy. Harley Staggers, for example, got his train in West Virginia. This was a case of inappropriate pressure to start a route, Parkersburg–Washington, with little chance of generating significant use by travelers." Reistrup believed that funding Amtrak should be on the same level as other transportation modes. "Let's try to equalize it, keep a level playing field. Fund them all, focus on the intermodal. All the truckers are using rail. Long-term funding is essential, not every two years." He emphasized that Amtrak should be allocated "enough to meet the service criteria and provide a minimal amount of food. Keep the network going. I really do feel we need this. Continue to serve the whole country. Keep places on the rail map. And do emerging corridors. But don't cut long-distance."

Is Amtrak needed?

Despite his history of cutting trains while at C&O/B&O and Illinois Central, Reistrup sees a need for Amtrak and believes the long-distance and rural services should continue. "Amtrak should serve both the unserved and underserved. We had 500 stations on my watch. They should be served. Most have no alternative transportation except for autos."

Did lack of a national transportation policy hinder Amtrak? Reistrup believes there was no difference at the time he was in charge. "We were evolving." Amtrak had good government affairs people/lobbyists. "You also need a good general counsel." But "we really ought to have some sort of commission on infrastructure. I'm talking about all modes. Congress can't do it."

Greatest Accomplishment

In retrospect, Reistrup was proud of what was accomplished. There was, of course, "The equipment. The Amfleet, I think, were really, really good." There were 492 cars. Fleet size was decided not by any real plan; it resulted from dividing the per-car cost of $333,000 into available funds; fleet size was not analytically based, another shortcoming that went to the issue of adequate funding of Amtrak.

The first Superliners were on his watch too. P-S built them and then closed the shop. And Budd closed shortly after building the Amfleet cars.[26] The Superliner contract was signed on April 1 of 1975, but the date was changed to April 2 to avoid April Fool's Day. [And thus are major business decisions made.] Regarding the F40s, "I was proud of them." He required that they have a particular type of wheel assemblies called Blomberg trucks. "They stuck to the rail." An old engineer named Staggers (not the WV senator) said, "GE's slip [their wheels] in the sand house." Translated from railroad lingo, this meant that the General Motors-built F40s had better traction than General Electric locomotives.

Reflections Upon Departure

Did Reistrup have second thoughts about leaving after three years on the job? "Not really. Let's get on with the next event. I was too young to have been president of Amtrak. I told them I would serve several years, so that was it. I enjoyed the job, all of it, even some of the entanglements with politicians." Did he have any advice about the future of the company? Reistrup suggested that whoever became president of Amtrak should possess a military background, if possible. If that person was an "airline type, then someone who's been in the trenches—face to face with customers." Customer satisfaction is important and a CEO should know what is going on at ground level. "Wick Moorman—that's the kind of guy you need."

As for Amtrak today: "I didn't think it would last this long. I'm really, really pleased—extremely pleased with the Northeast Corridor, but don't divide Amtrak in two. Amtrak should be whole: the Corridor and the long-distance trains. I am proud that we acquired the entire Corridor and began rebuilding the track structure and became a real railroad."

Following his service with Amtrak, Reistrup spent ten years with R. L. Banks, a consulting firm, four years as president of the Monongahela Railway (1988–1992), and was then a consultant on a wide variety of transportation projects. He was also a mentor and advisor to AmeriStarRail on NEC programs and a vice president CSX Passenger Integration, working with the Conrail breakup and coordination with the Massachusetts Bay Transportation Authority (MBTA) and the Southeastern Pennsylvania Transportation Authority (SEPTA) during the transition. Not ready to retire, he still does consulting work.

Following Reistrup was Alan Boyd. During the war, Boyd had been a pilot in the Army Air Corps. He was a member of the Civil Aeronautics Board under President Dwight D. Eisenhower and its chairman under President John F. Kennedy. During the Johnson administration, he was undersecretary of commerce for transportation. In 1966, President Johnson revived a long-discussed idea of streamlining the nation's fragmented transportation systems. Boyd led a group that studied the problems, wrote a bill to create the Department of Transportation and shepherded it through Congress. Signed into law on October 15, 1966, the department began operation on April 1, 1967 with Boyd unanimously confirmed by the Senate. He was the only secretary of DOT who possessed a transportation background. (Since its founding in 1966, two of the secretaries of DOT have been spouses of a Senate majority leader, and they possessed no known expertise in transportation.) Among his first decisions was to pick both Democrats and Republicans as aides, insisting that transportation was nonpartisan.[27] Later, he led Illinois Central from 1969 to 1976.

When elected president of Amtrak, he recognized the need for new equipment, and it was during his term (1978–1982) that the rest of the Superliners arrived. His administration was forward looking, respected by employees and frustrated by politicians who frequently meddled in his governance.[28] A close friend of Boyd, David Gunn said, "I learned a lot from him. Alan saw a role for passenger rail in transportation and for the national system. He didn't see it as a partisan issue as it is today. He enjoyed working in the rail industry and for Amtrak."[29]

Many believe that W. Graham Claytor represented the gold standard, Amtrak's best and one of its most effective stewards. A former Navy captain, secretary of the Navy, and deputy defense secretary, Claytor had the advantage of being a lawyer steeped in corporate law and government; was conversant with the Railway Labor Act. He also had run a Class I railroad, the Southern Railway; understood management of Class I relationships; possessed tremendous capacity to analyze operational, political, and financial issues; and knew what it took to run a first-class passenger operation. He knew railroad history and understood the balance between business and service. He was able to keep his eye on both.[30]

Cliff Black wrote, "From the service perspective, a frequent observation from Claytor was, 'As long as we are running passenger trains, we will provide the best possible service we can.' That was his mantra at Southern, and he tried to carry it with him to Amtrak, which was a much more complex and bureaucratic company from the passenger perspective than Southern. Graham was very straightforward about these things and openly testified that Amtrak

W. Graham Claytor Jr., Amtrak president, 1982–1993.   *Courtesy Amtrak*

was going to continue to lose money, but he would try to reduce the amount lost by increasing revenue and holding down costs where reasonable and proper i.e., while continuing to provide good service."[31] Those who recall working for Claytor said he was dedicated to making Amtrak run efficiently and was exceptionally passenger-focused. He was determined to see that Amtrak survived.[32] Upon his retirement, Claytor told his successor, Tom Downs, that "the president of Amtrak should take a solemn pledge similar to the Hippocratic Oath to do no harm."[33]

Claytor was a great source of advice for Downs and spoke with him frequently. "Graham told me, 'The secretary of transportation is the [Amtrak] shareholder; Congress is the banker. Pay attention to the banker—the customer is the key to the banker.'" This was instructive. When Downs was looking at cutting the Sunset Limited, which operated through Mississippi, the mayor of Meridian called Senate Minority Leader Trent Lott to complain. Lott called Downs and said, "I didn't know I gave a goddamn about Amtrak, but apparently I do." The train survived. "National interest is the key to survival. Three-day-a-week service diminishes the national effect and connectivity" (see appendixes 1 and 2).[34]

Tom Downs, whose entire male heritage on his father's side was involved in railroading, loves railroads and also wanted Amtrak to survive. He was hired as both president and chairman of the board (as was Claytor) which solidified the corporation's course.[35] His mission was "Safety, safety, safety. I told my senior executive staff: Think in understandable terms. The first objective is: don't kill the customers. Second: don't kill any employees. Third: don't injure customers or employees. The operating vice president saw that his mission was to run trains on time!"[36]

Downs was service-minded and rode every long-distance train at least once, and several times in some cases, often in a bedroom or roomette, meeting with every crew base to stay in touch with what was happening on his watch. "Whenever I attended some social function and people found out who I was and what I did for a living, I got to hear every tale of a 'trip from Hell.' I heard how bad our service was."[37]

As time advanced, the board became more political and quite a headache. "The Amtrak board became a dumping ground for friends of the [US] president; one member of our board had dated him in college."[38] She became the "spearhead of the resistance" to Downs's objectives. "If the president doesn't care one good goddamn, it's where he can pay off some friends to subvert governance."[39] Downs said that his board was the most political and was friendly to the president. "The board's mission was to kiss up to the [US] president."[40]

As a result, getting qualified people to serve on Amtrak's board of directors was a challenge. "Some board members didn't know the difference between a passenger car and a locomotive, a diesel engine from an electric." During a meeting about electrification between New Haven and Boston initiated during Downs's tenure, "Another board member asked, 'If electrification is so great, why doesn't Amtrak electrify the entire network?'" After a pause, Downs politely explained that Amtrak didn't own the tracks.

White House meddling led to the loss of Downs's job. The White House budget office called him and "insisted" that he had to publicly announce that Amtrak would be subsidy-free within five years. "If you don't say this, the president will say you will get zero for the next budget."[41] Tom Downs could not say this—but his successor, George Warrington, could. During this time Amtrak was at the end of difficult labor negotiations over productivity, wages, and work rules. Having exhausted all the "cooling off" periods, the Brotherhood of Maintenance of Way Employees was threatening to strike. If they did, Penn

Station and the entire NEC would shut down. Downs was trying to hold the line on pay increases and benefits, but the Clinton White House suddenly undercut him by unilaterally agreeing to the union's demands. This had the effect of compounding Amtrak's budget problems in the face of the recent "subsidy-free" mandate. "They didn't care, it was just politics."[42] The board fired Downs shortly thereafter.[43]

George Warrington was appointed interim president and became full-time a year later. He introduced the Acela high-speed trains and mortgaged Penn Station, generating about $360 million in cash at 18% interest, a move made out of desperation.[44] In his four years he did little to improve the company. He left abruptly in early 2002 with the company saddled with a $4 billion debt, returning to New Jersey Transit as executive director. He died in 2007. Warrington was succeeded by David Gunn, who knew railroad operations and how to manage them.

Exceptional Stewardship: David Gunn (September 12, 2019 interview)

> Dave Gunn is raw truth.
> Ronald L. Batory

In 2003, President Bush signed an enormous ten-year tax cut package followed by budget cuts that included Amtrak funding. Since Day One, America's Railroad had managed to survive existential threats due to both mismanagement and defunding efforts under successive presidential administrations. When David Gunn assumed the top position at Amtrak in 2002, the company was 31 years old and had survived the budget cut proposals of Democrat and Republican presidents alike: Jimmy Carter (the largest), Ronald Reagan, George H. W. Bush, and Bill Clinton. Party affiliation has never been a factor. As a budget line item, Amtrak funding was an easy target. Gunn's predecessor, George Warrington, had earned his place in railroad history by promising that the company was "on a glide path" to self-sufficiency in order to placate the Clinton administration and Congress. Gunn called this "happy talk," and Amtrak still was not being allowed the budget or the unfettered freedom to do its job.

Preparations

David Gunn was born, raised, and educated in the Boston area. His father commuted on the Boston & Maine Railroad, exposing young David to trains. He enjoyed traveling by train and though he was not a railfan as such, he

David Gunn, Amtrak president, 2002–2005. *Courtesy Amtrak*

knew he wanted to work in railroading. He earned his bachelor of arts degree from Harvard University and an MBA from the Harvard Graduate School of Business. Following a stint in the US Naval Reserve, where he had indicated "transportation" as his area of interest, he joined the Atchison, Topeka and Santa Fe Railway and worked on the *Super-C* piggyback service. Later positions were with the New York Central, right at the time of the Penn Central merger (he already knew Jim McClellan because McClellan was the NYC contact on *Super-C* service); Illinois Central Gulf Railroad, where he was assistant vice president; and then the MBTA, where he was the director of both Commuter Rail and Operations.

During Gunn's time at MBTA (1974–75) it was buying the B&M's commuter lines, and Gunn handled negotiations with B&M's bankruptcy trustees. "Even Amtrak is not as political as MBTA [was] in Boston." He was able "to negotiate a terrific deal, even a better deal than the one reached with Penn Central." B&M ran commuter operations on PC lines that had been the New Haven's and the New York Central/Boston & Albany's. "Penn Central was awful to deal with."

In 1979, Gunn went to Philadelphia as general manager/chief operations officer for the SEPTA, where he managed the daily operations for the third-largest transit system in the United States. In 1984, he became president of the New York City Transit Authority; in 1991, general manager of the Washington Metropolitan Area Transit Authority; in 1995, chief general manager of the Toronto Transit Commission. In 2002, Gunn became president and chief executive officer of Amtrak, and stayed until 2005.

Once a profit-making venture, public transit now is a government service. By the time he accepted the job at Amtrak, Gunn had a deep background in that field, and his knowledge of how to move people and deal with government agencies was of great help. Like Amtrak, transit had to be managed as a business, and being adept at this made David Gunn the right choice at the right time. He was known for his direct, honest, and decisive management style, but what made him effective were his background, experience, leadership acumen, and ability to attract talented personnel. He was also possessed of a wry wit that he put to good use. Outgoing, relaxed, and personable, he was widely respected and well liked among Amtrak employees and others in the rail industry. A dual citizen of Canada and the United States, he retired from Amtrak to the family farmhouse in Nova Scotia.

Motivations

Like some others who have led Amtrak, Gunn liked railroads and enjoyed being in the mix of daily operations. His brief tenure at Amtrak began with a phone call. "I had a call from [Amtrak vice chairman Michael] Dukakis saying Warrington had left and they wanted a replacement." This call came at a time when he was considering another job. "I had an opportunity to take a transit job in London at the same time as the Amtrak position was offered." When he sat down with his mother (she was living in Nova Scotia; all his grandparents were Canadian) and told her about the two opportunities, she was pretty straightforward about it. "My mother stepped in and told me that I was going to Washington." End of discussion. "I loved being active in the transportation area. When I go to a place, it becomes me. I'm possessive. I want to succeed. Once I got to Amtrak and understood its problems, my mission was to save the company."

Expectations

When Gunn arrived at Amtrak, he wasn't sure what to expect, although he knew the company was struggling and in fact was only a few weeks away from insolvency. "It was a crapshoot whether it would survive." The second

Bush administration wanted to get rid of it. Amtrak almost missed a payroll. The company needed a quick fix; nobody seemed to want it; DOT and FRA didn't want anything to do with it. It had no home. But Gunn was happy with the Amtrak board. John Robert Smith, the former mayor of Meridian, Mississippi, was chair. Gunn described him as "excellent"; Linwood Holton (former governor of Virginia) was on the board, as was Michael Jackson from DOT. The six-member board was rounded out by what Gunn described as "two political ladies" who were "not effective."

Warrington had left for New Jersey Transit, so Gunn spent two days in Washington doing interviews with Amtrak people to build a knowledge base. Of Warrington, he said, "He didn't give a rat's ass about anything but Acela; ignored track maintenance and other issues." Gunn made an observation to the board: "You have a big problem." Jackson, the DOT representative, said, "The [G. W. Bush] administration wants a caretaker." Gunn responded, "You need an undertaker."

The administration did not see Amtrak as a serious player in transportation. "DOT is a 'throwaway' department." The head of DOT should be somebody with a transportation background. "Alan Boyd was the only leader [of DOT] who knew anything about transportation. All the others are political hacks." Norman Mineta, the lone Democrat in Bush's cabinet, was DOT secretary when Gunn was at Amtrak and "was a political animal. His mission was to keep his job, and he was willing to do whatever the White House wanted." He and Gunn were at odds. "I wanted to make Amtrak survive. He [Mineta] didn't."

However, Gunn's expectations changed with time. He was "pleasantly" surprised at what Amtrak could accomplish in tracks, cars, and service quality, so his expectations rose as he saw what his various departments could do if they were given the needed resources. "Your expectations and hopes grow. In a positive way, I discovered how many good, competent, and committed people were at Amtrak." But did he know what he was in for? "Oh, yes, in the sense that I knew I had massive physical and financial problems. There was no organizational chart, no budget, no income statement, no profit-and-loss statement for the express business, and cash statements made no sense. It was a real mess." There were some serious challenges to confront. Warrington had bought into the idea that Amtrak would be profitable and kept promoting the fallacy of a "glide path to sustainability." Actually, "there was some worry on his part."

As far as Gunn was concerned, "I was over 65, and I needed two months to vest in Tier 2 Railroad Retirement. I knew it was serious business; I was worried about meeting payroll or the collapse of the company." But it got worse: President Bush replaced the board and David Laney (former chair of the Texas Transportation Commission under Governor George W. Bush who had raised more than $100,000 for his 2000 presidential campaign) became Amtrak's chairman.[45] "After a while he made it clear that the goal was to bankrupt the company. Jeff Rosen, an Amtrak board member, was an ideological DOT lawyer who also wanted to kill Amtrak." This worried Gunn, but he was not scared. He knew he would not be ruined if the company was lost, but a lot of people would be hurt. "Suddenly I'm responsible for the company." Amtrak people were his employees. The payroll pressure was the worst. Within two weeks of starting, he knew Amtrak would soon run out of cash. He went to the DOT, but the cash situation actually made them happy. So he confronted them with the fact that Amtrak owned the NEC and did all the dispatching. "Do you understand what happens if Amtrak stops operating? No Northeast Corridor, no New Jersey Transit, no SEPTA, either. Nothing. That woke them up. They got worried and got mad at me." This ended with two appropriations (a $100 million loan from DOT, followed by supplemental funding from Congress), and suddenly Amtrak had the cash it needed.

Having hardly begun his new job, already Gunn was disturbing the peace. As it turned out, he had to go to DOT for everything. In seeking additional funding, he found that "DOT's attitude was cut expenses and live with the cash you have. They wanted the whole thing to go away." Laney spent his whole time trying to "slice off the Corridor." This was after he told Laney what would happen if Amtrak was killed off, just as he had told the people at DOT.

When he arrived, there was "a lack of an operating focus by top management." Gunn reorganized the company, and by fall Amtrak had a railroad organizational structure and personnel titles. "Today," he said, "it has gone back to 'flavor of the month' titles. The railroad industry is old, and they've figured out how to make things work." He appointed good people to positions such as chief financial officer, marketing head, general counsel, and chief operating officer. "We had a competent bunch of railroaders. The Engineering Department was excellent. Give them the resources, and they can do the job." Still, no one had done a five-year plan, or even a comprehensive plan for the entire system. Amtrak got the money it needed because Congress gave it bipartisan support for specific things, but there was no long-term planning.

Missions

As he saw it, Gunn's mission was clear: "Run the company—the national system—in a safe, efficient manner, as economically as possible." The more immediate mission, though, was to survive the next two months and implement capital programs to put the system in a state of good repair. In testimony before the Appropriations Committee's Subcommittee on Transportation, Treasury, and Independent Agencies, Gunn testified that his immediate goals "were to maintain solvency, begin an incremental program of critical capital investment, create a lean organization with tight financial controls, and build a zero-based budget." In keeping with his matter-of-fact approach to his work, he added that, "Overarching all of this was [and still is] the continuing need to rebuild our credibility and so I have taken steps to end the spin and 'happy talk' press releases."

Gunn's mission and the board's mission were in harmony when he got there. But the board's mission changed when "the Laney crowd" was appointed and under him the new board's mission was to destroy Amtrak. "The last board [when Gunn was there] was the enemy, neither motivated nor competent. It was trying to kill the company."

"Part of an Amtrak president's mission involves transportation policy; he doesn't control it, but part of his job is to suggest changes to it. Right now there is no clear transportation policy. Nobody asked: 'What are you trying to accomplish?' There's nothing wrong with Amtrak's business plan; the problem is at the DOT level: what do you want? Waterways get 100 percent government money; airlines get the air traffic control system and lots of other government support. Highways have a trust fund." Amtrak is a budget line item that can be easily cut. "The other key factor is that the other modes are promoted and the freight railroads and passenger rail are not promoted."

"Government has screwed up the free market in transportation. It is not free enterprise. Governments do all the heavy lifting—fund, build, operate and maintain the airports, air traffic control, facilities, highways, manage the waterways. What is left is called free enterprise. The freight railroads are about as close [as possible] to being on their own. And passenger rail is an orphan."

Speaking of Amtrak's president at the time of our interview, Gunn said that Richard Anderson had no sense of the importance of the Mechanical and Engineering Departments. "He's on a mission we don't understand." Anderson never talked to Gunn. Part of Gunn's mission was to have good equipment, good facilities, and financial discipline and control. He reduced employment by 4,000; absenteeism ran 5-6 percent, "a good figure." Ridership was up, the subsidy was down. He stressed that management had to be organized, have a plan, and stick to it. "None of that is there today. Anderson doesn't understand this. He's never there."

Amtrak needed heavy car fleet maintenance; it needed scheduled overhauls. In further testimony before the subcommittee hearing in April 2003, Gunn remarked that "beginning in late 1998, the company began to defer capital [expenditures] to stay on the 'glide path' to self-sufficiency, the last great idea for Amtrak, and so among the activities that fell along the wayside was the repair of wrecked equipment." Gunn had Amtrak set up heavy overhaul programs at Beech Grove shops for the Superliners and Bear, Delaware, for the Amfleet cars. He also developed maintenance-of-way capital budgets to rebuild Amtrak-owned infrastructure, projects such as installation of 300 miles of new rail in the NEC over three years.

Service

Another part of the mission was providing good service. Gunn wanted a precise operation—a safe, comfortable, well-maintained property. He also wanted to be a good neighbor. In addition, he wanted cleanliness, an improved ride and quality of equipment and track; and an improvement in employees' attitudes. Gunn got out on the railroad to gather personal experiences—including on the long-distance trains—and spoke with the crews. "The Superliners are nice. I liked riding them. The Viewliners are junk." On the Capitol Limited there were "these awful pink blankets." He replaced them with blue or dark blue blankets. While this did not seem all that important, it was still part of the overall impression the experience gave passengers.

A lot of what Gunn saw and changed came from riding the trains and talking to employees. He had done this at New York's Metropolitan Transportation Authority and other places. "Talk to people. You learn a lot. Present management doesn't get out much." He was well aware that Amtrak had to provide food more efficiently, but he also recognized that it could not offer the same menu all the time. "Varying the menu had no additional cost; it just required more effort. [The] level of food service depends on the route—NYC to Albany, for example, does not need much. You need variety, but not a lot. It should be tasty and good."

Should Amtrak be expected to break even or make a profit on food and beverage service? "No. It's part of the service. Look at the performance of the train as a whole." For example, Gunn experimented with the food service and reduced the deficit on the Empire Builder. He kept rebuilt equipment on the train. The goal was to cut the overall deficit. Ridership and revenues rose much faster than the costs of providing the improved service. He noted that preplated meals might work out, "but you need more than that."

Part of the problem, and it is a big part, "is that Amtrak's current management does not understand what's required to buy railroad equipment. After the war, railroads could open a catalogue and pick and choose whatever they wanted for equipment, like out of a Sears catalogue. You can't order from a catalogue anymore." All of the traditional manufacturers are gone—P-S, Budd, and ACF. "What the railroad is losing is the institutional experience, so they don't know what a good design looks like. Airlines have a choice and can just pick from a catalogue, leaving the president to decide the color of the seats." Not so with Amtrak.

Support

In Gunn's opinion, "There is no real Department of Transportation that serves to support a true national transportation network with equitable support for all modes. It is the result of the politics of the last century, and the highway and air systems are overseen by people taking care of them—that is, private interests are calling the shots. It includes the Army Corps of Engineers too, serving the water transportation industry. Hedge funds are taking over the railroads, with a focus on the per-share profit for the next quarter. This may be the biggest threat to Amtrak, after its current known threats. Amtrak should be customer-driven. Amtrak needs to get along with the railroads, including Union

Pacific, [but] they're in the process of going out of business. [The late] Hunter Harrison and his precision scheduled railroading—PSR—are doing this. Live it up now and go out of business in ten years. There's no critical analysis of what Harrison did. Earnings per share rules, not whether the business is sustainable over the long term." PSR is about taking existing business and handling it in the most efficient manner and driving off the business that's inconvenient. "Railroad market share is constantly declining. Sounded great, but PSR is handling the business for the railroads' convenience, not the shippers."

Gunn says that Amtrak needs a secretary and a Department of Transportation that allocates resources in a logical way. It does not receive much support from the FRA. Joe Boardman, Amtrak president from 2008 to 2016, a good friend of Gunn's, was a bureaucrat and felt he had to be part of the administration. When Gunn was in charge, "Congressional support was good." The Amtrak board was his biggest headache and his greatest frustration—"DOT was by and large the enemy; [former Transportation Secretary] Elaine Chao is a classic example."

"If you want [political] support for the Northeast Corridor, you darn well better support the Empire Builder. Without long-distance trains you don't get national support. Breaking up the long-distance trains into corridors is absurd." When Gunn ran Amtrak, service to rural regions was as important as were corridors such as the NEC, Milwaukee, Northwest, California, Virginia, and North Carolina. To get support for the long-distance trains, "Mayor Roberts of Meridian, Mississippi, brought along Senator Trent Lott."

Is Amtrak Needed?

"Yes, if run well! It's trying to preserve what's left of a national system. It's a national system and deserves national support. We could end up with corridors that are not Amtrak's. Amtrak is the repository of what is left of the passenger institutional knowledge of the railroads."

"You cannot build a castle on a mud foundation. The mandate is valid: run the national system. If you have a national system you have to run it. A sense of direction is what's missing. Corridors solve major transportation problems in their areas. But it ain't gonna be done by private development." Besides, "there aren't that many [long-distance] routes, and they don't cost that much. And they provide important services. Even the poor old Sunset Limited is important." Assuming there is a rational national transportation policy, Amtrak would be the yeast for a whole bunch of rising passenger rail services. It would provide knowledge and skill to help create these services. "But it's being destroyed. We need an appreciation for what Amtrak people know."

What is the alternative to a viable Amtrak? "Flying—it's awful. Planes are airborne cattle cars. They cram as many people as they can into smaller seats with little legroom. Amtrak has enormous potential, but there's no advertising/marketing and no will to take advantage of the potential. Amtrak's goal is to make a trip pleasant."

Greatest Accomplishment

Gunn's greatest accomplishment, in his view, was in fiscal management and control, and controls over the employee headcount. And reporting too. "We spent enormous time on preparing the budget. This was not dictated—we sought goals and objectives of departments. We asked what was needed to accomplish those." There were a lot of capital projects, some unfortunately left undone. "It's never done, first of all." He wanted to make Amtrak and the systems he put in a little less destructible. "We got the operating deficit down, and at one point were almost about breaking even, but funding the capital projects was always going to be a government problem." The capital projects will always require additional government funding. "The expense of introducing replacement equipment means the company will never break even."

Transportation Policy and Funding

When it comes to transportation policy, it is clear that the country lacks a sense of direction other than to promote and subsidize aviation and highway construction. The historical approach has been to allow free market forces to address the issues rather than take the lead in planning for the future. "The highway infrastructure is at its limit. There are more cars on the road than the highways were designed to handle. They were designed in the 1950s and despite legitimate improvements for safety, governments have let congestion determine when and where expansion should occur. In some places, as in California, there is no more space to add lanes. And states are not in any position to fund expansion, let alone maintenance."

"The cost of infrastructure is a government responsibility. It's government's job to ensure transportation of people and freight. The goal should be to use the right mode in various markets. Rail is often the most economical and environmentally acceptable mode. Unlike Europe, we've allowed railroads to tear up much of their infrastructure. Atlanta, for example, has no room for passenger rail. Nobody is paying serious attention to infrastructure, and we don't have people who know how to make stuff happen physically. We're consumers and assume that someone else will do the physical work. They don't know how to do it. Transportation policy should be for government to figure out how to manage mobility. There is no sense that these [different modes] are tools." How can government level the playing field between highway, air, water, and rail? "Start with the mission of the secretary of transportation. Chao is clueless—about railroads, anyway."

Change

"The current board may be individually competent but as a group it isn't sure of what it's doing. There is no clear vision of what it wants Amtrak to be. There is some commitment to what a national system should be. Good operating managers are very scarce. Top management doesn't even ride the trains. Board members should know how to run a big company and have some knowledge of the railroad industry." Gunn's job required knowledge of managing and running a railroad. "The job of the Amtrak president is to run a railroad."

Reflections Upon Departure

In late 2005, Gunn strongly and vocally disagreed with board chair Laney about Amtrak's recent results and about forcing it into bankruptcy, as Laney had proposed in a Senate hearing. Given the opportunity to resign, reportedly at the direction of DOT secretary Norman Mineta, he refused. "They told me they had put a nice severance package together for me so I could leave with my head held high, but I had nothing to be sorry for, so I declined. I suppose if I had taken it I could have made out pretty well, but it was a matter of principle. I told them, 'You have to fire me.'"

They did, after which Gunn sent a letter to all employees saying that he had been fired. He also wrote a letter to Laney dated November 9, 2005 reporting on Amtrak's fiscal year 2005 results (which did not show a company on the verge of bankruptcy). "I think the goal is to kill Amtrak and have the residual remains of the Northeast Corridor in the hands of New Jersey Transit and other corridor/commuter operators."

Upon reflection, Gunn said he was "proud of what we had done; sad because I enjoyed the job." Unfortunately, Amtrak suffers from instability. There was some long-term leadership in the past: Boardman served eight years, Claytor, a bit less than 12. "Boardman really wanted Amtrak to survive, and he supported a national system. He was pushed out by Anthony Coscia, chairman of the board and a New Jersey politician.[46] Odds are you won't get a good president in this environment. They [the Trump administration] want someone to do their bidding. Anderson is doing that. The Trump appointees are not getting confirmed but are virulently anti-Amtrak."

David Gunn's Account of His Firing as President and CEO of Amtrak in 2005 (9/12/19 interview)

On March 16, 2005, David Gunn was at a meeting with board chair David Laney and other board members. The discussion centered on splitting Amtrak in two—the NEC and everything else. "This episode was a pivotal point in Amtrak history and it led to Dave's dismissal—David Laney's carrying out the dirty work of Norm Mineta, but more than likely his deputy, and a board subsequently bitterly divided. They never really understood the complexity and interrelatedness of the system as a whole," said Joe McHugh.[47] "Gunn tried to educate Laney that the success of the Corridor, which was so much more than Amtrak service, would not function if the construction people were not in the

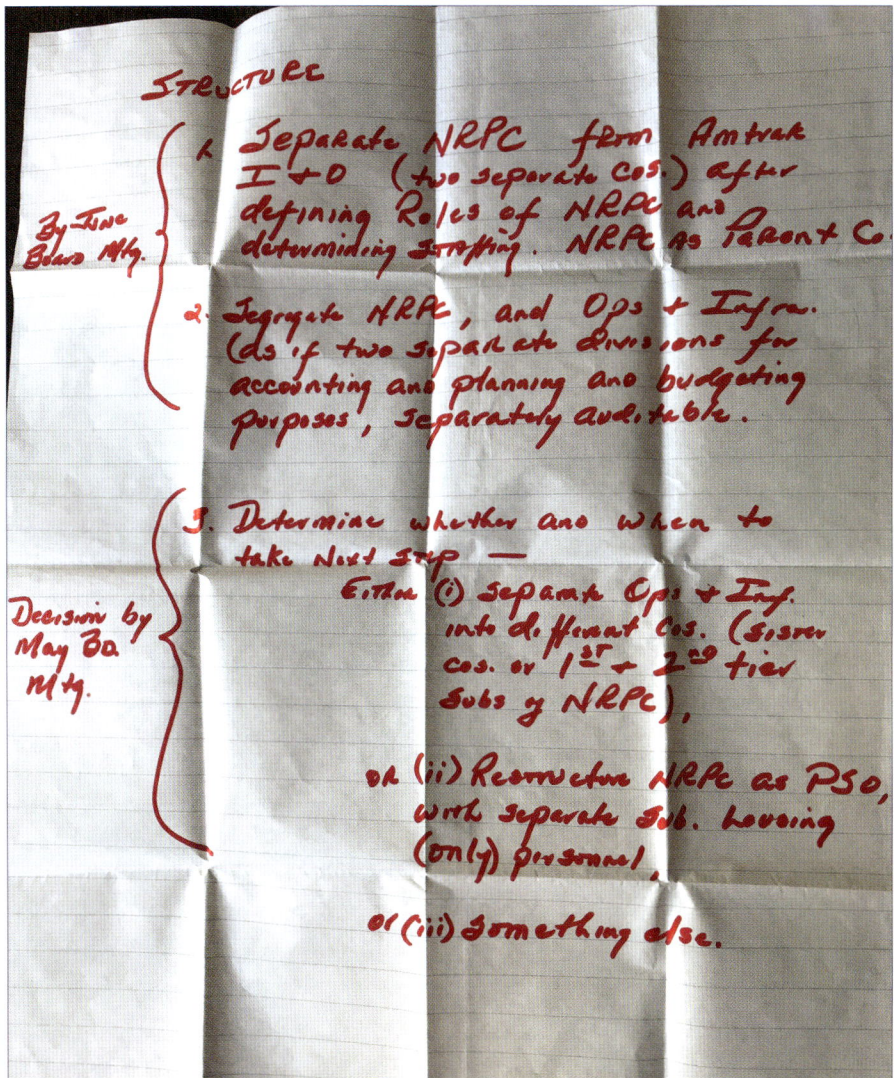

David Laney "wanted to please his bosses at the White House and DOT and so he worked behind the scenes to pitch the idea of privatizing Amtrak."[1] This flipchart page laid out Laney's plan. Cliff Black characterized it as "a devilishly designed deck-chair rearrangement."[2] What they wanted to do was break apart Amtrak by creating two companies—an infrastructure company and an operating company. David Gunn said: "It was driven by the ideologues at DOT, designed to destroy Amtrak—they didn't believe the government should be running passenger trains. Laney's objective was to get the Northeast Corridor out of Amtrak; sell off its [NEC's] assets [to the states?] while allowing the rest [Amtrak] to wither on its own. It was done so people wouldn't notice what they were doing."[3] (1. McHugh, January 22, 2021; 2. Email correspondence with Cliff Black, January 18, 2021; 3. Telephone interview with David Gunn, January 21, 2021. *Courtesy David Gunn*

same organization as the operating people."[48] But, Gunn said that Laney had no understanding of the impact this would have, since Laney was a lawyer [and, presumably, not experienced in railroading in general and passenger trains in particular]. Gunn left the meeting, claiming a dinner engagement.

Later that year, at a congressional hearing, Senator John McCain asked Gunn about the plan to split Amtrak. He told the senator, "It's a bad idea." Laney replied that the company was bankrupt and should be forced into [formal] bankruptcy. McCain replied, "But that's the end of Amtrak?" Laney replied it was. McCain then asked Gunn, "Do you agree with this?" Gunn replied, "No."

One morning some time later, Bill Crosbie, chief operating officer, told Gunn that "something was going on." Laney and Chief Engineer David Hughes (former Bangor & Aroostook president) had a lunch meeting in Philadelphia; Crosbie called Hughes, who said that Gunn was to be fired that day. When they met, Laney told Gunn he wanted him to resign. Gunn was adamant, saying he wouldn't, and furthermore, "If you want to fire me, fire me. I'm not resigning. Why am I being fired?" Laney replied that the "Financial numbers don't look good. Numbers are out of control." Gunn protested: "No, we're on budget." Laney: "Production is way off." Gunn: "No, it's up." [Laney presumably was referring to ridership, or possibly on-time performance, or ticket revenues, or all of the above.] Gunn: "I was curious about what excuse you had for doing this." He was given to understand that the chief of staff for Norman Mineta ordered it. So Gunn was fired, at which time he wrote the November letter outlining Amtrak's results for FY 2005 so there would be a comprehensive record of the positive direction in which the company was headed. He also issued a letter to all Amtrak employees stating that he had been fired.

Laney's public response was that "Amtrak's future now requires a different type of leader who will aggressively tackle the company's financial management and operational challenges."[49] As *Railway Age* reflected at the time, "In reality, Gunn was kicked out by the Bush administration appointees who had very different motives—namely, carving up Amtrak into pieces that could be 'privatized,' whatever that meant."[50]

In a subsequent interview on National Public Radio, Gunn put it bluntly, stating, "It's pretty clear that the administration's designs on Amtrak have been very different than mine. And the board is just a puppet for the administration and DOT. They're not an independent board. I was standing in the way of their plans to dismantle the company. The other thing that was happening was we were actually being fairly successful in bringing order and fiscal discipline to the company, which was making it more and more difficult to carry out their plan."[51]

In closing, Gunn made prescient observations before the subcommittee: "At some point, Congress will turn its attention to the reauthorization of Amtrak and it will be in this venue that the future of rail passenger service will be decided. In the year that I have been here, I have been struck by the amount of attention that Amtrak generates without real progress occurring in addressing the long-term funding problems that everyone knows exist. I realize that Amtrak is partly to blame for this paralysis of action; recurring crises distract us from the central issues that should be discussed. I know that Amtrak for too long had been engaged in the charade of pleasing its detractors by endorsing the concept of self-sufficiency. Let me be clear, however, that despite the best management

David Gunn's Six Myths About Amtrak

From testimony before the Committee on Appropriations Subcommittee on Transportation, Treasury, and Independent Agencies April 10, 2003:

Myth 1: Amtrak can be profitable.

• No national rail passenger system in the world is profitable. Without public subsidy, there will be no passenger rail transportation systems in the United States.

Myth 2: The private sector is dying to take over our services.

• Remember why we were formed. We are what is left of a once privately run enterprise.

Myth 3: Long-distance trains are the problem.

• This is perhaps one of the biggest myths. If you eliminate every long-distance train, your avoidable costs would decrease about $70 million a year, after about a year and a half of paying labor protection costs. On a fully allocated basis, after five years, you might save annually about $300 million. Focusing on this problem is not going to save Amtrak. This approach is a red herring.

Myth 4: Amtrak is a featherbed for labor.

• Our wage rates are about 90 percent of the freight industry and are even lower when compared to transit. Wages are not the problem; generating a higher level of productivity, that is the challenge. It is management's duty to seek such improvement.

Myth 5: The Northeast Corridor is profitable.

• The NEC may cover most of its above-the-rail costs, but it is an extremely costly piece of railroad to maintain. The NEC is not profitable and never will be. Sure, private groups might be interested in having it, but they would take it only with the promise of massive capital infusions.

Myth 6: There is a quick fix—reform.

• The word "reform" is like catnip to those interested in a quick fix to Amtrak. If the answer were quick and easy, we would have solved the problem long ago. What needs to be done is to tightly manage the company and its finances and begin to make incremental but critical improvements to plant and equipment.

---

that could be brought to this railroad, without support for a realistic investment over the next few years, we will always remain on the edge and the problem will grow worse, risking a real disaster either physically and/or financially. The lack of a detailed policy will soon produce unwanted consequences."[52]

After Gunn

When Gunn was fired, David Hughes was appointed interim president, followed by Alex Kummant, who ran into trouble with the board and who wound up serving only two years. William Crosbie, who had been chief

Joseph Boardman, Amtrak president, 2008–2016. *Courtesy Amtrak*

operating officer, was appointed interim president upon Kummant's departure. Since Joseph Boardman had been on Amtrak's board as FRA administrator (representing the principal shareholder, the DOT) he was hired as president in 2008 to replace Crosbie—just as President Bush was dealing with the national financial meltdown and ensuing crisis. In November, Barack Obama was elected president and there was some hope for Amtrak that soon proved unrealistic. Cliff Black, longtime Amtrak public spokesman, noted Obama's "support" was all a show. "[A] similar thing happened with Bill Clinton: much lip service about 'high speed rail' and passenger rail infrastructure during Clinton's first campaign. Famous photo of him wearing an Amtrak conductor's cap circulated widely during the campaign. Once in office, Clinton proposed slashing Amtrak's budget by more than half, to $400 million."[53]

Tom Downs recalled, "Clinton and Carter thought trains were all about nostalgia. Clinton's support was simply political calculation. Al Gore seemed to have a clear enthusiasm for Amtrak. He got the technology and Acela. His close friend [and former chief of staff] Roy Neel was [later] appointed to the Amtrak board."[54] Hunter Biden also was on the board at one time.[55]

Joe Boardman had been the FRA administrator and wanted the Amtrak president's job but had to sit it out as interim for a year before becoming permanent. Black wrote, "As Boardman was relatively unfamiliar with passenger rail operations and marketing, he put trust in his staff and generally let the railroad run itself. From the start, he was a strong advocate of the nationwide service and as time passed, he gained a better understanding of operations. He became a competent advocate for the company and its services, both in the media and on Capitol Hill."[56]

"Boardman was an extrovert, meeting with staffers, traveling on the railroad, talking with frontline workers, and soon developed his style and established his priorities. It was common for him to stroll unannounced into the Washington crew base and strike up conversations with conductors and locomotive engineers, communications and signal people and others. Although this habit was generally well-received by employees, it was viewed with some skepticism by management. He brought with him a keen sense of the importance of safety from the regulatory agency FRA, and although he scrapped the traditional railroad Safety Department, run solely by management, he encouraged the agreement-covered workers to establish their own safety program, which became 'Safe to Safer.' It was an unconventional concept that ultimately failed to produce the results he had hoped for in terms of lost-time injuries and accident reduction."[57]

Boardman had been president of Amtrak for five years and although he had his critics and contretemps with subordinates, he was given a three-year contract extension.[58] "Toward the close of his tenure, during several of Boardman's cross-country rail trips, he began to warn state and local governments that they would soon be required to carry more of the cost burden of Amtrak services. This made news that wasn't well received, but he was anticipating the effects of the PRIIA Act of 2008, whose provisions were beginning to come into effect."[59]

When Richard Anderson succeeded Wick Moorman as president, Boardman publicly criticized several of Anderson's cost-cutting initiatives that were so clearly harmful to the long-distance trains, including proposals to substitute bus service for some rail segments and drastically diminishing the level of food service. Black noted that "Joe Boardman was simply a good man whose intentions were admirable. He was friendly, cheerful, and filled with enthusiasm for the company he led. He carried out his job with fairness and a collegial sense of shared mission to keep Amtrak moving ahead."[60] He died of a stroke shortly after leaving Amtrak.

The company was at a turning point. What it required were stable and caring stewards. Instead, Amtrak's continuity of purpose was under threat from within—a board chairman and board members who had a different concept of a "national network" and who harbored motives and allegiances of a provincial nature.⁶¹

Transitional Stewardship: Charles W. Moorman IV
(August 7, 2019 interview)

Hello, I must be going; I cannot stay; I came to say ... I must be going.
Groucho Marx (*Animal Crackers*, 1930)

After leading Amtrak for eight years, the company's second-longest presidential term, Joseph Boardman was ousted when he came up against an Amtrak board that had changed course about where the company should be headed. The national passenger carrier was being directed to shift responsibility for passenger service to the states in order to reduce federal support for the long-distance operating budget and to focus attention on the densely populated NEC. This was yet another decision driven by politics. It would not be the last. Not having a replacement president ready to go, Amtrak's chairman began looking for somebody to carry out his and the board's agenda. Wick Moorman had just retired as chairman of one of the country's strongest railroads, Norfolk Southern, a combination formed by the merger of the Southern Railway and the Norfolk & Western Railway, and while he wanted to take a rest, to a degree he remained restless.

Born in New Orleans, Moorman grew up in Hattiesburg, Mississippi. His affinity for railroads began at an early age; he says he can only surmise that his mother dropped him on his head one day and, after that, "I was hooked." After high school he earned a bachelor of science degree in civil engineering from the Georgia Institute of Technology in 1975. As part of his studies, he took part in a cooperative education program with Southern Railway beginning in 1970, and while there gained appreciation for and knowledge base in the business of railroading.

Preparation

Upon completion of his degree, Moorman entered Southern Railway's highly respected management trainee program, after which he served as a track supervisor, and then a division engineer, relocating several times as his career advanced across the Southern and then Norfolk Southern systems. Along the way he married his wife, Bonnie, and raised a son and daughter. In 1987 he took a management buyout to pursue an MBA at Harvard University. Despite his having taken the buyout, the railroad asked when he would finish his degree. He interviewed with several companies, including CSX and Amtrak, but eventually returned to Norfolk Southern in 1989 as a planning director. He

Charles "Wick" Moorman, Amtrak president, 2016–2017.

advanced through a number of senior management positions in Transportation Planning and in 1992 was promoted to vice president of Personnel and Labor Relations. This entailed a moved to Norfolk where, after 18 months, he was appointed vice president of information technology. He spent seven years in that position working on, among other things, Y2K conversion and the Conrail acquisition. After IT, he ran an internal initiative on telecom infrastructure along with NS Strategic Planning.

In 2004 chairman David Goode advised Moorman that Norfolk Southern's board of directors was naming him the next president. The following year he was named chief executive officer, and in 2006 the board elected him chairman. In 2011, *Railway Age* named Moorman "Railroader of the Year," and *Progressive Railroading* gave him its "Railroad Innovator Award" in 2013. He spent four decades at the Southern Railway and Norfolk Southern, stepping down as CEO in 2015.

Joseph Boardman, who had been president of Amtrak since 2008, "retired" (was ousted) in 2016. While Moorman did not seek that position, the fact that he was retired and might be available prompted Anthony Coscia, Amtrak's board chairman, to call and ask if Moorman would help the corporation by becoming CEO. It was a difficult decision. Moorman was intrigued and realized that Amtrak required leadership and some significant change. He was experienced and knowledgeable and believed he could help, but he had just retired to spend more time with his family, for which his wife was more than ready. She had an *extremely* (Moorman's emphasis) dim view of the whole idea and consented only after he pledged to take the position on an interim basis with the understanding that he would be away from home for only three, or possibly four, days a week. With her approval, he accepted, becoming Amtrak's eleventh CEO effective September 1, 2016, with a clear understanding with Amtrak's board that he was only there on a temporary basis until a permanent successor could be hired.

It had been nearly 20 years since Amtrak had been given a president who possessed actual, hands-on, railroad experience. David Gunn had been the last.[62]

Motivations

Moorman liked railroads generally but also passenger trains. While he was happy in his retirement from Norfolk Southern, he still had a drive to work on something constructive. He saw a new opportunity when he was asked to take on this assignment, believing it would be "interesting, but also fun." Admitting to a bit of ego, he remarked, "I was perfect for the job." Personable, affable, and with a predisposition to good humor, he believed that passenger trains were making a comeback, becoming more popular. Freight trains lack the appeal of passenger trains, which are the public's connection to railroads. "Amtrak is important and public service is important. I felt I could be good at it." In fact, had he not been president and chairman of NS, would he have taken the job as Amtrak's CEO? "Yes, I am sure I would have, for the same reasons."

Expectations

When he took the job, Moorman did not know what to expect. Upon arriving at the office, he had a lot of investigative work to do. He knew Joe Boardman slightly and had read about Amtrak in *Trains* and *Railway Age* magazines, but he feared that learning all the good and bad about Amtrak would take time and that "just understanding the problems might take me more than six months [a reference to how long he might stay with Amtrak when he first considered the position]." There were lots of surprises, and he realized that he really had a short amount of time and had to learn a lot quickly. He needed people he knew could understand the challenges and whom he trusted, so he brought in several NS retirees to do deep dives in critical areas such as safety, labor relations, engineering, and technology. These investigations highlighted critical areas such as IT, where the IT staff was capable given good leadership, "but large amounts of money were being wasted in poorly managed projects being run by unqualified managers in user departments."

"But there were still three months of 'What!!??'" He discovered to his dismay that Amtrak was poorly organized in some areas and occasionally chaotic. There were also managers who clearly were not effective, although the majority of the management team was competent and working to make the organization succeed. There were some elements of management "flavor of the month" in an organization which clearly needed to get back to basics. In addition, he was surprised by some unforeseen problems, such as structural issues with the underwater tunnels serving New York's Penn Station. Still, the issues didn't faze him. "It was fun. I didn't stress out."

Missions

Sticking to his position that he took the job only until a full-time executive could be chosen, Moorman clearly recognized his mission: "Fix what you can and help find the next person." Just as important, he and the board believed that the job of president and CEO had to be elevated so the person chosen would be seen as a "real CEO," not a placeholder. Amtrak had suffered from a series of place holders who adversely affected the company's success. In his view, the company needed long-term competent leadership at the top in order to be sustainable.

Amtrak is sometimes thought of as a quasi-governmental agency, but it was actually incorporated as a for-profit corporation. Moorman recognized the situation upon taking up his post. "We may have a crummy business model, but we can be a good corporation." It was a point that he made emphatically and consistently to every group, internal and external. He told people that Amtrak is in many ways really no different than any other government contractor, but instead of being able to charge for its services to make an adequate return, it has to rely on direct appropriations.

As a corporate CEO, Moorman was directly responsible to the Amtrak board. Its mission and his, he believed, "were in perfect alignment." Board members had some business experience—an important fact, in his estimation. Their mission and his was to "Ensure that Amtrak is a well-run corporation. This is a business. Secondly, promote passenger transportation across the country." Amtrak's original mandate was to provide a national transportation system, but, he asked, "How exactly do you define a national passenger service?" This is an important question that the current Amtrak management has to address. In his view, the mission of an Amtrak president is to "Promote the use of effective transportation across the country in the places it makes sense. That can include some of the long-distance routes but not necessarily all of them." When considering Amtrak's original mandate, should long-distance trains be continued between major population centers such as New York–Chicago, Chicago–Seattle, and Chicago–Los Angeles? From a strictly business perspective, "Some, yes, but there are places where a combination of bus and train makes sense."

"You can put good buses on routes. On the Santa Fe, for example [Chicago–Los Angeles], the train has lots of passengers between Chicago and Kansas City. Put on a bus west of KC to whatever is the eastern endpoint of a train coming east from LA. The people you disappoint—those riding the train on the whole route—are few. You can run a great bus and save a lot of money. There are ways to serve underserved communities, which is one of the primary arguments that is offered in defense of parts of the long-distance network, and not spend a lot of money."

The Work

His first task was Amtrak's safety culture. "The gap between Amtrak and the Class I's was substantial." The safety record had deteriorated over several years following the implementation of Safe-to-Safer, a program derived from behavior-based principles. "It was well-intentioned but implemented very poorly and in such a way that supervisors were taken out of the process." In addition, supervisory training in safety and other operating practices was practically nonexistent. He knew that creating a positive safety culture is a long-term process, but also that it needed to get underway.

There were problems other than safety that needed attention. Moorman told a group that had questions about dining car service, "Look, I'm a plumber. I'm trying to fix the big problems you don't see." That was part of his mission: Fix things and get out. And there was still more to do across the entire organization. Some things could be done quickly and some could not. "I've seen good companies. I know what good looks like. This is not good." Change was necessary across all departments. With diligence all of it could be done. Management had to get its hands on expenses, cut operating costs to enable capital spending.

Some needed change centered on work rules. HR and Labor Relations were badly organized and out of touch with the company's needs. "Amtrak's Engineering Department was poorly organized and spending a lot of money. It's hard because it involves maintenance of the railroad in the NEC, and capital expenses. It needed different leadership. There's still work to be done, but much has been done. It's a process of many years."

While Moorman was in a position to make changes, he made substantial organizational revisions and let more people go than he did while he headed NS. "It was simply necessary." Amtrak's employment had expanded over the years, and it was difficult to manage, to determine who was responsible for the people working on the trains. The Amtrak bureaucracy was too large and cumbersome—"but it is better now, although [then-current president/CEO] Richard Anderson still doesn't like it. It's probably no worse than in any other large corporation." There were some frustrations, but Moorman didn't believe he was under much pressure and felt free to make changes he thought were for the best. In the back of his mind, "I knew I was an interim president. What were they going to do? Fire me?" He wanted to cut operating costs, improve the effectiveness of capital expenditures, and create a safety culture. While reluctant to criticize his predecessor, Moorman said, "Most of what was needed could be done easily. There were things to be improved everywhere. Positive change was possible." But much had been ignored by previous management.

Service

Because he was an interim president, Moorman didn't have much time to travel Amtrak's trains and usually traveled coach when he did. He made a trip or two on the California corridor trains and on the Acela in addition to riding most weeks from his home in Charlottesville, Virginia, to Washington. However, even on trips to Washington before taking the Amtrak job, he was struck by the state of its equipment. "The carpets were dirty, the seats were worn and tired, it wasn't awful, but it wasn't very inviting." It became clear after he took the job that Amtrak had a history of cost cutting in areas that most impacted the customer's experience, both on the trains and in the stations. He asked some of the management team what might be done to enhance car interiors, and they quickly gave him a proposal for an interior refresh of the Amfleet II equipment at a very reasonable price. "They obviously saw the need as much as I did, and we quickly found the funds by cutting back on some non-passenger-related programs." Onboard service is crucial to pleasing passengers, the key elements being "a decent, clean car and seat; clean lavatories—Richard Anderson is fanatical about this; good lighting; no rattles; on-time performance; and good crew announcements."

Looking back can be instructive: Robert R. Young believed passenger service should attract passengers; Ralph Budd said a train trip should provide a good experience that encouraged repeat patronage. Part of that good experience is convenience and a certain level of comfort. Moorman says Amtrak's management should keep asking, "Within reason, how do we improve the quality of onboard services? That is a good start."

What does he think about food and beverage service? Historically it was provided at a loss, since railroads at that time believed feeding passengers was essential to providing good service. Should Amtrak be expected to eliminate losses on food and beverage service as mandated by its re-authorization legislation (Section 11207 of "The FAST Act", which passed in 2015 as H.R. 22)? "Running a modest deficit is not a sin. When it comes to food, Amtrak is between a rock and a hard place." By law it had to eliminate food and beverage losses by December 2020, but it could not fire people, the major cost of such service, and could only "attrition them out." For first-class passengers, the cost of meals is taken from ticket revenue and put into the dining services account. That helps, but it does not eliminate food and beverage losses.

Moorman noted that dining cars are too expensive for the majority of coach passengers and that the average passenger is aboard for two meals' worth of time. The café cars get closer than diners to covering costs [and seem to provide adequate services for those travelers].

Another important element of service is on-time performance. Amtrak controls all NEC traffic, and there has been much time-keeping there, along with significant work to improve ride quality and Wi-Fi availability. As for the long-distance and most state-supported regional/corridor trains, the Class I's have forgotten that Amtrak relieved them of their passenger service obligation. Amtrak payments to host railroads are a fraction of what they earn from freight traffic, and there often are delays of Amtrak trains. Of all the railroads, BNSF does the most to run Amtrak on time, and while at NS Moorman told his people it was going to do the same. The corporate attitude there was: "If you run [passenger] trains, (1) take care of liability, which Amtrak does; (2) provide capacity required to avoid delays; and (3) pay us a modest return."

Support

When Moorman was appointed, there was much approval from employees and the rail-focused media. "At FRA, and on Capitol Hill, everyone was happy I was there and very supportive of me. Right at the end of my tenure, Elaine Chao, DOT secretary, came in, and while she and her staff were personally supportive, it was clear that the senior DOT people had ideological issues."

Congress mattered too. "Today there is nowhere near the animosity of the past. Congress is generally more supportive; there's good support. People on the Hill were saying 'thank you' to me." But with a successor appointed, Moorman's mission was over and the mood changed among some members.

Is Amtrak Needed?

Moorman is supportive. "Yes. Amtrak should be the advocate for and operator of passenger rail where it is wanted and makes sense economically and socially." This is generally in urban corridors. Yet railroads view Amtrak as an annoyance due to capacity issues. Regarding the long-distance trains, do national demographics have (or illustrate?) a need for them? Moorman believes that Amtrak has become a fixture in the national transportation picture but remains a budget item subject to elimination, unlike aviation and highway modes. Questions about its mission are still in flux 50 years after its creation.

Greatest Accomplishment

"We started a significant process of change across the company. I helped to recruit a great successor. Richard Anderson knows a lot about moving people and was an outstanding CEO at Delta Airlines." There are parallels between Amtrak and the airlines. Moorman stayed on for six months after Anderson was appointed, and they were co-CEOs for that period. He supported Anderson's efforts to reduce the federal subsidies to the company.

Political opposition to Amtrak is much less than in the past; however, "It will never be what it can be unless it's a well-run company." Moorman believes that current management has worked hard to improve Amtrak and that those efforts are paying off, as evidenced by 2019's fiscal and ridership results.

Transportation Policy

"For many years, the country had a de facto policy—build highways. It's only fairly recently that issues of severe overcrowding, diminished funding through the Highway Trust Fund, urban air pollution, etc., have created more discussion around a more 'balanced' policy and have elevated the discussion about the role of passenger rail." He noted, however, that the lack of a national transportation policy had little effect on him while he was at Amtrak. Regarding the freight railroads, they should be regulated in a way that enables them to maintain and grow their infrastructure. He is not shy about stating that trucks need to be taken off the highway [and loaded onto the railroads]. "By and large, Amtrak is viewed by freight railroads as a nuisance. The higher the opinion people have of Amtrak, more of it will wash over the freight railroads."

In Moorman's view, it is a fallacy that long-distance trains would thrive if their frequency went to two per day. Matters complicating this idea have to do with capacity problems on the freight railroads and where to get and how to pay for additional passenger cars—the same dilemma passenger-carrying railroads faced in the late 1960s.

Funding

Transportation in the US will always be mainly car based, but the Highway Trust Fund is too low, and we need adequate funding for all modes. "We must fix infrastructure. Really, highways are not on a level field. The system is way underfunded for its needs." The NEC needs funding to maintain existing infrastructure and to grow. "We need a thoughtful plan looking at today, but also 20 years in the future."

Change

As for changes needed at Amtrak, Moorman said, "First would be to change the process for appointing board members," which today does not consider the skills necessary to effective corporate board membership. "Ineffective boards always lead to bad leadership. There have been long periods of poor management [at Amtrak] such that operations and service have degraded. David Gunn saved Amtrak. He was fired in three years because the board wanted him to do things he wouldn't do. Joe Boardman was a very good person, but he lacked not only the background, but also the leadership skills to be an effective CEO."

How has Amtrak turned out? "It's good that it's still around. There's a national need for it to fill." It's important to keep in mind that Amtrak is "actually a marginal success from the standpoint of those who created it and hoped to keep the concept alive in the US, but a failure to those in government whom the policy makers assured that it could become profitable."

"In the employee base there has been a strong preservationist culture—'we'll need it someday.' But when change comes it won't be the way you think [it will]." He believes that the organization's receptivity to change has grown over the past three years.

Reflections Upon Departure

Wick Moorman wishes he had had more time to do more "fixing." He misses it; he was having fun and it was challenging. "I don't miss the CEO role, but I miss the railroad and being in the thick of it and having a voice. I still check the track and watch trains go by." He agrees: a railroad gets in your blood and you never really leave.

If he were to advise future boards about hiring a new president, he suggests the candidate be "bright, with a coherent vision, able to work with others, somebody who knows the passenger transportation business, who possesses integrity and leadership skills, but also has the ability to execute with Amtrak's constituencies, including Congress."

While still wanting to be "engaged," Moorman has turned his energy into spearheading historic rail preservation projects.

Stewardship in Perspective: Robert Clifford Black IV
(September 26, 2019 interview, with subsequent telephone conversations and emails)

Once you are caught in a lie, you lose credibility, which is nearly impossible to restore.
Cliff Black

In order to gain a sense of perspective about other presidents, we turned to Cliff Black who served under seven Amtrak presidents.

Amtrak was ten years old when Cliff Black arrived there. Alan Boyd led the company and was another capable and experienced railroad executive who moved it forward by purchasing new equipment and adding services.

Cliff Black. For three decades, the voice of Amtrak in the news media.
Doug Riddell

Preparations

"Cliff" Black was born in 1943 in Atlanta, Georgia, where his father was stationed in the Army as a transportation officer. Cliff later lived in Troy, New York, West Hartford, Connecticut, and Washington, DC, but also has family roots in New York State and Colorado. A Vietnam-era veteran of the US Air Force, he attended Hobart College in Geneva, New York, and American University in Washington, DC.

His college years were interrupted when he enlisted in the Air Force in 1962 and became a teletype and crypto operator in Turkey and in the Air Force Special Security Office in the Pentagon. Honorably discharged in 1966, Black briefly worked as a car salesman in northern Virginia, then completed college at American University, earning a BA in English. He taught English at the Landon School in Bethesda, Maryland, from 1971 to 1980. In 1981, Black was hired as a consultant in Amtrak's Public Affairs Department and joined the staff in September 1982. He remained until he retired in 2010 as chief of corporate communications and moved to Winona, Minnesota, with his wife, Jeanine.

Black always had an interest in railroads because his father worked in railroading but also was a published academic historian. After college, Cliff developed teaching and speaking skills and taught high school English for nine years. He did some consulting on railroad issues and did research at the USRA. Black said that it was "inculcated through the news media that Amtrak was constantly failing" and that its enabling act said it was to be run for profit. When he went to Amtrak in 1981, its Public Affairs office was affiliated with its Government Affairs office and the two had to coordinate messages "because that was our lifeline." Black discovered that his military training was applicable to working at Amtrak, but he liked Amtrak better. Endowed with a keen sense of humor, good looks, an affable personality, and an ability to speak, spell, and write in complete sentences, Black became the asset Amtrak needed.

Motivations

As a consultant, Black saw how the company functioned and decided that if offered a job he would be interested. When the opportunity came, his motivation for accepting was partly fundamental—he was married and had a growing family and bills to pay—and also was interested in transportation and liked what he was doing for Amtrak. "I considered the media my audience. You had to nurture those relationships."

Expectations

At first, Black was in an entry-level position where he had to learn about the passenger train business, but he also got to participate in developing policies that expanded and improved Amtrak. There were about eight staff employees in the DC office and others in California and Chicago. Policy issues such as Capitol Hill contacts and state-supported trains were coordinated with the DC office. "I started out as just a grunt writer." He worked with Bruce Heard on the 10th anniversary celebration on May 1, 1981, his first "real" project. The second was the new Arrow reservation system, including development of a newsletter and conducting employee training on using the system. He admits it had a rocky start, despite Amtrak's IT person saying publicly that it was "flawless." It wasn't. Early on, he learned, "trust but verify" and "check your sources."

There still was a lot to get used to. Given Black's academic background, the massive Amtrak bureaucracy surprised him, but he saw it as mostly necessary. One aspect that gave him pause was that, in a way, some viewed Amtrak as an employment agency and mainly a political animal due to its federal (and some state) funding. Perhaps this should not have surprised him; this was the nature of the beast. David Stockman, President Reagan's head of the Office of Management and Budget, began "an ideological little game: Every time someone buys a ticket, the government hands out money." The Reagan administration wanted to cut Amtrak in half and its people were always hostile.

Their attitude was, "The lower the administration's budget for Amtrak, the better," but it usually ended up with more funding. This surprised Black at first but he figured it out: "[Congressional] Constituents liked their trains." Even if they didn't ride, "they wanted it there." This remains true today.

Though still a consultant, in 1981 Black started answering media inquiries and eventually became an Amtrak spokesman. In May, Amtrak decided to reduce management employees by 10 to 15 percent in each department. Someone warned Black, "Don't come to work tomorrow" because pink slips were being handed out. Keeping a low profile, he worked sporadically from home for several months. Despite the layoffs, he remained as a contractor, and the relationship eventually became his career. His brother-in-law was former Johnson White House advisor Harry McPherson, who had worked on some Democratic political campaigns with Clark Tyler, an Amtrak Group VP with responsibility for marketing, government affairs, and public affairs. McPherson had set up the interviews that resulted in Black's consultant work. Still in that role, he returned to the office in the fall of 1981 and in September of 1982 became a full-time staff member.

In 1982 Alan Boyd—in Black's words "a rock of a guy"—left, and W. Graham Claytor Jr. arrived as president/chairman and CEO of Amtrak, a deus ex machina. Claytor was conservative and was acceptable to the Reagan administration. Claytor announced, "I'm not firing anybody," but he immediately froze all management hiring until he could get the lay of the land. Of Claytor, Black remarked there was "not a false bone in that guy's body." Claytor told upper management that if there was someone they absolutely had to have in their departments, get the person's resume and Claytor would conduct a personal interview. Black learned that he had become full-time in part because Claytor was a "closet" historian and knew the elder Black had written a book on Civil War railroads. It was just as well that he was no longer a consultant. Years later, David Gunn reviewed a list of all consultants and fired them wholesale. Gunn said, "If your management team can't handle it, get a new team."

Perspective

Black was a survivor not because he was conniving, but because he was talented, articulate, a quick learner, and sincere. His superiors recognized his talent, and his work benefited both his bosses and Amtrak overall. His long tenure at Amtrak provided him with a perspective few others could claim. He was close to those at the top, got into every aspect of the corporation, its departments and operations, and had to speak on its behalf. The people to whom he spoke believed what he was saying. He was credible. Did a credibility gap ever exist? "No. Once you are caught in a lie, you lose credibility, which is nearly impossible to restore. I learned that fast [from the difficult switch to the Arrow reservation system in 1981]." The FDA consent decree [covering food handling practices and rodent infestations] was an example of how we applied complete, voluntary revelation of truth to a thorny matter as the best defense.[63] I like to think there was no credibility gap with me. The lies we are hearing now are damaging—for example, the idea that millennials want prepackaged meals and don't want to talk to others [and thus presumably don't need the setting of a dining car, which encourages communication among strangers]. I was not concerned about credibility. Only occasionally did I feel uncomfortable. Part of the job was to publicly deal with complex issues, so I expected to get tough questions. However, I quickly learned that a response of 'I don't know' is not a sin," provided it is not overused. Some issues could be tough, uncomfortable, and stressful. "But sometimes the adrenalin is useful and you rise to the occasion. If you say 'I'll get back to you,' do it."

Since Black represented not only the corporate leadership, but also the employees, he had to develop relationships with them too. He served seven presidents. "Depending on the person in that office, my relationships varied from formal to casual, but always professional. Some presidents I became close to, even to the point of becoming social friends. Others were more distant, but I inevitably had access to them. Some of them sought my advice; others I was more likely to furnish unsolicited advice. I constantly tried to convince them to talk to the news media on positive stories so that they could comfortably face the cameras in crisis situations."

When Black arrived at Amtrak he had to write some speeches for Alan Boyd. While he found Boyd "friendly," they were not close. "Still, I had his confidence. Boyd had an uncanny ability to remember names, including those of frontline employees. He was a pillar of respect."

"I stood in awe of Graham Claytor, mainly because of his accomplishments." Theirs was a formal relationship, "but friendly enough. He was brilliant at problem-solving, understood politics, law, railroads, and business. When he rode the trains, he walked them end to end." Employees got to know him and trusted and respected him.

Tom Downs was "a personal friend, mercurial, but enthusiastic. He enjoyed Amtrak. Tom had had experience as a manager of large bureaucratic organizations, including as transportation commissioner for the State of New Jersey and as city manager of Washington, DC. His work in New Jersey prepared him for the political vicissitudes of passenger rail when he worked—sometimes frustratingly—with the Port of New York and New Jersey. I recall that one of Tom Downs's greatest assets was his thorough sense of fiduciary responsibility for protecting the taxpayers' investment in Amtrak. He was enthusiastic in his role, had a strong moral compass, and wanted to do a good job. He was easy to work with and had Amtrak's interests at heart."

Downs hired Mercer (a consulting firm) for cost-saving studies, and its report eventually resulted in the elimination of the Desert Wind and Pioneer trains. "He also created the NEC Strategic Business Unit. The SBUs were another Downs creation, I believe another manifestation of the Mercer report.

I liked working with Tom Downs, and he led the company with a positive and hopeful panache. 'We're on a roll!' was a frequent Downs exclamation. He was realistic about labor costs and fought the labor organizations on their push to gain parity with the Class I freight railroad agreements. The freights bargained together as one and made pay and work rule agreements that applied only to them. They were profitable companies, while Amtrak was not. Downs's realism and fiscal prudence eventually cost him his job, as the labor issue rose to a head with a threatened strike by the BMWE [Brotherhood of Maintenance of Way Employees], which would have shut down the NEC. Northeast Corridor Business Unit president George Warrington arranged with the Clinton White House to accede to BMWE's demands, and Warrington became acting president shortly thereafter."

"Warrington was a politician, a practiced poseur, and kept two sets of books, which led to a crisis resulting in his voluntary departure from Amtrak." His mantra was that Amtrak was on a "glide path to self-sufficiency." This was plainly false. "Despite his transit background, he didn't know railroads and didn't seem interested in learning. He was a showman, given to highly produced, glitzy presentations for both public and employee consumption. However, internally, he was often aloof with lower-level managers and employees. To his credit, his administration oversaw the creation of the highly successful Acela trains that essentially put the airlines' shuttle flights out of business. He rarely rode trains except the Acela, so when he traveled on business, he often flew commercial airlines or chartered private planes. He left abruptly when Amtrak was on the edge of financial collapse and was a few months from being unable to make payroll."

Warrington was succeeded by David Gunn. "Gunn was very down-to-earth. There was nothing pretentious about him. I saw him wear a formal business suit only once. He was terrific, similar to Claytor in some ways. Totally competent. In 2001, internal politics had pushed me out of Corporate Communications in Washington, but room was made for me at the Philadelphia office of the Northeast Corridor Communications office, to which I commuted by rail from my home in Washington. When David Gunn came on board as president in 2002, he immediately abolished the so-called strategic business units—which included the Northeast Corridor SBU, which was semi-autonomous, with its own president. Chicago and LA were the other two SBU headquarters. I was left without a position. Corporate VP of Operations Stan Bagley secured a slot for me in the Amtrak Police Department headquartered in Wilmington, Delaware. This was only about eight months after the 9/11 attacks, and the company was alert to possible anthrax contamination from US Postal Service shipments on Amtrak trains. Several postal workers had died from such contamination, and mail laced with anthrax had been sent to some lawmakers in Washington and elsewhere. The Amtrak Police Department needed a media relations person to deal with the possible fallout from any contamination of the trains, which had the potential of shutting down the entire system. Fortunately, that never happened."

"Despite that assignment, I still did considerable work in the Washington corporate office at Washington Union Station, since I knew the railroad well and David Gunn needed the support of a communications officer with that knowledge. I received frequent calls from the chief of Corporate Communications, Bill Schulz, to meet Gunn and take him to various sites on the railroad or at editorial board meetings with media outlets. I also routinely drafted news releases for corporate, particularly when the subject involved railroad operations."

Black's old corporate office remained available to him, however, including his files, telephone, and computer. "It was an odd arrangement. When Bill Vantuono (of *Railway Age* magazine), Don Phillips (transportation columnist) and Dan Machalaba (*Wall Street Journal*) all wrote to David Gunn asking him to reinstate me at corporate, Gunn was astonished to hear I was not at corporate since I had already worked with him regularly from the time he arrived in summer 2002. Shortly thereafter, I received a call from Pat Shaw, Gunn's executive assistant, that I was to return to my office in Corporate Communications as director of Media Relations. Gunn's informality was disarming and only thinly veiled his fierce determination to do what was honest, frugal, and correct as the caretaker of a large corporation. He was a great leader. We became close friends and remain in contact today." Gunn was direct and sparred publicly with board chairman David Laney, even in Senate hearings. "His realistic approach was his downfall."

When Gunn was abruptly fired under the false pretense that Amtrak had poor financial and service performance, David Hughes, a former president of the Bangor & Aroostook Railroad and former chief mechanical officer of Amtrak, was appointed president, albeit in a temporary capacity. Hughes was preoccupied with operations and engineering, and Black had little interaction with him. Hughes was succeeded by Alex Kummant, a former Union Pacific executive who also had held positions at Sunbeam and Honeywell. "Shortly after taking over, Kummant showed he had power and guts by sacking several high-level managers. I had been director of Media Relations and he made me chief of Corporate Communications." He and Black got along well and held editorial board meetings with Eastern newspapers. "Kummant had railroad experience, which was a plus, and his business background motivated him to try to make Amtrak more efficient. After all, he was David Laney's choice to succeed David Gunn." Kummant was there for two years but was "besieged" by the board, with whom he often disagreed. "He was not happy in the role and became a little dismissive with some staffers and reporters who asked ill-informed questions. He always treated me well, and I appreciated his confidence in me."

Amtrak board membership changed several times in this period, and Joseph Boardman was hired to replace Kummant. Boardman was a bureaucrat, a former FRA administrator. Under Governor Pataki, he was New York's transportation commissioner and once ran the Binghamton bus system. "He was amiable and pleasant. Intelligent." While they were not pals, Black and Boardman had a very respectful and professional relationship. Boardman liked meeting and speaking with the "line" workers and brought Doug Riddell (a former radio announcer in Virginia and Amtrak locomotive engineer whom Boardman befriended) into management as an official photographer. "Boardman liked his job but was insecure." Who at Amtrak wasn't?

One of Boardman's more unpleasant tasks was to warn the states they might have to start paying more for their in-state service and perhaps even for long-distance trains. Unfortunately, during his tenure, "Boardman dismantled the Safety Department's existing structure and turned over much of the responsibility to the employees, but without a well-defined mission. This is not to say that Joe didn't care about safety; he did. Whenever he spoke to employees or to the public, safety was mentioned prominently." To his credit, Boardman cared about the company and its mission. Shortly before he died, Boardman criticized Richard Anderson for proposing and then threatening to put a bus segment in the middle of the route of trains #3 and #4, the Southwest Chief. But before Boardman was forced to retire, Cliff Black decided the time was right for him to retire.

Missions

Although he was not in a position to make corporate decisions about operations or marketing, Black still had the task of improving Amtrak's mission through "education, via news media, and by supporting the Government Affairs Department and clarifying the subsidies issue."

Early on, the "subsidy" issue bothered him. He often had to question, once again, why federal funds allocated for highways and airways were an "investment" but for passenger rail generally and Amtrak in particular they were a "subsidy." The answer stemmed from the original premise that the company would be profitable. "Many felt at the time that the creation of Amtrak was simply a painless, orderly way to eliminate intercity passenger train service in the US, since knowledgeable observers knew it would never be profitable."

In Black's view, Amtrak's mission should be "To provide high quality, safe, convenient, comfortable, [and] timely intercity passenger rail service in markets where it is warranted by either population density or need due to few other options." This includes the vital, active participation of consistent and competent employees. "I don't know what the economic environment will be five years from now," Black said, but for now, Amtrak's mission seems to be "hold on, run a skeletal long-distance system supported by regional services. The NEC is another matter entirely."

Much also depends upon the attitude and mission of Amtrak's board, which gets most of its marching orders from the presidential administration. "The board has a fiduciary responsibility to protect and promote the company. It should oversee the functioning of top management and seek knowledge about passenger rail operations from management. Ideally, at least one board member should be an active or retired railroader. With Graham Claytor, he was the board! Claytor enjoyed declaring that he was 'doing what he thought was best for the company, and if the board disagreed, they can fire me!' For a time, board meetings were open to the public, but they were merely pro forma to endorse decisions made after private deliberations. Public access to board meetings was eliminated around 1997. In other Amtrak administrations, the board eventually became more and more of a political animal, with political operatives being seated by both major political parties. They fired Tom Downs and David Gunn, both for political reasons."

The board members should learn from management about the operations of the passenger railroad—not from just the Amtrak president, but also the executive staff. The Senate confirms board appointments nominated by the [US] president and others, in "an involved process." President Trump has appointed at least two Amtrak board candidates who are "demonstrably anti-Amtrak."

"According to the Rail Passenger Service Act, the enabling legislation that created Amtrak, board members should have knowledge of, or experience with, transportation and a familiarity with fiduciary responsibilities. Specifically, have some railroad knowledge and experience—how railroads are run; also proven managerial skills with a large corporation; and know how to hire good management, with a track record of doing this. Good executive staff is important; they should have the trust of and a good relationship with the people under the executive staff. Anderson's executive staff has largely an airline background."

"In terms of structure, the board should have a chairman, and that office could be filled by the Amtrak president and CEO. Other board members should head committees in areas where they have expertise."

Over the course of Black's Amtrak career, board members and chief executives changed. This affected not only the current operating model but its future too. Changing missions shifted priorities. Decisions were well intended but sometimes disrupted continuity of service. For example, the mission and agenda of Alan Boyd was introducing the Superliners; Graham Claytor's was improving the revenue-to-cost ratio; Thomas Downs: Mercer and labor; George Warrington: Acela, branding, and image; David Gunn focused on balancing the books and maintaining a state of good repair; David Hughes: Engineering; Alex Kummant: cost recovery and businesslike operations; Joe Boardman's was safety and shifting costs to the states (PRIIA 2008). Decisions changed one president to the next in accordance with the mission and agenda of each. Boyd, for example, was "a guy to be reckoned with—thoughtful before saying anything. He had the confidence of Congress and maintained good relations with the freight railroads. He was competent; he was a former secretary of transportation [the first, in fact] and president of the Illinois Central—a railroader. His mission: acquire the Superliners, deploy them, show a future for long-distance trains; make sure Congress was on board [with the idea of having new equipment and how it would be used]; he held open houses for Congress members at Washington Union Station when significant new Superliner car types, such as diners, sleepers and Sightseer Lounges, arrived from Pullman."

Starting with Downs, there began a shift away from having a person at the helm who possessed a railroad industry/institutional background and more toward administrative. "Economic and political forces were beyond the control of the president of Amtrak. The good years were when management knew passenger service and the railroad industry. Under Boyd, people began to think it desirable to grow and maintain a national train network. Representative [John] Dingell of Michigan was a great supporter." Political support became an increasingly key factor.

Would Amtrak run better if politics wasn't involved? "Yes, but you have to have top-notch management. Politics is an important part of Amtrak. Congress is a snake pit populated by sometimes nasty people." Although politics prodded Amtrak and shook it up when needed, there was a downside: personal grudges or agendas. "A good example was [Representative John] Mica of Florida. He attempted to initiate Amtrak's demise by inserting into its reauthorization legislation the requirement for the food and beverage service to eliminate losses by December 2020. While a seemingly reasonable goal, it was patently unrealistic."

On the other hand, could Amtrak work without the political component? "You would be throwing Amtrak to the lions of public transportation—subsidized air and highway—if you took politics out of it." Black believes that unless the approach of national transportation policy changes, Amtrak will always be subjected to the whims of politicians.

Service

The day Amtrak began operations, what had been the railroads' passenger business became a quasi-public corporation providing passenger service operated on a business model—of sorts. Both the service and business models changed over time.

At the outset, the service model was a continuation of what the company had replaced albeit with an "under new management" banner. This was a standard of service that people expected, but as time advanced it devolved to what the company could afford. What constitutes good service, in Black's opinion? He had the opportunity to see what worked and what didn't.

"Service" can mean transportation for towns and cities or customer service aboard the trains, but performance of a service is what matters. Black sees service as "impeccable safety, on-time performance, consistency of [onboard] service (a perennial problem), courteous, competent employees—airline flight attendants are consistently competent, why aren't Amtrak's?—clean functioning equipment, and decent track conditions."

Providing onboard service and amenities is complicated and requires management to consider several factors that can determine whether passengers will travel aboard Amtrak trains. "Well, there was, and is, aviation competition, private auto factors, cost, logistics [e.g., servicing of equipment], and optimal utilization of staff, among others. The 'market' and what it needs and wants. Whatever is provided needs to have consistency in its delivery. Many things have been tried and pulled." (This leads one to question whether millennials should be the arbiters of what the market "needs and wants.")

With management's recent decision to eliminate time-honored traditional dining services aboard its long-distance trains, the question becomes what level of service passengers are likely to expect aboard a train. Black believes it "varies widely from a 'news butcher' to full-service dining and business class/sleeper class. But it should be consistently courteous and competent across all product lines. This is still an unsolved problem." Crews today, based on interviews during recent Amtrak travel, are embarrassed and dispirited by the changes in dining and food services.

Black, who says he "almost exclusively" traveled on Amtrak trains, including the overnight long-distance ones, in "line space" (accommodations in which the public travels) and only occasionally on the office car, said he regrets seeing the cuts in service since he retired. "When I ride Amtrak, I sometimes get embarrassed."

What about making a profit on providing food and beverage service? "No, but ticket revenue obtained by offering good service should be recognized as helping offset food service losses. This is an age-old problem." He believes passengers need good full-service diners on long-distance trains.

"Amtrak is a business but more importantly, it's a business that's a service. There has to be a balance, and the people who are shelling out the money [Congress] need assurance that it's being spent wisely. A well-run business brings that necessary discipline. Rail passenger service is different from an airline which carries its passengers for a relatively short duration. Trains have to have a better onboard experience."

Support

Political support from members of Congress varied but improved over time, especially once members realized their constituents wanted passenger service. Senator Angus King (I-ME) was initially skeptical of voting in favor of Amtrak passenger service, but when he recognized the popularity of the Downeaster between Boston and Portland, he became a believer. Service was later extended to his home town of Brunswick, the home too of Bowdoin College.

In Black's view, support for Amtrak presidents from the federal bureaucracy was "considerable." He cites safety oversight from the FRA, Northeast Corridor Improvement Projects funding from DOT. There was some "ruler vs. ruled" tension between those agencies and Amtrak, due to their regulatory roles, but generally Black feels it was a supportive relationship. However, in answer to a question, he said, "Yes, DOT is mainly highways and aviation."

From Congress, there was considerable support from both parties. Black mentions Trent Lott, R-MS; Kay Bailey Hutchison, R-TX; Frank Lautenberg, D-NJ; Patrick Leahy, D-VT; Daniel Patrick Moynihan, D-NY; Jim Florio, D-NJ; Tom Carper, D-DE; Steven LaTourette, R- OH; Silvio Conte, R-MA; and, of course, "Mr. Amtrak," former Senator and Vice President [now, president] Joe Biden, D-DE.

Is Amtrak Needed?

Amtrak's original mandate was to provide a national service. In Black's opinion this still is valid. "Largely, yes, except for the now-stricken requirement to be operationally profitable." There is a need. "Yes, in corridors, and some long-distance routes to provide underserved locations and supplement intermediate-distance routes on portions of those long-distance routes. Success will be heavily dependent on the condition and availability of freight railroads. But there is also a need for a second round trip on once-daily routes." In addition, rail service is needed "where intermediate markets are underserved by other modes and where some economy of scale can be achieved through overlaying short- and medium-distance train routes. Competing air and auto transportation costs and viability will also play a role." Some point to Canada, where VIA Rail serves underserved communities that lack air service and, in some cases, highway access. "Yes, but the Canada model is failing," Black said, and for similar reasons as in the United States—government policy. But also, "Amtrak needs clean, functional equipment and good track."

Transportation Policy

Although Black was not in a position to recommend a transportation policy, he recognized the need for one that allowed for a "judicious investment in all forms of transportation in markets and regions where it made sense. One of balance, shared facilities, interconnectivity, rail where it made sense, other forms where they made sense. High-speed rail plans like California's failed one are a good example of too many cooks spoiling the broth: consultants, lawyers, politicians, construction companies. It should have been run from the beginning by one managing entity, with considerable authority but oversight from a board-like group."

Unfortunately, Amtrak is still viewed as being different from the transport of people by car, bus, and air. "It's a sad legacy from its enabling legislation that stated it would be profitable, a ridiculous claim in view of the reason it was established in the first place: private sector losses and bankruptcy trying to operate passenger trains in the face of heavily subsidized competition. In heavily traveled corridors, Amtrak is considered different in a positive way: it is far more convenient and efficient than the usual competition of highway and air. Even on long-distance routes, it is 'different' because of the low stress factor and the opportunity to get relief from a crazy cyber world."

"Amtrak needs large-scale popular support, which is translated into needed government support by elected officials, local, state and federal. It is at the grass roots level that these things succeed or fail. Large-scale public support brings needed government support, and the money follows. Amtrak is easy to criticize because it is a line item in the federal budget. Other modes have trust funds and would have to be de-legislated to stop their funding flows. While it would be nice to excise the injustices of the imbalances inherent in the current funding model, including the self-interest political factors, creating a coherent transportation policy in today's political environment may be an unrealistic goal."

Change

Black says Amtrak's role in the future remains to be seen. "Currently a focus on environmental quality may have some effect on shifting resources to 'sustainable' forms of transportation, which currently includes rail. I doubt high-tech pie-in-the-sky technology like maglev and hyperloops will gain any traction in the foreseeable future as they are simply too expensive and fraught with technical problems, and there is little advantage to them in terms of practicality. Even the Asian and German inventors/builders of maglev have essentially given up on it."

"A great deal of effort has been made to create some sort of overarching identity or 'branding' of Amtrak, but efforts to provide consistently excellent customer service always failed. That needs to change. A huge order, but it should be a major push by management. True, the company runs a railroad, but it does so for the benefit and pleasure of people, not inanimate commodities, which the freights carry. Many very fine employees serve Amtrak customers, but service delivery is uneven. On-time performance is another factor that needs to be improved—it's a perennial challenge."

How Amtrak's leadership is chosen should change. "I don't know how it's done now, but I agree it should be changed." Leadership should have "railroad experience and a passion for passenger rail; high fiduciary skill and integrity; a vision for the company's future. You need somebody like Gunn who has an eye for management talent and for motivating people. Also, fiduciary responsibility." Anderson is not widely supported by the employees. "Gunn was 'loved' at all levels, from car knockers [equipment maintenance personnel] on up." Interviews with long-term employees from Red Caps (who assist passengers with luggage) to service attendants confirmed this.

How should management treat the NEC versus the long-distance trains? "Really, there are three Amtraks: (1) NEC, (2) regional/state supported, and (3) long-distance trains. Because they are different types of services, they should be operated differently with different options of service, such as first class, business Class, Economy class, and so on, but the competence and professionalism of employees must be consistent throughout the range of services. That is the big challenge."

Headaches and Frustrations

"The advent of universal cell-phone use. Unauthorized comments to media, resulting in '24,000 Amtrak spokespersons [employees]' who give out inaccurate information to the media; the two-in-the-morning phone calls from the Centralized National Operations Center (CNOC) in Wilmington was another." Black failed "to make mainstream media understand and report the reality that all forms of transportation are subsidized." It is still a problem. He was annoyed with Representative John Mica, in particular, who said, "Amtrak is a Soviet-style railroad." Black was never sure what he meant by this. Unfortunately, Mica's attitude regarding Amtrak had long-term repercussions, even after voters relieved him of his seat in Congress.

Greatest Accomplishment

Cliff Black believes his greatest accomplishment was "maintaining my integrity with management and the news media, and the confidence of my staff." In addition, he points to in-house employee communication; great confidence in him on the part of management; and the Graphics Department's work on menus, literature, and flyers. "If you don't stab people in the back, you'll be okay."

Reflections Upon Departure

Black admitted, "I loved it." It was "exciting, never dull. No two days exactly alike, constant challenges, high stress, sometimes exhausting, but a company that did things with big complex machines over a continent-spanning system, 24 hours per day. There were some very fine people at Amtrak, and some whom I know remain, though most have retired or taken a buyout due to concern over new directions under [former president] Anderson. Anderson may be the person the company needed to find a new direction, but his vague understanding of passenger rail tradition and history is both a benefit and a liability. He is angering a lot of traditionalists, and that has had the effect of raising the volume if not the content of the ongoing debate about the future of passenger rail in the US. But the issues have been brought to the forefront, and that is a good thing. But one has to reflect upon how damage inflicted under Anderson will be repaired by his successor." A lot of people are focused on bad trends—bad food, poor service, the idea of cutting the NEC off from the rest of the system. "Maybe Amtrak needed a kick in the butt. But Anderson's solution may not be the right kick. It will be fascinating to see where it leads."

He has some regrets. "The big regret: [the continuing objection that] Amtrak is 'subsidized'—other transportation is 'invested' in. Amtrak is the intercity passenger rail system, in addition to being a single corporation." He admits he was unable to change this perception of "subsidy" of Amtrak vs.

"investment" in other modes. He wanted to get Amtrak into the mainstream of transportation systems. "The FAA covers the aviation system, FHWA covers the highway system. Why not intercity passenger trains? It's a system too. To refer to it as 'subsidized' doesn't recognize it as a part of the national [transportation] system."

There were improvements Black felt should have been made, such as "acquisition of sufficient new equipment; [achieving] the state of good repair and right-of-way in various places; onboard staff training/hiring practices. New baggage cars were ten years late; sleepers overdue." There also was "bad stuff"—"Derailments, loss of life: Bourbonnais, Illinois [a truck carrying steel violated grade crossing warnings and stopped on the tracks]; Chase, Maryland [an impaired freight locomotive engineer violated a stop signal]; Big Bayou Canot, Alabama resulting in 47 fatalities and 103 injuries [an inexperienced towboat crew's barge struck a bridge]. The annual claims budget is in the millions." Black is quick to point out that Amtrak personnel were not responsible for any of these tragedies. After a high-profile incident, Black often had to pull together a news conference. "But it protected me from sadness and depression." He had to show that the organization was caring and competent. Credibility always mattered.

There was "good stuff" too: almost everyone knew the brand name, even if they were often misinformed about it. "We're really a player now. When I was there, we still were an experiment. We're a company to be contended with." He was proud of what Amtrak had achieved: trying high-speed rail, for better or worse; Turbos; and finally Acela, which "put the nail in the coffin of the air shuttles." When he departed, he had mixed feelings. "I'm happy about many things and concerned about others. Much had changed in my 29 years there, much of it good. It had become a more modern, well-known corporation. Acela was a crossword puzzle word. But the sense of shared mission among employees had diminished as the 'me' generation gained popular currency. Toward the end of my tenure, new hires were not particularly interested in Amtrak's product, just the job, which they increasingly considered to be a step on a pay-raise ladder."

The prospect of being laid off at a moment's notice played a role in this. While vice presidents routinely came and went, Black survived nearly 30 years. "That was a rarity," he said. "The sadness was largely personal: I had been through a lot and had many positive experiences. I truly loved my work there, but I still regretted that Amtrak remained the 'government subsidized passenger railroad' in many otherwise neutral news reports and stories. I worried about where Amtrak was headed. Freight railroads were emboldened; TSA [Transportation Security Administration] rumbling about security checks; Joe Boardman warning states they would have to take on more of the cost burden."

Black stays somewhat in touch with former colleagues. Some have left, some were very disillusioned about the direction of the company. "It's not happy—not a happy place to work. It will change soon; it cannot go on like this. Or it will disintegrate into small business units, get picked up by some states. Environmental concerns should help. Amtrak has a card in that game." He remains skeptical about the new non-stop Acela service between New York and Washington [currently thrown into purgatory by the coronavirus because much of the Metroliner and then Acela traffic was to intermediate stops]. "I hope it works. We tried it over and over again and it always failed."

"We have airline-style crowds now," with, for example, boarding by groups of customers. Black believes in the need for the passenger rail "tradition." Rail passenger service has been around for about 190 years—roughly 1830 to 2020. At the age of 50, Amtrak is 26 percent of the history of United States railroading. It is a big part of our railroad history. "Anderson may be the unalloyed bottom-line person the company needed, but it's dangerous." When Cliff was at Amtrak, the company's core values were "safety; revenue-to-cost ratio; state of good repair; new high-speed train sets (Acela); cost recovery; [we] had some success covering more of costs out of revenues. But accounting has been questioned." The "fatal crashes were awful, [but] it was a great career. It was a terrific ride."

The View From The Train—So, Just Who *Is* Traveling Aboard Amtrak?

> I don't take a night journey on a railroad for the sake of duplicating the experiences and conveniences of my own home: when I travel I like to get into some new kind of difficulty, not just the same old trouble I put up with around the house.
>
> E. B. White, "Progress and Change"

It is easy to focus on the roles played by politicians and railroad managers and officials who are engaged in making sure Amtrak remains to serve the American public. But in so doing, it is easy to overlook the most important player in Amtrak's tale—the passengers. So just who is traveling aboard Amtrak long-distance trains?

The answer may or may not seem obvious: some high-, but mostly low- and middle-income people; the young, elderly, or retired, some physically challenged, and some religious folk. It is the American public, and each person has his or her own reasons for choosing Amtrak over the car, the bus, or the airplane. During the research and writing of this book, the authors traveled by car when necessary but mainly by air, bus, and train, the country's primary public passenger modes. We questioned fellow travelers on many topics, with a focus on why they were taking a flight, a bus, or a train. In the interest of transparency, we acknowledge that the interviews were hardly scientific, but the responses were revealing nonetheless and are food for thought. Ages of the forty-five people we interviewed ranged from the mid-teens to the early 80s.

The Amtrak experience can be affected by various outside factors in addition to the condition of the specific train, its route, and its crew. This can lead to a range of opinions and responses in an interview. Convenience played a large part in what people told us, as did generational differences. A common observation was that people on an airplane did not converse with their seat partners unless they knew each other; people on a bus were the same. On the train, much the same seemed to prevail. People riding in the coaches were either asleep, looking at phones or laptops, or otherwise not interacting unless they were with friends or family. In café cars, where patrons can choose a seat at a table, most try to sit alone. In dining cars, Amtrak has continued the long tradition of the steward seating people. (Imagine how quickly the story in *North by Northwest* would have fallen apart if Cary Grant had not been seated with Eva Marie Saint on the 20th Century Limited.) This naturally tends to initiate conversation with tablemates. That said, in one instance, by no means uncommon, we watched a 20-something man who came in wearing headphones connected to his phone, didn't say a word to anyone other than to order scrambled eggs, ate them, and got up and headed back to his coach.

People choose a travel mode based on convenience, cost, type and quality of service, and, sometimes, necessity. On one of our flights people were focused on saving time. The airplane's advantage in this regard is irrefutable. Given the complexity of the air transport system, it is miraculous that there are so few major delays. Nobody liked the security measures, but they understood why they are necessary. Generally, there is nothing all that attractive about flying—if one's flight arrives on time and safely at its destination, then air travel is basic transportation. One businessman said that while he does take the train on occasion, he was taking the plane because the train did not go directly to where he lived outside of Cleveland, and even then he had to connect to another flight in Detroit.

We conducted interviews over several days aboard Amtrak's Lake Shore Limited, Silver Meteor, Empire Builder, Coast Starlight, Texas Eagle, California Zephyr, and Southwest Chief between March and November 2019 and February and March 2020. Passengers included a mix of younger and older travelers. All enjoyed travel by train, citing various reasons. Several said they simply wouldn't fly—period. One under-30 described flying as "getting the job done" while another used words that cannot be printed here without the censors' intervention; he did not like the experience and complications such as stress, security lines, lost luggage, seating discomfort, weather and/or mechanical delays, and lack of amenities. One retired airline captain and his wife said they gave up flying altogether despite their ability to get a discounted fare because "it wasn't the way it used to be." They like Amtrak travel because it gives them the ability to see America, a point often repeated by others. Many find it relaxing since there is no time crunch (unless one has to make a connection in, say, Chicago). "If the train is a couple of hours late, so what?" said one.

One passenger aboard the Texas Eagle who was devoted to flying stated she was taking the train to try it out. "I hate delays, so I always fly." As the train was five hours behind schedule, she said the train didn't measure up to her standards. She admitted to liking the comfort and ability to move around and talk with others, and she had indeed met a person she enjoyed and with whom she had eaten meals in the diner. She seemed to be enjoying herself, and when asked about flight cancellations and delays she responded that the airline she flies does not encounter many delays.

Another passenger, returning from a conference, did not want to fly because, in her words, "flying is awful." Another passenger, in his 20s and attending a trade school, was taking the train—by coach—during a school break, traveling between Pittsburgh and Vancouver, B.C., solely for the purpose of taking the train. He said he couldn't afford a sleeper but was happy traveling by coach and was enjoying meeting people. Aboard the Empire Builder, two oil rig employees, when asked at breakfast what they would like to order, in unison replied they wanted beer. This was at 6:30 a.m. and, when told that was not on the menu and could not be ordered a la carte, they each settled for scrambled eggs and bacon.

Breakfast options on the Lake Shore Limited were different from those on trains operating west of Chicago. The Lake Shore menu in 2019 and 2020 was a little below the quality of what one would find at a low-budget motel. Amtrak initially advertised this embarrassment as "contemporary dining" and later as its "flexible dining." Passenger reviews contained a mixture of disapproval and disappointment. One passenger on the Empire Builder, who had traveled on the Cardinal a week or so earlier, was an Amazon employee in his late 20s returning from a meeting in Washington, DC. He thought breakfast aboard the Cardinal "was fine." This was the exception.

Many pointed out that Amtrak goes where national air carriers don't or won't go, leaving many markets to smaller airlines that charge exorbitant and unaffordable fares (and in many cases receive surprisingly high per-passenger federal subsidies to keep the service running). Amtrak is cheaper.

Another passenger who said she flies "a lot," responded that with the exception of the miracle of flight, there is "nothing special about flying; it is purely functional." And there are those who cannot fly for one reason or another. Many who cannot fit comfortably in airline seats or have certain medical conditions take the train because it is their only reasonable option. Some travel by rail for other reasons. Almost daily, Chicago Union Station hosts members of religious communities who take the train exclusively. Bus may be an option, but not always, and taking the train is preferable.

Almost all travelers we interviewed replied that they enjoyed being able to have a sit-down meal on a train, along with the social experience of meeting new people while dining. A few had traveled aboard the Lake Shore Limited where "first-class" sleeping car passengers were given boxed meals—dubbed by Amtrak as the new "flexible dinners," an "enhancement" to the travel experience. Most described the experience as "disappointing," though one gentleman said it was "better than nothing" (probably not a good quote to use in advertising the service). His wife, who was picking at her dish, said, "It isn't bad, but it isn't good, either." Media reports, by contrast, seem to parrot Amtrak's positive publicity statements about these dinners.

Several who said they travel Amtrak frequently commented on the fact that, while train personnel were most often cheerful and solicitous, dining car staffers were inconsistent in their demeanor. Most liked the Sightseer Lounge cars, with their extralarge windows, but found snack items terribly expensive. A high school student traveling from Tucson to Springfield, Massachusetts, said she has never flown and was taking the train, in coach, for the first time, a journey of three days. She said the food was too expensive but had brought her own. What she had sampled in the café cars was "okay." (Conducting our own research, we bought a cheeseburger, a bag of chips, and a beer for $17.)

Several people were traveling by train for the first time because they thought it would be a different experience and would be fun. One young woman was indeed enjoying it and said flying was not memorable unless it was a bad experience; she believed that more people should ride the train. Although she would be flying home to Boston from Portland, Oregon, it was because of cost and the time factor—she had to get back to college. Another young person responded that she was traveling to Syracuse, New York, aboard a train from New York City because of a snowstorm. She was a customer relations agent for Delta Airlines. When asked what she did as a customer relations agent, she responded that she "apologizes a lot." Informed that the former president of Delta was president of Amtrak, she smiled and then laughed. "Is he charging for carry-on luggage?"

Trains also cater to those who come from overseas and want to see America. A woman in her mid-20s from Australia who is employed in the Australian trade office was traveling the California Zephyr to see and visit parts of the United States. Beginning in San Francisco, she traveled to Reno and Tahoe to ski, then was traveling to Chicago for a few days while planning to fly back to visit Los Angeles before returning home to Canberra. She was traveling in a roomette and enjoyed the scenery and meeting and talking with people. In contrast to what Amtrak has purported as an excuse for its flexible dining regimen she protested, "We're a social bunch." Asked if she enjoyed flying, she replied, "Does anyone really enjoy flying? You put up with it. Extra charges for bags, no legroom—it's annoying. It's a necessary evil." On a previous trip she took Amtrak's Acela. "It was time efficient, easier than flying."

She said she was traveling Amtrak as "a lark—why not give it a go?" and was surprised when people she met in Tahoe thought she would be bored by it, but that she thoroughly enjoyed the experience. She was surprised that so few there seemed to know about the train, and was enjoying the California Zephyr. "It's fun. The scenery is great." Would she recommend the trip? "Yes!"

Many felt that Amtrak needed more routes and more money to make improvements in the equipment, which seemed old and worn; a few suggested that Amtrak needs to advertise the benefits of train travel, and service should be available for more people.

Riding a bus was for one passenger memorable only for the uncomfortable seats, the bumpy ride over an interstate highway and streets, and was made purely by necessity of cost and inability of Amtrak to reach her destination. For many, a bus ride is not memorable, is made without the benefit of amenities; it is purely a functional exercise, like flying, to go from point A to point B.

The View Aboard the Train

Interviews with train personnel revealed that David Gunn and Joseph Boardman were crews' favorite leaders, both of whose primary attribute was concerns about employee welfare and the quality of Amtrak's service. When Wick Moorman was appointed president, many employees expressed hope for the future, but it didn't last.

A good leader must be trusted. This is particularly important when it comes to employees with direct contact with passengers. Any organization lacking a high level of trust and respect for leadership will suffer low staff morale, inevitably leading to a lower quality of service than the organization's customers have a right to expect. Unfortunately, our interviews revealed that morale has declined while even discouraged staffers still try to do their jobs as best they can in trying circumstances. Better leadership can build on this base of employee commitment.

Interviews were conducted with sleeping car and coach attendants, dining car crews, and conductors. All were willing to talk even though they said that Amtrak policy forbids interviews. (We trust that this will be perceived as real concern on employees' part about Amtrak's future and not just griping or rule-breaking.) Most expressed disappointment over policy changes and job losses following the appointment of Richard Anderson, while a few said it was to be expected, as in their view that was all he had accomplished while president of Delta Airlines. Most expressed frustration with the inability to have input into changes and frustration with equipment issues that crop up. Each indicated that they often had to ignore some given policy to make the passenger experience better. For example, in the single-level dining cars, the person in charge is supposed to stand at the kitchen door and hand packaged food to passengers, but most said they ignore that policy and serve the dinners to the passengers because "that is what passengers expect and deserve for the price they are paying."

Onboard staff are at the front line of the passenger experience. It is they who have to salvage the shortcomings of management decisions, policies, mistakes in judgment, equipment failures, and be creative in maintaining pride in operation. It is difficult to achieve passenger satisfaction without support from above.

The onboard staff being interviewed usually was composed of veterans of Amtrak, serving more than ten years and some who have worked upwards of thirty. Most had worked in different capacities, such as coach and sleeper attendants, but also served in the diners. As cuts were made in the rosters, they moved around accordingly on the basis of their seniority. Of those who had worked for more than ten years, they observed they were career oriented and liked working and meeting passengers.

But there are many problems that one does not readily recognize. Amtrak needs career employees who are invested in the company and who want to make it succeed. Amtrak's continual fight for scarce capital funding and its insecure future handicap efforts in hiring. Recent state drug-use laws, especially those dealing with marijuana use, have negatively impacted hiring. In one case, according to one employee, out of fifty applicants, only three passed the drug test (the trucking industry is likewise impacted). "Amtrak will hire anybody;" said one career sleeper attendant, "but marijuana and other drug problems have hurt us when trying to hire people." The work is often hard, and on the train can be of long duration covering a week, "but they like the six days off, so they hang on."

"There is a lot of turnover," said another. "Many don't last the first 90 days. If they last more than 120 days, then chances are good they'll stay." Too many today are not looking for a career, only a "job." In some instances, this has resulted in poor onboard service because there is little employee "buy-in" while management cuts and lack of job security have only validated the belief that working for Amtrak is not a good career choice.

Management cuts in employment have resulted in the workload being added to other employees. The positions are cut, but the tasks remain and the burden of workload is shouldered by those who have other duties. Essential tasks don't get done and service suffers.

Dining staff uniformly disliked the cuts being made in employment, but more so for the diminishing effect on passenger service aboard the cars. The declines in food quality, such as the amount and number of salad ingredients gradually reduced over time, seem petty. Not all passengers have a historical perspective, so what they get aboard Amtrak diners meet their expectations.

The same could be said about the sleeping car experience. "Taking the train used to be a novelty," said one attendant. "The company tried little things to please passengers and make it seem different, like putting a small mint on the bed after it was turned down. They gave out small amenity packs to sleeping car passengers in special zippered packs. They gave them route guides and newspapers in the morning. They cut all that stuff. They even stopped printing timetables. What's with that?"

Employees made observations about the decline in passenger behavior, also. "First-class passengers generally cause fewer problems," said another attendant. Alcohol consumption creates problems so that on the Empire Builder conductors have to announce that disturbances and foul language will not be tolerated. Attendants are not all trained to deal with such behavioral problems. Some passengers are not as sanitary as others and create havoc in the lavatories; some get sick; sometimes passengers are unruly and there aren't mechanisms for getting help in a timely basis from train crew members.

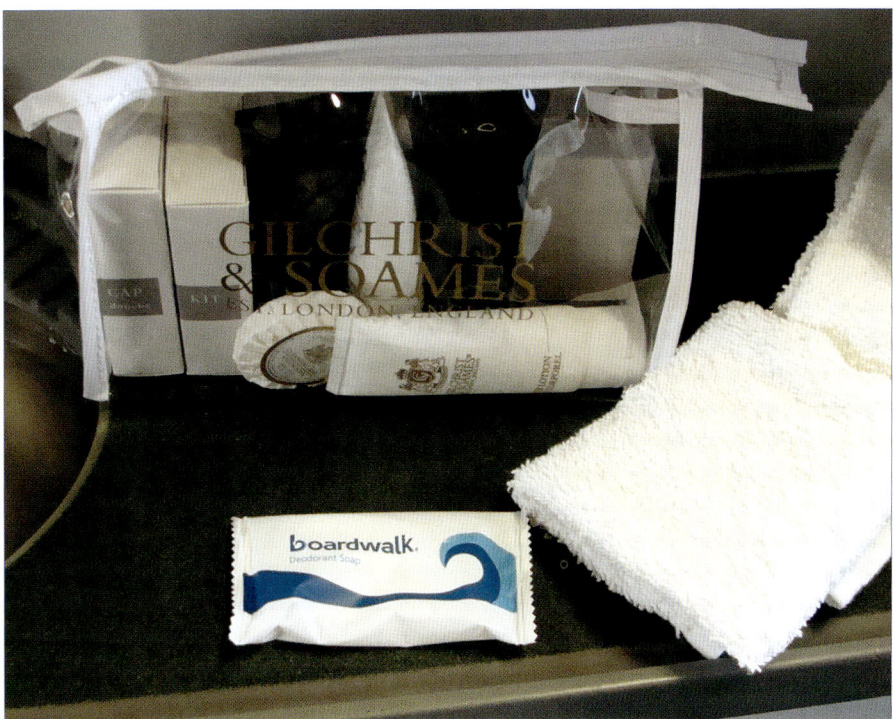

A zippered Amtrak amenity pack. *Geoffrey H. Doughty Collection*

Equipment problems and failures are not easily resolved, and it is up to the train's onboard staff to try to repair or somehow deal with the problem and customer complaints. Employees are never sure of what will happen next. People were bringing aboard emotional support animals, and some would not follow the rules about how they are to be transported. In one case, after repeated attempts to elicit cooperation from the passenger failed, the passenger was put off at the next station.

One career diner employee has a hospitality background and responded to an ad that read, "Work on a train." When he was hired, he was told "not to expect to retire from Amtrak—it won't be around." That was in 1988. He complained that there wasn't any consistency in the food delivery. The supplier, a concessionaire, reportedly is inconsistent in the delivery of items needed on the menu, or oversupplies the food, creating waste. When the "new" menu was introduced in 2020, many of the items on the menu weren't delivered to the train (California Zephyr).

Many employees expressed the belief that management does not trust the employees, although several made reference to specific managers whom they liked and respected who possessed leadership skills. "But, they retired" and were replaced within the past couple of years by people who had no railroad experience. Several employees expressed frustration with the managerial "command and control" nature of Amtrak, advocating that it is the frontline employees on board the trains who make Amtrak function. "Management doesn't ride the trains. They don't know what goes on out here. It's demoralizing." said one attendant.

But it is not just the delivery of foodstuffs. One sleeper attendant told the tale of showing up for work in Chicago only to find that his car had not been outfitted with any towels, requiring him to requisition them for the run. "Where's the supervision?" he asked.

Overall, the career employees want to retain their employment and want to do a good job and give passengers a pleasant experience, but continual retrenchment hurts morale, and they don't feel as though they are given the tools to do their jobs to the best of their ability.

The View from the Towns and Cities Being Served

Not surprisingly, city/town/village councils see a need for Amtrak service to their community. Thomas Horsman, Sandusky, Ohio's city planner, responded by saying, "Sandusky has consistently had the highest Amtrak ridership per capita in the state of Ohio, which shows that train service is a great asset to our region. I don't own a car, so I use public transit and if I have to travel I take the train."

Mayor Stephen Wood of Rensselaer, Indiana, said that his community paid into a fund to keep the Hoosier State train that operated on days the Cardinal didn't. His community did not get support from local state representatives or the state's governor. "He took $6 million for Amtrak and gave it to the airport." Amtrak started out with high hopes, but the trains were always late. On-time performance was an issue. "The train was never on time. Iowa Pacific did a great job." But, he said, "The state's focus is on highways. You have to move people—the highways are overloaded." Although a small local college went out of business, "People would use the train to go to Chicago if it was reliable."

Noelle Weishaar, city councilor of Rensselaer, Indiana, replied: "It's a vital link of transportation options for our community. We are a rural community with little to no transportation options. Amtrak is vital to link us to travel to larger cities and bringing people to our community."

Carolyn McAdams, the mayor of Greenwood, Mississippi, replied, "Absolutely! It [Amtrak] is already here and provides people the opportunity to travel to Greenwood inexpensively. Elimination of Amtrak passenger service "would have an adverse effect on our tourism and sales tax. Greenwood is fortunate to have the train stop and have new passengers board but some actually decided to stay and visit Greenwood for a few days before continuing their trip." Greenwood is the second-largest ticket fare in Mississippi. Last year [2019] 14,700 people stopped in Greenwood as their destination on their way to Memphis or Chicago. "That is [according to] Amtrak."

Rachel Smith, assistant to the mayor of Walnut Ridge, Arkansas, replied that the city "has no air or bus services available in this area." Amtrak is an important link for this community.

The city manager of Waterloo, Indiana, Pamela Howard, stated that Amtrak serves 22,000 passengers annually, the most for any city in the state. They "take pride in our depot that serves as a waiting spot for the rides of Amtrak. We are hoping with a downtown redevelopment that we will have a coffee shop that may serve the passengers waiting on the train. There are people from all over the world that ride the train out of Waterloo going to Chicago, New York, and Washington, DC."

The mayor of Dodge City, Kansas, Brian Delzeit sees a need for Amtrak and "communicates and meets with elected officials in Washington regularly about the importance of Amtrak service and other issues." Highways and air service are available but not bus service.

Neil Segotta Jr., mayor of Raton, New Mexico, stated that the state of New Mexico is less supportive of Amtrak "but not a hindrance. The closest major airports are Denver and Albuquerque, both 225 miles. The closest commercial air service is Pueblo, Colorado—110 miles. Santa Fe and Colorado Springs Airports are approximately 150 miles from Raton. Bus service is available with numerous buses connecting with [the] Southwest Chief in Raton daily." He continued by saying, "Raton, New Mexico, is a part of a multistate local agency coalition that has successfully leveraged three TIGER Grant awards and has compelled New Mexico, Colorado, Kansas, BNSF, and Amtrak to participate financially also."

Senator Angus King (I-ME) travels by Amtrak's trains between Washington, New York, Boston, and Brunswick, Maine. "As a longtime advocate for smart, forward-thinking transportation policy, I am concerned about the state of the nation's public transportation infrastructure. We have not been good stewards of this infrastructure of our country, and we have reached the point where we need trillions of dollars of new investment to repair, upgrade, and build from scratch the means of transportation that will give our twenty-first-century country the growth and opportunity it experienced in the twentieth century. My conversations with my colleagues have illustrated that there is universal agreement on the importance of funding this necessary exercise—the challenge is what we decide to fund and how we pay for it. The obstacles here are not simple 'liberal' versus 'conservative' ones alone—rural states (like much of Maine) have very different needs than more urbanized states, geographically larger states must distribute a transportation network over larger land masses, and coastal states have the added consideration of more waterways. I believe my colleagues are acting in good faith, but all too often, we don't bring up conversations surrounding infrastructure unless we are responding to a harmful incident that results in negative consequences, news coverage, and widespread concern. The goal we should have in mind is to make transportation policy a venue for proactive growth and opportunity, instead of reactively plugging the holes of crisis. We all use roads, rail, airways, and waterways, and we all have a responsibility to press for our best vision of what they are and can do to help us all get where we need or want to go.

"In general, because Congress set Amtrak up as a quasi-public corporation, I believe that we should allow the corporation the latitude to conduct business with an appropriate level of freedom from government overdirection. That is the standard we have generally operated by in our economy over most of the course of Amtrak's life. That is not to say that Congress should not have an important role in setting direction for Amtrak—the federal government owns nearly all the stock of Amtrak and corporations have responsibility to their shareholders. The problems that we encounter often occur when members of Congress ask Amtrak to take actions that go in opposite directions; for example, to both cut costs (and thus require less subsidy) but also to preserve historic levels of service, particularly to underserved rural regions. If we can be consistent in what we ask of Amtrak, I anticipate that passenger rail service can be part of our national transportation network for years to come."[64]

Maine Senator Susan Collins, who chairs the Transportation, Housing, and Urban Development Appropriations Subcommittee, also has supported Amtrak. "I believe members of the Senate are keenly aware of Amtrak's challenges and its importance. With the growth of our nation's aviation system and the Interstate Highway System, passenger rail service has become more challenging to sustain, but it is critical that we do so. I believe that Amtrak is part of the solution to reduce congestion in the Northeast and to reduce emissions. Amtrak is also essential for numerous rural communities throughout this country that have limited alternative transportation options." She added, "In my role on the Appropriations Committee, I will advocate for funding for all modes of transportation. As the Senate Commerce Committee and the House Transportation & Infrastructure Committee develop a long-term surface transportation bill after the FAST Act expires next year, I believe they must: (1) allow Amtrak to continue to become more efficient and provide better service, (2) continue to invest in infrastructure, and (3) not sacrifice service to rural communities that have few or no other transportation alternatives."[65]

The Travel Experience

There was a time when the Pullman Company boasted that it safely transported more than 100,000 customers a night across America, making it the country's largest hotelier. Pullman was a for-profit company in the business of providing safe and comfortable parlor and sleeping car service. It also maintained its fleet in eight company shops strategically located around the country. Pullman had its own laundry for towels, dining car tablecloths, and napkins, sheets, pillowcases, and blankets. It had its own rules of employee conduct. Mirroring Ralph Budd's comment about a completed trip being remembered with pleasure and encouraging future trips, Pullman's level of service was intended to retain customers. Admittedly, times were different in Budd's day, and for that matter, George M. Pullman's.

By the mid-1950s, Pullman was trying to meet the competition head on with advertisements that spoke to the stress-free aspect of Pullman travel. *Geoffrey H. Doughty Collection*

Unfortunately, as competing transport modes gradually drew rail travelers away, the Pullman Company had no future, and its lofty standards of service became anachronisms. But had the company survived just two more years, it would have been in the best position to operate a national rail passenger network. Amtrak inherited the mantle of providing sleeping car service to those who still traveled by overnight train. But partly due to the tenuous nature of its founding and attitudes of its "host" railroads, Amtrak's ability to provide a consistent, reliable, and pleasurable travel experience has always been handicapped by its unpredictable funding and, all too frequently, by its own management.

Railroad passenger service has myriad interconnected parts. When Amtrak began in 1971, many of the institutional and traditional aspects of Pullman's operation were ingrained in the onboard personnel who transferred from the railroads to Amtrak employment. To Amtrak's detriment, however, the invaluable institutional knowledge of those career employees was lost when they departed because Pullman was no longer there to provide "basic training" to new Amtrak hires.

To onboard service personnel Amtrak offered opportunities for advancement, but the company had to establish its own training, work methods, and rules and had to create its own service culture. This was not necessarily a difficult thing to do, but over the years, significant and frequent leadership changes and lack of adequate funding that would have allowed the company to mature hampered a positive and healthy growth. As a result, the quality of service became inconsistent and, unavoidably, so did the passenger experience.

Unpredictability of onboard service can range from lack of a hospitality mindset in the dining car to lack of sleeping car supplies, frustrating passengers but also company personnel trying to do a good job with what seemed to be little if any support from headquarters. For decades, Amtrak dining crews were notorious for often rude and ill-tempered service. Dining car crews do have the most difficult jobs on a train. They are on their feet most of the time, are short staffed (due to management's cuts), and have to deal with a public whose behavior is subject to many variables. But, it must be noted that during the past decade, dining staff demeanor has vastly improved.

The dining experience does not have to meet the standards of a gourmet restaurant, but it should be better than that of a fast-food chain. Amtrak management should desire to excel and do more than meet the minimum standard of what people expect. To do this it should demonstrate its advantages compared to air and highway travel—and an important part of this is to offer something more than a seat, cold cereal, or a prepackaged meal.[66]

Equipment

For the time being, travel by train remains a part of the country's social fabric, and our personal experiences and interviews reinforced the belief that long-term employees want Amtrak to succeed as a mode of passenger transport. But as these words are written, Amtrak is facing the daunting challenge of replacing much of its rolling stock. While VIA Rail Canada invested in complete rehabilitation of its 1950s Budd-built heritage equipment on its long-distance flagship *Canadian* and some other services, Amtrak chose to purchase new equipment to replace its heritage fleet. There was logic in this because, as we have seen, that fleet came from several builders and had compatibility problems

A P42DC locomotive and Horizon Fleet cars in Chicago-Milwaukee Hiawatha service. *Kevin J. Holland*

in addition to its unpredictable patterns of in-service breakdowns due to age and deferred maintenance. When it came time to renovate the equipment, individuality of the cars made harmonizing of the fleet a "mission impossible."

Most of the VIA cars, by contrast, were from a single fleet built at the same time, and it was easier to retrofit plumbing, electrical, and other components in a uniform and economical manner. Amtrak did not have that luxury.[67] Furthermore, it did not seem to have a long-range plan, especially in light of the fact that many believed it would not be around for very long. That attitude changed once it seemed Amtrak might actually survive, but in the meantime equipment failures took their toll, and the company badly needed entirely new cars. Those cars were a welcome change and gave hope that a new generation of travelers could be lured away from autos and airplanes. One reason was that they were all-electric; no more steam-generated appurtenances. Locomotive-supplied power now handled fleet-wide lighting, heating, and cooling in a much more predictable manner. There is wide agreement that the Amfleet coaches have been a great success, and they and their café-car brethren remain the backbone of the coach fleet.

Overall, the Superliner cars for some of the long-distance trains also worked out well, though they had some issues; they were inspired by the Santa Fe's successful two-level El Capitan cars from the mid-1950s. The car bodies were stainless steel like the heritage fleet and were just as durable, but on the interior many components such as sink handles, door latches, and other elements were made of lightweight materials such as aluminum where the heritage fleet universally used materials such as steel and brass. The lighter material's fragility became a problem. Another was the sleeping car door latches and buffers, which seemed to work well when installed during construction. At 80 miles an hour, though, they often rattled loudly. Small matters, perhaps, but little annoyances can diminish the quality of the ride and, therefore, the passenger experience.

The single-level Viewliner sleepers eventually joined the fleet, and the last of the heritage fleet—some rebuilt dining and baggage cars—were finally, and only recently, retired. For its fleet, Amtrak created uniform maintenance procedures and schedules for each car type. However, maintenance suffered over time due to budget reductions. Further, some seemingly passenger-friendly innovations such as "ice-cold" water spigots and small TVs—a bad idea in any case—had to be disconnected (the video players feeding the televisions were not designed for rail travel). Complex piping created plumbing problems in both the Superliners and the Viewliners. The first of the Superliners arrived just over 40 years ago and the Viewliners 25 years ago, and many are showing signs of wear and suffering accelerating failures. It is a vicious cycle.

First impressions are critical to the success of any customer-focused enterprise, and quality of housekeeping makes the first impression for a passenger boarding a train. The passenger experience should not include inoperative toilets, cars with empty water tanks, dirty lavatories, ragged blankets in sleeping cars, balky temperature controls, or dirty interior windows. Repetitive failures leave passengers with the impression of a company that either cannot make things work or does not care to. Cuts in supervision, especially in the Mechanical Department, have caused much damage to passengers' experiences and have caused huge amounts of waste (speaking of which, all the throwaway food service items for which Amtrak has opted mean full trash receptacles on board and large bags of solid waste dropped off at intermediate points—not a pretty sight). The perception of Amtrak as a political bouncing ball that could at any time be kicked off the field of play does not communicate a sense of an enterprise trying its best. By contrast, well-maintained equipment that is fully functional, along with proper housekeeping—before boarding passengers and during the trip—would create a stable and structured state of good repair and sound practices. Passengers would find life aboard the train a more pleasurable experience that would encourage another trip, and crews could be proud of the service they offer.

Regrettably, after 50 years, a serious question remains unanswered: What should we do with Amtrak?

Part Three Notes

1. "E. G. Budd Sees No Saturation Point in US Travel," *Railway Age* 120, no. 4, (January 26, 1946), 247.
2. Telephone interview with Tom Downs, August 25, 2020.
3. Goodwin, Doris Kearns. *Leadership in Turbulent Times* (New York: Simon & Shuster), 2018, 18.
4. Johnson, Bob. "Amtrak's Money Mystery," *Trains* magazine, (January 2019), 54.
5. Downs, July 30, 2020.
6. Downs, September 1, 2020.
7. Perl, Anthony. *New Departures* (Lexington, University Press of Kentucky, 2002), 108.
8. Perl, 108.
9. Perl, 106.
10. The for-profit language was modified in PL 95-421, October 5, 1978, when Sec. 301 was amended

to insert "operated and managed as . . . a for-profit corporation." The Congressional committee that wrote it stated in the report language accompanying the bill that: "This amendment recognizes that Amtrak is not a for-profit corporation." Email correspondence with Mark Singer, October 10, 2020.

11. Perl, 110.
12. In August 1970, the Post Office Department was reorganized as the United States Postal Service with the intent of making its operations more "businesslike." Historically, the presidentially appointed postmaster general was most often a campaign supporter of the president. Starting in 1971 under President Nixon, the postmaster general was then appointed by a board of governors whose members were appointed by the president. Amtrak's enabling legislation occurred two months later and shares similarities in these respects. The two agencies' offices were located at L'Enfant Plaza in Washington, DC.
13. Downs, June 25, 2020.
14. Telephone interview with David Gunn, July 30, 2020.
15. Rush Loving, *The Men Who Loved Trains* (Bloomington: Indiana University Press, 2006), 342.
16. Downs, June 25, 2020.
17. Downs, September 1, 2020.
18. Richard Pierson, "Roger Lewis, ex-General Dynamics Chairman, Dies," *Washington Post*, November 15, 1987, www.washington post.com.
19. Rush Loving, *The Men Who Loved Trains* (Bloomington: Indiana University Press, 2006), 131.
20. Rush Loving, *The Well-Dressed Hobo* (Bloomington: Indiana University Press, 2016), 189.
21. Telephone interview with Robert VanderClute, May 29, 2020.
22. Downs, June 30, 2020.
23. Email correspondence with Cliff Black, January 4, 2020.
24. Telephone interview with Bruce Heard, June 27, 2020.
25. There is nothing in the original legislation (PL 91-518, October 30, 1970) that states Amtrak is a two-year experiment. Some believe the initial funding was expected to last two years. However, Sec. 404 (b)(1) states that "The Corporation must provide the service included within the basic system until July 1, 1973, to the extent is has assumed responsibility for such service by contract with a railroad." Furthermore, (b)(3) states: "If at any time after July 1, 1973, the Corporation determines that any train or trains in the basic system in whole or in part are not required by public convenience and necessity, will impair the ability of the Corporation to adequately provide other services, such train or trains may be discontinued under the procedures of section 13a of the Interstate Commerce Act." This, more than anything, gave rise to the incorrect assumption by many that Amtrak was a two- or three-year experiment. Certainly that was the hope of many detractors, including the Nixon administration and some of the freight railroads. They thought it was hopeless and would likely collapse after July 1, 1973. Singer, October 10, 2020.
26. And the fifty long-distance Amfleet II cars much later. Also, Budd built the prototype Viewliner shells—two sleepers and a diner—then ceased operation as the Budd Company in 1985, changing to TransitAmerica under owner Thyssen doing contract work on subway cars and (unsuccessfully) bidding on large orders. It finally closed entirely in 1987. The three prototype Viewliners were completed at Amtrak's Beech Grove, Indiana, shops after a delay of several years. Black, October 9, 2020.
27. McFadden, Robert D. "Alan Boyd, Who Set Department of Transportation in Motion, Dies at 98," *New York Times*, October 20, 2020, sect. A, 24.
28. Downs, June 25, 2020.
29. Gunn, October 21, 2020.
30. Black, July 3, 2020.
31. Black, July 3, 2020.
32. Black, January 4, 2020.
33. Downs, June 25, 2020.
34. Downs, July 10, 2020.
35. After Downs was fired, the two positions were separated allowing the chairman to dominate board decisions and dictate direction of the corporation. Downs, September 28, 2020.
36. Downs, June 25, 2020.
37. Downs, August 31, 2020.
38. Downs, June 25, 2020.
39. Downs, June 25, 2020.
40. Downs, June 30, 2020.
41. Downs, June 25, 2020.
42. Downs, June 30, 2020.
43. After his departure, Tom Downs became executive vice president and CEO of the National Home Builders Association; executive director, National Center for Smart Growth and Education, University of Maryland College Park; president and CEO of the Eno Foundation; and chairman,

North American Board of Veolia Transportation.
44. Email correspondence with Joe McHugh, January 22, 2021.
45. "Reshaping, Rebuilding Amtrak," *Railway Age*, March 2017, vol. 218, no. 3, 12.
46. Appointed as an Amtrak director in 2009 by President Obama, he was elected chairman in 2013. A lawyer and former chairman of the Board of Commissioners of the Port Authority of New York and New Jersey, he has no railroad background. Reputedly he desires to separate the NEC from Amtrak and have it controlled by New Jersey Transit.
47. McHugh, January 22, 2021.
48. McHugh, January 22, 2021.
49. "Reshaping," 12.
50. "Reshaping," 12.
51. "Reshaping," 12.
52. Testimony before the Committee on Appropriations Subcommittee on Transportation, Treasury, and Independent Agencies, April 10, 2003.
53. Black, August 22, 2020.
54. Downs, August 25, 2020.
55. Appointed by President George W. Bush, he served as the board's vice chairman from July 2006 until January 2009, resigning in February 2009. Black, August 29, 2020.
56. Black, July 6, 2020.
57. Black, July 6, 2020.
58. Some industry observers suspect his contract extension was coincident with the appointment of Anthony Coscia as chairman and there was nobody in waiting who had Boardman's connections with FRA. In time, Boardman's national system bias was in conflict with Coscia's corridor bias, reducing long-distance service, and shifting costs to the states. Hence, Boardman was given a short-term contract extension of three years while internal politics played out. Those internal politics led to his resignation.
59. Black, July 6, 2020.
60. Black, July 6, 2020.
61. Black, August 22, 2020.
62. "Reshaping," 12.
63. Don Phillips, transportation writer for the *Washington Post*, wrote about the matter on June 13, 1992: "Amtrak and the Food and Drug Administration have agreed that mice should not travel by train—with or without a ticket—and that Amtrak needs to do a better job of refrigerating and handling food."
64. Email correspondence with Senator Angus King, December 18, 2019.
65. Email correspondence with Senator Susan Collins, July 19, 2019.
66. Politicians sometimes stand in the way too. A classic example is the campaign of former Representative John Mica (also discussed earlier), a Florida Republican who saw Amtrak subsidies as a drain on the American treasury. His efforts to curtail subsidies were legendary, and it was he who proposed that as part of Amtrak reauthorization bills, the money-losing beverage and food service had to end losses by December 2020. This provision, buried in the bill, drove the Anderson administration to eliminate full dining service on some trains and degrade service on others, even aboard brand new and attractive dining cars, in 2018-19. The problem is perpetuated because Congressional members often do not acquaint themselves with the details and provisions of proposed legislation.
67. Many of the Heritage cars were successfully converted to HEP before toilet holding tank mandates required their retirement. Black, October 9, 2020.

Amtrak's purpose should be to attract passengers.
It's that simple.
>   William C. Vantuono, from an interview with the authors

The Road to the Future

4

The fact is that Amtrak has had to endure a half-century of increasingly unfavorable perceptions of its purpose, performance, and legitimacy. There have been bright spots, for sure—the success of Acela and Auto Train services, expansion of the route network, online reservations, the automated reservations helpmate "Julie," and greatly increased ridership. And while much focus has been on the NEC, excellent intercity service, such as that in New York State, is often overlooked. Amtrak's New York City–Buffalo–Niagara Falls Empire Service is comfortable and relaxing; the scenery is superb; and the crews are uniformly friendly and accommodating.

The long-distance trains generally provide good service, but they trend toward *basic* rather than *excellent*. Passengers aboard any mode of transport must accept the possibility of delays, mechanical problems, and other hard-to-avoid slip-ups. When mechanical problems occur on trains due to inadequate supervision and funding, onboard crews generally try their best to provide as pleasant a passenger experience as possible, often beyond the call of duty. Service to passengers is their livelihood and they take it seriously. Some dysfunction has come about because Amtrak actually has dropped the ball, but ongoing negative government and media attitudes surely do not help, and lack of trust in upper management takes a toll.

The variable level of quality in Amtrak's dining service is a good example. Bill Howes recalled that when he was at C&O/B&O, "If the sleepers had fewer than ten passengers, the diner had two crew members and two menu entrees. It was simple to prepare and to 'do it right.' The crews were told, 'If you think you can do more and do it right, okay.' Cooked-to-order steak was okay if done right. Much to my surprise, the crew added steak almost every trip. There were three or four entrees plus steak—steak generated the highest tips. They did it and did it right. Amtrak hasn't done it right."[1]

In 2018, Amtrak introduced its "contemporary dining" regimen, unconvincingly justifying its microwaved meals in cardboard boxes with an undocumented premise that the millennial generation desires such food and beverage aboard its trains. An additional argument that millennials do not wish to interact with other passengers in a dining car setting may be true in some cases, but they are not the only people who ride trains. Basing the company's food and beverage service protocol on such specious precepts is simply foolish. As a result, the brand-new single-level Viewliner dining cars are not utilized in the manner for which they were built—to provide traditional, quality meal service.

When the changed meal policy was introduced, a crew member handed the passenger a boxed meal, a minimalist service. This saved on staffing costs, but quality of the rail experience and customer satisfaction suffered badly. When passenger complaints flooded the company, management pivoted slightly by introducing its "flexible dining" regimen, suggesting with a degree of élan that passengers should "experience" the new service. While the packaging and presentation were changed, the quality of the cuisine remained essentially the same. Disposable plastic plates, knives, spoons, and forks became standard dinnerware while being promoted oxymoronically as environmentally "sustainable." Such actions and pronouncements erode Amtrak's integrity, and degradation of the dining experience has been a huge disappointment. As Bill Vantuono quipped, "Cold boxed food for sleeper passengers is not cutting it."[2]

We can learn lessons from the past without trying to repeat it. Bill Howes remembered that when NYC refurbished its 20th Century Limited in 1962 for its sixtieth anniversary, the railroad "really made an effort."[3] NYC was led by Alfred Perlman, no friend of the passenger train, but the Century was still making a modest above-the-rail profit, so he did not protest. Female sleeping car passengers were given a corsage; men were given a boutonnière and a morning newspaper. Some traditions were maintained. Shoes, left in a small receptacle in each bedroom and roomette, were accessible from the aisle, and the car's porter shined them overnight. Flowers in a small vase adorned table settings in the dining car. For the company's employees the train served as a symbol of pride. They did it right.

Cutting expenses in a labor-intensive operation is a mighty task. Amtrak's management chose first to trim at the edges, eliminating the small, sometimes elegant amenities of travel that people did not anticipate but found pleasant, such as a morning newspaper, or complimentary coffee and/or juice brought to the passenger's room, or a shoe shine.[4] Their cessation happened gradually and it was left to onboard personnel to explain these moves to passengers, in another step in the descent toward the mundane. Saving money was the goal, but as Ronald Batory points out, "Money is not about how much is spent but how wisely it is spent."[5]

In an article for *Passenger Train Journal*, the former chief of Amtrak's West Coast Product Development, Brian Rosenwald, was quoted saying, "In a real or perceived financial crisis, not much consideration goes into what I would call the 'value proposition,' meaning what customers are willing to pay for

"Boy, they really meant it when they said 'No Frills.'"
Warren Miller, The New Yorker. Copyright Condé Nast. Used by permission

the long-distance-train experience. Cutting amenities is usually the easiest thing to do, but a loss of even 1 percent in sleeping-car ridership completely negates those savings. Improving financial performance for long-distance trains requires two parallel and very challenging efforts: addressing the primary cost drivers for those trains, which include labor productivity and cost along with equipment utilization, and, even more importantly, figuring out how to increase ridership and revenue, particularly during off-peak periods. The latter issue," he concluded, "is tied to the quality of the product offered to existing as well as potential customers."[6]

"When I took over the Starlight," he recalled, "ridership had experienced three years of decline, largely because Southwest Airlines had entered our market. My idea was to create a superior on-train experience, since we couldn't compete on speed." By the year 2000, cumulative ridership and revenue both had grown roughly 70 percent.[7]

The Amtrak story is haunted by the specter of money. Amtrak budget cuts unfortunately seem inevitable and began on Day One back in 1971.[8] Management's focus on reducing avoidable costs is part of its responsibility—indeed, any public service must be provided in a businesslike manner—but cuts at Amtrak are coming at the expense of passenger comfort and travel enjoyment. Can the quality of onboard service be improved? "Yes," said Bill Vantuono. "VIA Rail[9] does it; why can't we? Better onboard service can be achieved."[10]

Air Travel in the 21st Century

Of course, travel by air has become de rigueur and is a vital link between population centers; it has, however, become basic transportation whose only advantage is speed. And this assumes no weather or mechanical interruptions. "Travel's a curse," says innkeeper Thénardier in *Les Miserables*, but all travel is an adventure, so delays, while inconvenient, should be taken in stride. Comfort is another matter.

Ironically, it was passenger train advocate Robert R. Young who said in the 1950s that in their efforts to attract passengers, railroads must emulate the marketing model of the airlines. Some tried, but the airlines ultimately captured the long-distance travel market and largely assigned the passenger train to the history books and the ocean liner to cruise ship status. In today's market, however, like the railroads in the early 1920s, airlines simply have no incentive to attract more passengers. In-flight services and amenities such as beverages, meals, and wide, comfortable seats have become viewed as unnecessary expenses.

Commenting on ABC News in April 2019 about flying in the 21st century, United Airlines President Oscar Munoz told senior transportation correspondent David Kerley that airlines are reaching a breaking point with shrinking seat sizes. "I think we are nearing a point certainly that we can't do that anymore." Munoz acknowledged having to stay competitive with peers and match many of their moves, but he admitted passengers may have had enough. He recognized that the experience of air travel, for many, had evolved from exciting to painful.[1] "It's become so stressful," he said, "from when you leave, wherever you live, to get into traffic, to find a parking spot, to get through security. Frankly by the time you sit on one of our aircraft . . . you're just pissed at the world, and improving the flying experience won't ultimately depend on what coffee or cookie I give you."[2]

At one time, the public was willing to accept narrower seats and the absence of free meals, snacks, and beverages. These were superfluous to a traveler whose motivation was to get to a destination as quickly and cheaply as possible. What society lost were the pleasure and social benefits of travel; the adage that "getting there is half the fun" no longer influences a traveler who does not care about the travel experience.

When the Civil Aeronautics Board regulated the airlines and their fares, they competed by offering improved flight experiences and comfort. With deregulation, the airlines focused mainly on cutting fares to attract passengers, and a "no frills" experience became the standard. Unfortunately, most people seem to endure rather than enjoy flying. Often chaotic security screening, nonrefundable fares, change fees, vacuum-packed economy seating, small bathrooms, and baggage charges that encourage pushing the limits of carry-on bags, along with a clientele that often seems unfamiliar with appropriate travel dress and behavior, all combine to make air travel unappealing. Is this progress? Young certainly did not envision this when he suggested railroads emulate the airline industry.

Notes

1. "United Airlines CEO Says Aviation Industry Needs Changing," ABC News, April 23, 2019.
2. "United Airlines CEO Says Aviation Industry Needs Changing," ABC News, April 23, 2019.

Vantuono adds, "Astronaut Jim Lovell once remarked about the 1960s space program, 'It wasn't a miracle; we just decided to go there.' Decided to and did. We can if we decide to. But, there's no grand vision for anything, really."[11] Today even top management seems unable to stop thinking about Amtrak as a *business* that suffers *losses* from running trains that need subsidies to keep operating—and focused specifically on the cost of providing long-distance services. From outside Amtrak—Congress, media commentators—as well as inside, there has been ongoing discussion about eliminating or at least radically altering Amtrak's long-distance network, even before the coronavirus pandemic. This would ignore Amtrak's mandate to maintain a national network and would discriminate against a large portion of the nation's population.

Amtrak maintains that "only" 3 percent of passengers are riding end-to-end on long-distance routes, apparently citing this as a reason to consider cutting back or eliminating the trains altogether. This 3 percent figure may be factually correct, but the premise is misleading. If 100 passengers board the Empire Builder in Chicago, it should be expected that far more than three passengers will get off in Seattle. The "3 percent" argument ignores the intermediate travelers—those riding Chicago to the Twin Cities, Minot to Whitefish, Williston to Essex, Spokane, or Seattle. There likely are days when 100 board at Chicago and twice that many get off in Seattle. Arguing that less than full-route ridership counts against long-distance trains is like saying that the interstate highway system should be abandoned because only a few drivers travel the entire length of each route. Long-distance trains serve multiple city pairs, and ridership often will turn over several times between endpoints. Like the interstates, the long-distance trains provide a valuable means of connectivity among cities and towns on their routes that often have no access to other public transportation.

Is Amtrak a Business or a Service?

While we have described Amtrak as providing a public service, it really is a hospitality program that provides a service. It must not be solely considered a business. "If Amtrak was run purely as a business," says Cliff Black, "presumably it would shut down, just as the private freight operators were about to do prior to the passage of the Rail Passenger Service Act. If Amtrak were operated purely as a service, it would require an infinite amount of money simply in order to provide perfect service. So the two have to come together, ideally in the middle."[12] As for the freight carriers, they would be content if Amtrak were to cease operations, so long as they were not required to take over its operations and functions.[13]

Restaurants and hotels are businesses that provide a service singularly designed to attract customers. Most budget hotel corporations recognized at some point that a free breakfast would attract customers. Although the quality of breakfasts varies among hotel chains, it has proven to be a convenient way for overnighters to start their day, and it attracts a loyal following to a particular brand—along with "reward" and incentive programs to encourage repeat customers.

Government services are different. The National Park Service, for example, charges entrance fees to help offset the cost of conducting its operations, but it has never been operated with the intent of making a profit. The US Postal Service also charges fees and has been viewed by some politicians as a for-profit corporation. However, it has never made and should not be expected to make a profit.

Unfortunately, Amtrak's frequent management changes have left the corporation in a state of continual vacillation between operating as a service and as a business. Average CEO tenure was about four years. The quality of its leadership, in both character and/or skill, has been like a carnival roller coaster, hurtling between the appalling (Lewis) to the brilliant (Reistrup, Boyd, Claytor, and Downs, who tried to keep it a viable enterprise by investing in it), to the poor (Warrington, who didn't care), back to superb (Gunn, who strove to straighten out its flaws), to frustrated (Kummant, who was hired as a placeholder), to Boardman, who wanted the job and was a fast learner but whose efforts were often unfocused and subverted by a new board chairman. How did some of the less qualified get the top job? The answer lies in the intangibles: personal ambitions and political connections. It is easy to see why Amtrak has bumped along.

After Boardman departed, Amtrak had three presidents in four years, all placeholders. As in the Nixon years, the business side dominated the Amtrak board's point of view, centered on cost control and reducing the federal appropriation. Although these are commendable goals, it has come at the expense of service quality and passenger satisfaction. As a former successful businessman, US Senator Angus King observed, "No business will improve its bottom line by degrading service."[14]

How Much Damage Was Done by Richard Anderson?

When hired by Amtrak's board of directors, Richard Anderson had recently retired as chairman of Delta Airlines, having made it one of the most successful in the industry. But, like Roger Lewis, he had no railroad experience whatsoever. As was his legacy at Delta, his brief tenure at Amtrak will be remembered for the cost-cutting he imposed on the company and for the buyouts of seasoned management, a mistake that excised the company's institutional knowledge and with it the experience gained over time of what worked and what did not.[15] His aim was to reduce the federal appropriation and make Amtrak more businesslike (both admirable goals, if challenging). Reduced supervision in the Mechanical Department negatively impacted maintenance, and downgrading the quality of food and beverage service affected passengers' enjoyment of the travel experience. His contentious and acrimonious management style did not help matters. Employee morale suffered. Perhaps Anderson's biggest failing was, as Tom Downs points out, that "People from an airline or some other business do not understand the irrational nature of railroads and those who love them."[16]

Anderson, like Wick Moorman before him, brought in former colleagues to run various departments and functions. They may have been competent in their various fields of expertise, but the disadvantage was that they were there for the short term and had no stake in Amtrak's future or loyalty to Amtrak or its employees. Most of Anderson's hires were from the airline industry, including a safety manager; while their experience in general was in transportation, they knew little or nothing about railroads. They were brought in to make changes but not to innovate in ways that would make rail travel more attractive. Instead of making it superior to traveling by bus, car, or airplane, Anderson's emotionally detached guidance made Amtrak's primary policy a focus on cutting costs, fare pricing, and adding fees—much as the airlines had done. Printed timetables had already disappeared in 2016, along with route guides, coloring books for children, complimentary newspapers, and amenity kits for sleeping car passengers. What remained to be cut were meals prepared on board, the final step in stripping down the rail travel experience.

But a question remains as to who was behind Anderson's draconian policies. Was it the board chairman, Anthony Coscia? Executive vice president Stephen Gardner? Would Anderson's successor, retired air freight executive William Flynn, be able or allowed to repair the damage and restore the attractiveness of travel by train? It did not take long to find out.

A New Direction?

Flynn's presidency was too short to allow any improvement efforts and the coronavirus pandemic so reduced ridership that acting in survival mode was the order of the day. Acela service was devastated, and on October 1, 2020, long-distance services were cut to triweekly.

Then, following the November 2020 election of Joseph Biden as US president, events at Amtrak headquarters moved swiftly. William Flynn was promoted to CEO, while executive vice president Gardner was elevated to president. In an article in the December 2020 issue of *Railway Age* titled "Gardner Ascends to Amtrak's Presidency," what many suspected came about:

> It was only a matter of time before Gardner was named President, as many industry observers had commented following Flynn's appointment, and during the tenure of Richard Anderson, Flynn's predecessor. Gardner, it is widely understood, has been making most of the major decisions and quietly setting policy in his role as second-in-command.
>
> Gardner is a lifelong Democrat and skilled political operative who joined Amtrak in 2009 following a stint on Capitol Hill developing rail and transportation policy for the US Senate Committee on Commerce, Science and Transportation and for Senator Tom Carper (D-Del.) and others. Early in his transportation career,

he held various positions with Guilford Rail System (Pan Am Railways) and the Buckingham Branch Railroad in Virginia. He is widely recognized as the principal author of PRIIA (Passenger Rail Investment and Improvement Act of 2008). By 2017, he had garnered enough experience to be appointed to Amtrak's top spot, but "there was no way he'd get the job as long as there was a Republican in the White House, and as long as Elaine Chao was Secretary of Transportation,"[17] according to one Capitol Hill transportation insider. "When Democrat Joe Biden, a staunch Amtrak supporter and long-time Amtrak customer, became President-elect, that set the wheels in motion to give Stephen Gardner the throttle. It's not surprising that the Amtrak board didn't wait until Inauguration Day."[18]

What does Gardner's promotion portend for Amtrak? In the view of one retired railroad executive, "Gardner has worked diligently to dismantle the Amtrak long-distance network from the inside, and many believe he is largely responsible for the reduction of train services to triweekly." And while his public statements seem to value the long-distance network, decisions undermining it seem contradictory. "As a former legislative aide to a Democratic congressman, he knows the political landscape very well and has used that knowledge to his advantage. Since recent CEOs have been placeholders, it has given Gardner the ability to effectively become the chief operating officer with little direction from his superiors."[19]

In addition to its severe economic challenges, Amtrak also is burdened by erroneous public statements about profitability of the NEC; a shift of focus to state programs; the effects of three-day-a-week service on ridership and revenues; and behind-the-scenes moves of its leadership.

The "Amtrak Problem"

In David Gunn's view, "The problem with Amtrak is that it has run out of Jim McClellans."[20] That is, it does not have true rail passenger service advocates determining its fate. Tom Downs adds, "Alan Boyds and Graham Claytors too."[21] They were the Renaissance men who knew how to do it all, who understood passenger trains and how to get people to travel on them.

Some critics want to solve the "Amtrak problem" by privatizing it; as we have noted, they simply do not understand that this cannot work. Privatizing it means killing it. Bill Howes noted that "Amtrak was created in 1970 and implemented in 1971 as an expedient to deal with a bunch of perceived crises (the most serious of which depended upon who you talked to). Very little thought was given to its long-term mission or role in advancing any national policy (should one eventually emerge) governing the country's mobility. Amtrak finds itself in essentially the same position today. It is an organization trying its best to hold onto the ball until the country decides where to place the goalpost and determines whether the run to the goal can be realistically accomplished through private enterprise, a private-public (taxpayer-supported) partnership, or exclusively public means. To the extent that Amtrak was or is expected to be a successful for-profit business in support of national transportation policy objectives, it has failed due to (1) the lack of a coherent national transportation policy on this subject, (2) the inherent economics of rail passenger service as a mature business saddled with obsolete or inefficient practices, and (3) political dogma and meddling."[22]

Wick Moorman echoes this sentiment about a lack of coherent policy. Amtrak "has no clearly defined mission," other than to provide a national service. "Politics and money underlay transportation policy. It [Amtrak] did the best it could with the money it was given."[23] But, Tom Downs added, "How can you have a failure of policy when there is no policy?"[24]

"Putting Amtrak under the aegis of 'transportation policy,' is actually being kind," says Cliff Black. "Its creating documentation had the characteristics of a late-night scheme among tipsy dreamers writing on a cocktail napkin. I don't say this to disparage the efforts of the creators, because they were under tremendous time pressure and political oversight, so they did what they could under the circumstances. When you create an entity in a hurry in order to take over a failed business model with the expectation it too would fail when its puny $40 million seed money ran out in three years, and cobble it together in a few months, it's hard to call it transportation policy."[25]

Amtrak's many supporters, and especially members of Congress, have different priorities and ideas for what Amtrak should be. Transportation of people, however, is too important to be left to the shallowness of partisan politics. So, even though a coherent and balanced transportation policy remains elusive, Amtrak's operations nevertheless can be improved. There is a way, and it is not that difficult.

Recommendations for Action

Although Amtrak can be seen as a failure of transportation policy—or the result of a failure to develop one—that does not mean Amtrak itself has been a failure. It has survived thus far in spite of itself, as Tom Downs has opined, "because of its customer loyalty."[26] One must also add because of dedicated Amtrak employees who want it to succeed and prosper and, it must be said, because at least some Congressional friends did not want to see it disappear.

Defining where and how Amtrak goes from here requires identifying and solving the problems that have plagued "America's Railroad" from its start. Correcting Amtrak's flaws will entail major transplant surgery to install a president, a board chairman, and a board who recognize Amtrak's value and who will ensure its success.[27]

Writing of Amtrak's creation, Jim McClellan presciently observed, "If the passenger train was to have a fighting chance, it needed a pro-passenger management with nationwide responsibility and a nationwide identity."[28] This remains true 50 years later.

Governance

The history of Amtrak's governance is a story of the board chairman versus the Amtrak president, where each got tired of the other; it was never given the governance structure it needed.[29] Aside from Amtrak's founding legislation, the primary problem today is "the chairman and the board of directors," says David Gunn. "They want to kill it."[30] Rush Loving characterized it as a political contest: "When the liberals are in power, they try to obstruct anything the labor unions oppose. If the conservatives are running the show, Amtrak must battle against a fixation that has dominated conservative thinking since the days of Richard Nixon. Many Republicans think it is wrong for government to spend money on passenger trains, even though they have no qualms against pouring millions into highways, airports, and air traffic control systems."[31]

The Rail Passenger Service Act of 1970 defined board appointments and sought a cross section of members whose purpose was to provide judicious oversight while ensuring and furthering the goal of a national passenger rail network. In recent years, however, the Amtrak board has become intensely politicized. In David Gunn's view, some current members of the board possess "limited competence" while others are actually anti-Amtrak.[32]

"Board members," says Cliff Black, "should learn from management about the operations of the passenger railroad—not with just the Amtrak president, but also the executive staff."[33] Rush Loving wrote that the process by which board members are chosen "must be freed from the politicians—as Congress did for [the] USRA [in the run-up to creating Conrail in 1976]. If the board were reconstituted in such a way that neither Congress nor the White House could influence it, Amtrak would have unfettered opportunity to change the way people travel in the corridors of the Northeast, the Midwest, and the West Coast."[34]

Furthermore, as Wick Moorman points out, "The chairman of the board should remind new members that they have a fiduciary responsibility to see Amtrak succeed, not closed down."[35]

Board of Directors

The board's leadership selection procedure should be depoliticized, eliminating meddling from the White House and Congress. The US president has the authority to choose board members and the chairman of the board, but state governors, congressional members, AARP, rail passenger associations, the traveling public, and other stakeholders should demand accountability in their nomination and confirmations.

Members must not be political hacks or friends of the US president. They must be nonpartisan and possess specific expertise in passenger rail transportation and/or hospitality, safety, labor relations and human resources, risk management, and principles of good governance. Board composition should include one or two railroad presidents, a representative from a state with significant passenger rail services, a commuter agency, consumer and union representatives, and a finance and legal expert. They must abide by the 1970 Congressional mandate regarding Amtrak's mission. Term limits should apply (two two-year terms; the chairman and board as of 2020 were holdovers from the Obama administration) so that members do not make the board their life's work.[36]

Echoing Wick Moorman, Tom Downs adds, "It is imperative that board members be instructed on their fiduciary responsibility to see that Amtrak succeeds."[37]

Leadership

By contrast, Amtrak's president should accept the position with a long-term commitment and focus and has to be on the job daily. Recent Amtrak presidents have been part-time employees, a move that seems to reflect short-range thinking and a lack of commitment on the part of the board and the president. They have been retirees who are in the office only one to three days a week, have had brief contract terms of three years, and have been reduced to "caretakers" and figureheads, not stewards. Amtrak requires able and devoted leadership that sees its job as a seven-day-a-week assignment.

An Amtrak president must possess foresight and keen vision for the company and be free of self-serving purpose, ideally have a rail-based background in rail finance and/or operations, possess a record of skillful administrative talent, recognize the importance and value of its employees, be trustworthy and able to manage people and attract and hire qualified career management without reliance on consulting firms to do the job, demonstrate interest and care in supporting the national network, have familiarity with government, and be accessible. The president's mission must be to promote safety and provide a service that attracts passengers (simple math: more passengers mean more revenue and less federal support) while being run on a business model that recognizes the unique character of carrying passengers by rail.

A persistent problem of leadership has been the reinventing and refining of programs with no lessons learned from past successes and failures. For example, Graham Claytor, Tom Downs, and David Gunn's attempts to bring clarity to Amtrak's accounting were all scrapped by successive administrations.[38] The company's repository of reliable corporate memory has been depleted through buyouts of seasoned employees. The advantage to Amtrak of this valuable institutional knowledge and experience of what works and what does not has been needlessly squandered for short-term gain.

What the US President Can Do

Presidents of the United States have greater problems to address than the future of Amtrak, but they are responsible for appointing its leadership, and Amtrak's flaws will persist if the president and his closest advisors do not act in its best interests.

In addition to the secretary of transportation, the president can appoint board members who have varied expertise in business, hospitality, state or regional transportation, labor, human resources, and consumer protection, and direct them to grow the business using sound business practices while improving operational expertise and market appeal of first-in-class national long-distance and regional passenger service.

What Congress Can Do

All too often, congressional opponents with political influence have determined Amtrak's direction as a matter of political doctrine. Congress needs to face the facts: Amtrak will never make a profit and will need continuous financial support as a public service with an underlying business model. For more than 50 years, Amtrak has been handicapped by short-term funding and reauthorization measures.

While Amtrak's flaws can be traced to the founding legislation, there have been many changes through subsequent reauthorizations whose effects have been both positive and negative. Amtrak's problems are complex—like the rail industry itself—but are not insurmountable. Its more serious shortcomings are those requiring the company to be a profit-making enterprise while eliminating loss. Congress must first change the law, but also it must reform the reauthorization procedure so Amtrak is a permanent fixture in passenger transportation committed to operating a full national system of long-distance service and the NEC. The idea of a separate NEC must be finally put entirely to rest.

Congress should also:

- Address the manner by which board members are nominated. Amtrak board members should be selected by a bipartisan congressional committee or, preferably, one composed of Amtrak stakeholders (e.g., the National Governors' Association, the US Conference of Mayors, senior citizen advocacy groups, environmental organizations, the travel and hospitality industries, or the Rail Passengers Association) who would recommend individuals for the president's consideration. This committee could also testify at Senate confirmation hearings.
- Approve a long-term permanent funding plan for both Amtrak and state-supported intercity passenger operations that would give the corporation the same funding priority as highways, aviation, and waterways.
- Assess America's current and future mobility needs and determine where and how rail passenger service will help meet those needs.
- Fund rebuilding of critical tunnels and bridges along the NEC.
- Permanently remove the language under the "FAST Act" requiring food and beverage service to "eliminate . . . operating loss," which passed in 2015 as H.R. 22, in particular Section 11207, Food and Beverage Reform.

- Clearly and succinctly prescribe policy only, and leave operational details to management.
- Initiate a massive reinvestment program to replace and repair passenger equipment.

The federal government should establish a trust fund for capital improvements on host railroads that will improve both passenger and freight services. There is nothing wrong with investing public funds in privately owned infrastructure since doing so will yield significant public benefits. Doing so, however, will need to overcome a legitimate concern on the part of the railroads that such aid will come with "strings attached." The best way would be to avoid most such strings and negotiate and agree upon the specifics and purpose of any that are attached.

What Amtrak Management Can Do

Service

After 50 years of operation, Amtrak has been unable to develop any reputation for high-quality service. What reputation exists is mainly one of continual service degradation, more recently described in Orwellian terms as "enhancements" or "reforms" whose only achievements have been to sour the travel experience.

Amtrak cannot afford customers who try it once and vow never to return. Service policy can no longer rely exclusively on cutting costs. Restoring some level of quality and making it clear the company wants people to travel on its trains would not be unreasonable, especially when compared to the competition's lowest common denominator concept of travel. Doing so will attract passengers. Well-designed hospitality and passenger amenities should be deployed to make travel attractive. Amtrak can improve food quality by returning to freshly cooked meals prepared on all long-distance overnight trains. It has to remember the point made earlier, that the cost of lost customers is almost always higher than the cost of enhancing services; negative media accounts of the rail travel experience have to be made a thing of the past.

Payments to Host Railroads

Host railroads must be paid compensatory rates for track usage that reflect the true cost of accommodating Amtrak trains. Payments to the railroads could take account of any tax credits or deductions for the railroads' investments in capacity improvements as well as capital and maintenance costs borne by Amtrak. Fair and reasonable existing agreements between various railroads and rail commuter authorities can provide a model for negotiations between Amtrak and its host railroads.

Accounting

Amtrak must review its accounting to make it more transparent, find another accepted methodology if generally accepted accounting principles prove unworkable for Amtrak's unique situation, initiate procedures that reflect actual costs by seat-mile, avoid assigning costs to operations that do not logically incur them, provide a framework for measuring passenger satisfaction, and provide regular performance reports detailing ridership, revenues, operating costs, safety statistics, and any other data useful in evaluating the company's performance. Charges to state- and authority-run corridor and commuter services for use of Amtrak tracks, equipment, facilities, and employees, must be reasonable.

Marketing

To attract passengers, Amtrak must identify markets and develop a strategic plan to attract passengers, including media advertising. It must restore aggressive marketing to the public and tour groups; restore printed timetables; make them easily accessible on its website; and make the website as easy as possible to use by people unfamiliar with rail travel.

Amtrak "Reforms"

Unfortunately, most efforts to reform Amtrak have not resulted in actual reforms or improvements; just the opposite. Amtrak's own effort to reform itself through the creation of the Amtrak Reform Board was foiled when that board was abolished under Richard Anderson. Unfortunately, "reform" efforts still consist of attempts to shift away from long-distance trains (in violation of the 1970 founding legislation) to a focus on operating only the NEC and state-run corridors. It is clear that the public and the states served by long-distance trains want them to continue as the critical core to which corridor operations connect.

Host Railroads

Host railroads' managements have forgotten the complexity and burden of passenger service that they relinquished to Amtrak in 1971. The railroads should treat Amtrak as a customer, not an inconvenience, and operate Amtrak trains on schedule. They should recognize their advantage in having to deal only with Amtrak, a single entity, rather than the multiple providers of long-distance passenger service that likely would result if Amtrak were privatized or reduced only to state-run corridors. They should work with Amtrak and come to mutually agreeable business arrangements for access based on those with state-sponsored agencies.

Part Four Notes

1. Personal interview with William F. Howes, February 12–13, 2019.
2. Vantuono, January 31, 2019.
3. Howes, February 12–13, 2019.
4. Shoe-shining continued under Amtrak, ending in 1983.; Black, October 9, 2020.
5. Email correspondence with Ronald L. Batory, February 21, 2021.
6. Zimmermann, Karl. "Where Have All The Flowers Gone?" *Passenger Train Journal*, Vol. 37, no. 2, 2014, Issue no. 259, 44.
7. Zimmermann, 44.
8. Howes, February 12–13, 2019.
9. VIA Rail Canada shares similar problems with Amtrak when it comes to funding and the manner in which politicians view its value as a service.
10. Vantuono, January 31, 2019.
11. Vantuono, January 31, 2019.
12. Black, July 3, 2020.
13. Email correspondence with Mike Weinman, June 6, 2020.
14. Senator Angus King, quoted in the *Portland Press Herald* (ME) online discussing Postal Service cuts August 7, 2020.
15. Wrinn, Jim, "Changing of the Guard at Amtrak," *Trains* magazine, July 2020, 3.
16. Downs, June 25, 2020.
17. Chao resigned in early January 2021, before secretary-designate Pete Buttigieg could even be confirmed.
18. "Gardner Ascends to Amtrak's Presidency," *Railway Age*, December 2020, 6.
19. Email correspondence, November 20, 2020.
20. Gunn, October 12, 2020.
21. Downs, October 13, 2020.
22. Email correspondence with Bill Howes, July 27, 2020.
23. Telephone interview with Wick Moorman July 27, 2020.
24. Downs, July 31, 2020.
25. Black, July 18, 2020.
26. Downs, July 16, 2020.
27. Telephone interviews with David Gunn and Cliff Black, July 30, 2020.
28. McClellan, 188.
29. Telephone interview with Joe McHugh, January 4, 2021.
30. Gunn, October 12, 2020.
31. Loving, Rush, *The Well-Dressed Hobo* (Bloomington: Indiana University Press, 2016), 192.
32. Gunn, July 30, 2020.
33. Black, January 4, 2020.
34. Loving, Rush, *The Well-Dressed Hobo* (Bloomington: Indiana University Press, 2016), 192–193.
35. Moorman July 27, 2020.
36. Downs, October 13, 2020.
37. Downs, October 13, 2020.
38. Downs, October 6, 2020.

> If you wanted to kill off Amtrak, setting up three-day-a-week-service would be the way to do it. All of Amtrak.
>
> Thomas Downs, from an interview with the authors

Epilogue

Saving Amtrak

Like the passenger railroads of the 1950s and '60s, Amtrak's management's focus has been on cost control, not courting passengers. Amtrak's financial problem is not an expense problem—it is an income problem. Like the airlines, Amtrak does not market its services anymore; it relies on fare pricing and waits for passengers to show up at the gate. There is, however, more to this than management's lack of a strategy.

Generally speaking, Amtrak's supporters are advocating for a change of attitude by the federal government that mandated its creation and an improvement of support so that an important and vital part of the passenger transport infrastructure can be sustained and made available to a wider base of the population. As competing travel modes and travel space become saturated, long-distance passenger rail travel will be in greater demand—and not just three days a week.

The current voices in favor of saving Amtrak are not coming from inside company headquarters. Amtrak's politically driven governance seems intent on reshaping the corporation with a focus on the NEC and using the coronavirus pandemic and reduced ridership as a convenient cover for dismantling the rest of the network a little at a time—except for the state-run corridor services.

Cliff Black noted,

> A subtle political game is going on here. You'll recall that several members of the Amtrak board [of directors] have been there longer than the bylaws recommend, or even permit, I believe. Some New York politicians want Amtrak's Sunnyside Yards for New York's control, and I suspect board chairman Anthony Coscia (from New Jersey) would like control of the NEC for New Jersey Transit. Consequently, they are inclined to favor federal investment in the NEC infrastructure to the exclusion of the long-distance system, for which they

appear to have little interest. It's all about control (ownership) of infrastructure and real estate. The long-distance trains are merely collateral damage of that struggle, and it seems the Andersons and Gardners would be pleased to have them out of their hair.[1]

Although it is pretty obvious that there is a compelling reason for the Northeast Corridor's Boston–New York–Washington service, some have questioned the need for Amtrak at all. Curiously, there is no such debate when the subjects are highway and aviation support. The debate climaxes when the subject becomes establishing a compelling argument for Amtrak's long-distance trains.

In Tom Downs's view, that compelling argument is pretty simple: "It's a marketable service. People want it. Long-distance trains generate revenue in the sleepers and can come close to paying for the service, but the political 'corridor culture' dominates."[2] Thus, Amtrak continues as a victim of the Washington ethos of favor-trading where what the people want is simply ignored.

There are approximately thirty-two million or more annual Amtrak customers who tell us that passenger trains still have a place in the national transportation infrastructure, even though more people today travel by car or airplane. "People choose Amtrak's long-distance service for the experience even though it often costs more," says Downs.[3]

One does grieve for what we have lost, and it is not nostalgia or a desire to live in the past as has been alleged by some. We mourn losing the civility of travel. This is not elitist. There was a time when the lowliest coach passenger could afford a decent dining car meal while seated at the same table as a corporate CEO. Private sleeping accommodations, of course, cost more than coach, although the Slumbercoach concept made such services available to more people, but the diners, the lounges, and the dome cars were all truly egalitarian. All passengers were welcome and were treated equally.

There has been some discussion about introducing competition: Would Amtrak be innovative and strive to offer better service overall if it were to have others competing for its routes and services? Would a competitor expect to, and could it, make a profit given the complexity of running passenger trains? While no clear answer has developed, it is quite clear that no such competition has developed. It should be noted that the Brightline service in Florida is analogous to the NEC, a corridor operation in a densely populated area, and thus is not really an Amtrak competitor. The same will be true of currently planned or under construction high-speed services.

One author, in a 2004 book that grasps at an astounding number of straws to argue why Amtrak must die, proposed Canada's Rocky Mountaineer as a for-profit model for "reforming" Amtrak.[4] Running on three different routes from Vancouver into the Canadian Rockies, the train has been an unalloyed success (though suspended as this is written but expected to restart in the summer of 2021). It provides well-maintained accommodations, excellent crews, and unmatched onboard services. But egalitarian it is not. Transportation it is not. It is an excursion train. People ride it for the experience, not to get from point A to point B. Translated into US dollars, per person fares begin at around $1,500 for a two-day trip and $1,950 for a four-day one. Many people can afford this, but many more cannot. Simply proposing a luxury excursion service as a replacement for intercity transportation is irrational.

Although efforts to kill Amtrak seem relentless, there is some hope. Writing in *Passenger Train Journal*, Kevin McKinney pointed to several pieces of legislation in the congressional pipeline in the summer of 2020. One is the INVEST Act (Investing in a New Vision for the Environment and Surface Transportation), providing $494 billion over five years to make infrastructure investments in surface and rail transportation.[5] One amendment buried in the INVEST Act bill, titled the TRAIN Act (Transforming Rail by Accelerating Investment Nationwide), authorizes $29.3 billion over five years: $16.2 billion for the National Network and $13.1 billion for the NEC. Section 9 amends section 301 of the Rail Passenger Service Act, recognizing that Amtrak is not a for-profit corporation and clarifies its mission to serve the public interest in providing reliable passenger rail service. In addition, the "Amtrak Board of Directors would be realigned to better reflect both the interests of passengers and reflect geographic diversity." Furthermore, McKinney writes, while the initiatives are the most "significant leap forward in forty-nine years," the important aspect is that the measures "are being introduced and therefore might see passage at a later date."[6] However, this is a small step only. The legislation has to be passed, not consigned to the graveyard through inaction or diluting.

Congress has, on balance, made it clear year after year that it wants Amtrak to continue. It has always come up with at least enough funding to keep the company alive—sometimes barely, sometimes better, and sometimes with nonsensical limitations and mandates. Even so, while Congress's wish is clear, it is easily distracted.

During the Amtrak presidencies of Anderson and Flynn, the coronavirus crisis in early 2020 devastated ridership and became the "perfect storm," giving cover for Amtrak's management to initiate cuts in long-distance services. America was distracted by the pandemic, social unrest, international relationships gone awry, and a heated election. Amtrak's announcement of curtailed service generally went unnoticed by the public and media. But the cuts in long-distance services had been planned well before the virus had even emerged.

In early November 2019, the authors were informed by an Amtrak official of a meeting where Amtrak management would unveil its plan, "Amtrak 2.0," to reduce the long-distance trains to two Florida trains (Silver Meteor and Auto Train) on the East Coast, one on the West Coast (Coast Starlight), a three-day-a-week Empire Builder and California Zephyr between Chicago and the West Coast, and to eliminate all the rest of the country's long-distance trains. The plan was later modified, but thrice-weekly service is a death sentence for

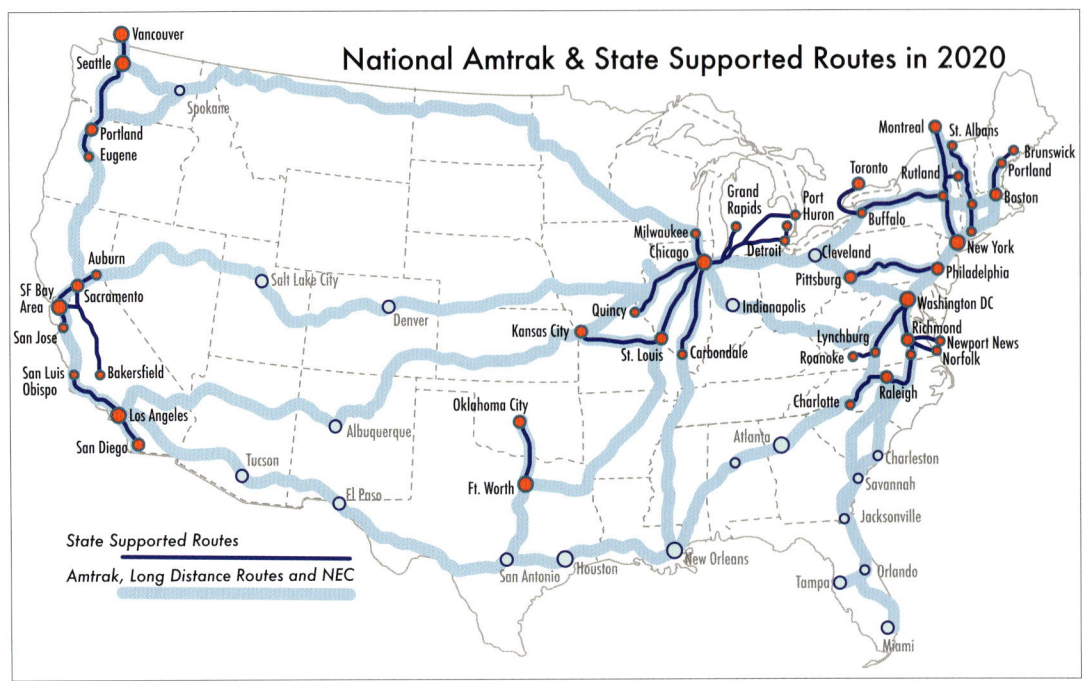

Map: Christopher Swan

trains because connections are disrupted and planning for trips is made more complicated. As a further insult to the traveling public, Amtrak buried online timetables for each of its trains, making it even more difficult to plan a trip. Stephen Gardner, executive vice president at the time, was viewed by some as the guidance counselor behind the 2.0 plan.

These clearly are actions of people who want Amtrak to expire. How are potential passengers to plan trips without easy access to schedules? And if trains run three days a week, they do not run four days a week. Most travelers planning trips have specific timeframes in mind. If they call Amtrak and find a desired train runs one or two days later than they expected, they will not travel by train. And how does a three-day-a-week train cover seven-day-a-week costs, especially if the three-day-a-week schedule is reducing passenger loads? Furthermore, can Amtrak's management be believed when it says it wants to continue long-distance service and will reassess its prospects using a metric that analyzes future bookings six months in advance of a specific date? Even if trains are fully booked for those three days, there is a very good chance that many more passengers are being left behind. Has anyone thought this through? The answer, unfortunately, is probably yes, someone has, but for the wrong reasons.

To Save or Not to Save

Since President Biden's election in November 2020 and subsequent economic infrastructure proposals in 2021, Amtrak management's position on long-distance trains has performed an abrupt about-face. Management now says that the long-distance trains are an essential part of the network and service should be expanded. But when the political winds shift again, conceivably so could Amtrak's plans, demonstrating the historic instability of Amtrak's 'vision' of purpose and the need for a coherent and consistent passenger transport policy.

Many of the people interviewed for this book revealed a desire to "save" Amtrak, perceiving a clear and present danger and an existential threat. Some believed this threat is strictly political machination; others that it is all about money and/or bankruptcy; and still others that there is a "fifth column"—namely the chairman of the Amtrak board and its president, Stephen Gardner. Some suggested Amtrak should be scrapped and started over or wonder for whom it would be saved. Eliminating Amtrak would require congressional action—passage of a law doing so. Then another law would be necessary to create a "new" Amtrak, but there are enough long knives out in the current Congress that a new Amtrak would never be created. In Tom Downs's view, "Amtrak should be saved from the venality of politicians. Several presidents [of Amtrak] have tried to save it, but realized they can only fix Amtrak incrementally."[7]

Upon his retirement, echoing of Ralph Budd, Amtrak President Graham Claytor summed up the matter when he confessed to Tom Downs, "When I came to Amtrak I was convinced I could save it, but finally came to the conclusion that only the American public can save it when they say they want it."[8]

Epilogue Notes

1. Black, August 22, 2020.
2. Downs, July 10, 2020.
3. Downs, July 31, 2020.
4. Joseph Vranich, *End of the Line* (Washington, DC: AEI Press, 2004), 155-157.
5. The bill provides $319 billion for the federal-aid highway program under the Federal Highway Administration, $105 billion for transit programs under the Federal Transit Administration, $5.3 billion for highway safety programs under the National Highway Traffic Safety Administration, $4.6 billion for motor carrier safety programs under the Federal Motor Carrier Safety Administration, and $60 billion for rail programs.
6. Kevin McKinney, "Three Congressional Proposals Boost Passenger Rail Funding," *Passenger Train Journal*, 284, no. 3, 2020, 7.
7. Downs, July 31, 2020.
8. Downs, June 25, 2020.

Appendix 1: Tracking Amtrak

State Rail Programs

Over time, several states stepped forward to provide services connecting with the national network while also relieving some of Amtrak's financial burden. Recognizing the need for rail transport to connect communities, states developed a variety of approaches, with some encountering political barriers, but overall they have been successful. Although not all state ridership gains have kept up with population growth, these services have helped Amtrak survive, and its current network would not exist but for the participation of

Table A.1

Passenger miles per train mile (not all Amtrak trains shown)

Service	2003	2011	2019
Acela	142	192	192
NEC regionals	179	203	255
Lake Shore Limited	209	139	212
Cardinal[a]	105	125	118
Auto Train	326	361	330
Silver Meteor	174	232	197
Crescent	155	167	130
Empire Builder	193	170	163
California Zephyr	186	162	157
Southwest Chief	187	196	165
Texas Eagle	148	185	148
Sunset Limited[a]	157	133	117
Coast Starlight	260	218	199
Long distance avg.	180	184	168

Source: Compiled from data supplied by Amtrak to Rail Passengers Association.

[a] Train operates only three days a week.

Table A.2

Revenue per train mile (not all Amtrak trains shown)

Service	2003 ($)	2011 ($)	2019 ($)
Acela	91.77	147.32	182.36
NEC regionals	55.54	100.53[b]	124.19
Lake Shore Limited	22.86	21.48	38.81
Cardinal[a]	11.39	19.77	24.17
Auto Train	73.57	110.68	128.81
Silver Meteor	25.84	38.90	39.10
Crescent	22.05	30.43	31.32
Empire Builder	19.08	28.24	28.29
California Zephyr	19.90	25.88	28.40
Southwest Chief	19.06	27.78	25.81
Texas Eagle	15.70	25.93	22.90
Sunset Limited[a]	13.91	17.79	17.65
Coast Starlight	28.41	39.96	41.88
Long distance avg.	21.32	31.80	34.47

Source: Compiled from data supplied by Amtrak to Rail Passengers Association.

[a] Train operates only three days a week.
[b] This figure is for 2013. The 2011 NEC regional data was unavailable.

states funding equipment, stations and other facilities, staffing, operating costs, and promotion for the many regional services that complement Amtrak's Northeast Corridor (NEC) and long-distance routes. Thus, understanding the value of the state-supported component of Amtrak's national network will enable a better picture of passenger rail services in the United States.

Following Amtrak's Day One in 1971, it took only a few days to secure state support for adding a service—the extension of the New York City–Buffalo route to Chicago. New York and Ohio later disagreed on funding issues and the service ended, at least until Amtrak restarted it as a basic system train some years later. To date, eighteen states have supported new Amtrak services or started other services their citizens wanted. Some states tried supporting passenger rail and failed; still, others can be considered failures for never having tried at all. State-supported services are regional in nature, some in densely populated areas, such as Amtrak's NEC and Connecticut's New Haven–Hartford/Springfield line, while others serve both large cities and more rural areas; these include the Pennsylvanian, the Empire Service, and Virginia's routes. Some state operations are identified as Amtrak services, while others have their own state-themed identities. Three are international, serving the Canadian cities of Montreal, Toronto, and Vancouver. With one exception, all these routes connect at shared stations with Amtrak long-distance or NEC trains, offering passengers easy transfers between services. The exception is the Downeaster between Boston and points in Massachusetts, New Hampshire, and Maine; because of the city's railroad geography, it must use North Station, while Amtrak uses South Station about a mile away.

Table A.3

Trends in percent share of passenger-miles (trips greater than 100 miles, by travel mode, excluding commuter and ferry data)

Mode	2000 (%)	2011 (%)	2018 (%)
Auto	78.88	79.84	76.83
Air	15.97	13.26	15.05
Bus	4.98	6.74	7.99
Train	0.17	0.16	0.13
Total	100	100	100

Source: Bureau of Transportation Statistics, bts.gov/content/us-passenger-miles.

Table A.4

2019 Fiscal year key indicators for state supported services

Measure	Amtrak system[a]	State supported[b]	% of Amtrak total
Fare revenue	$2,354,313,000	$533,535,000	23
Ridership	32,716,000	15,436,000	47
Passenger-miles	6,487,245,000	1,983,085,000	31

Source: Data supplied by Amtrak to Rail Passengers Association.

[a] Fares only; excludes nonpassenger revenue and state contributions.
[b] Excludes separate payments to Amtrak under the Fixing America's Surface Transportation Act and the Passenger Rail Investment and Improvement Act.

Reflecting the long-term imbalance in transportation funding, rail patronage, while posting impressive net growth through 2019, represents a modest proportion of all intercity passenger-miles (autos and airlines, of course, dominate).[1] This is a national average. One of California's state-supported routes, to cite an exception, has an estimated 3 to 5 percent passenger-mile market share.[2] Several states are investing heavily in passenger rail and know that continued connectivity to Amtrak's national network is essential to their long-term success.

Table A.5

Amtrak passenger-miles average growth per year (comparing 2005–19 and 2011–19 fiscal years)

Sector	Average passenger-miles growth per year 2005–19 (%)	Average passenger-miles growth per year 2011–19 (%)
State supported	2.84	0.31
NEC	2.09	1.65
Long distance	−0.18	−1.46
System	1.23	−0.09

Source: Data provided by Amtrak through Rail Passengers Association.

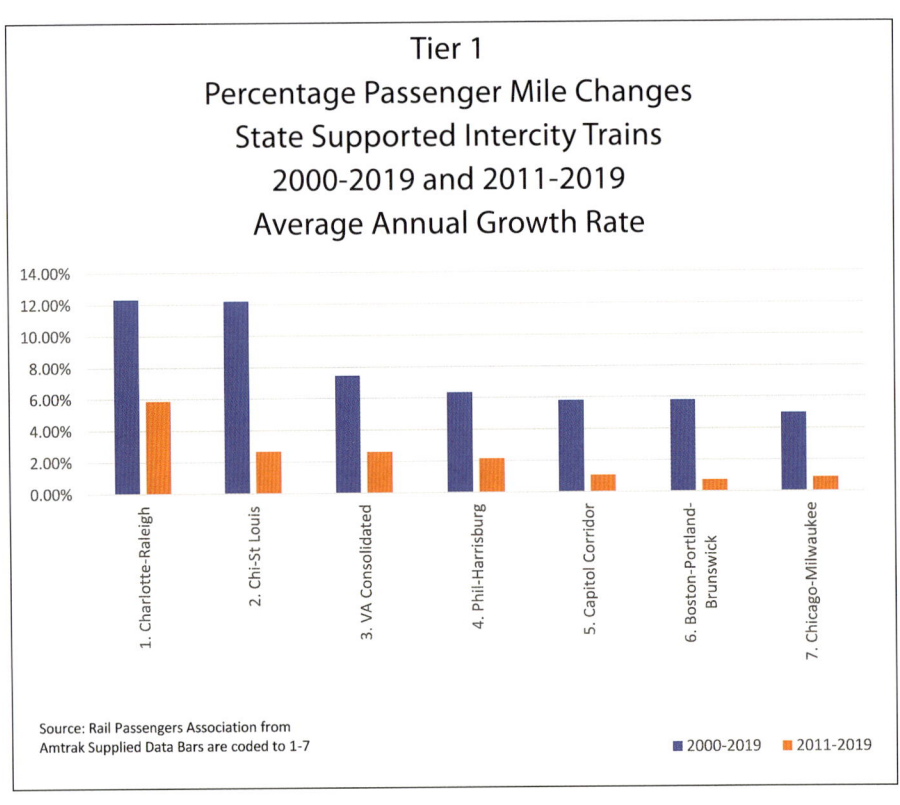

Tier 1 Percentage Passenger Mile Changes		
Service Name	2000-2019	2011-2019
1. Charlotte-Raleigh	12.32%	5.87%
2. Chi-St Louis (a)	12.20%	2.67%
3. VA Consolidated (b)	7.47%	2.62%
4. Phil-Harrisburg	6.34%	2.17%
5. Capitol Corridor	5.82%	1.07%
6. Boston-Portland-Brunswick	5.81%	0.74%
7. Chicago-Milwaukee	4.99%	0.89%

In addition to fare revenue, twenty-one agencies in the eighteen states provided a further $234.2 million to Amtrak in 2019. That additional boost would take the state portion of Amtrak's fare revenue to 33 percent.[3]

Passenger-mile growth leveled off in all categories of Amtrak's business and then showed slight declines.[4] Between July 2005 and July 2019, United States population growth was 6 percent.[5] Intercity rail passenger ridership is not keeping up with population growth.

State-supported intercity passenger services showed almost no growth from 2011 through 2019.

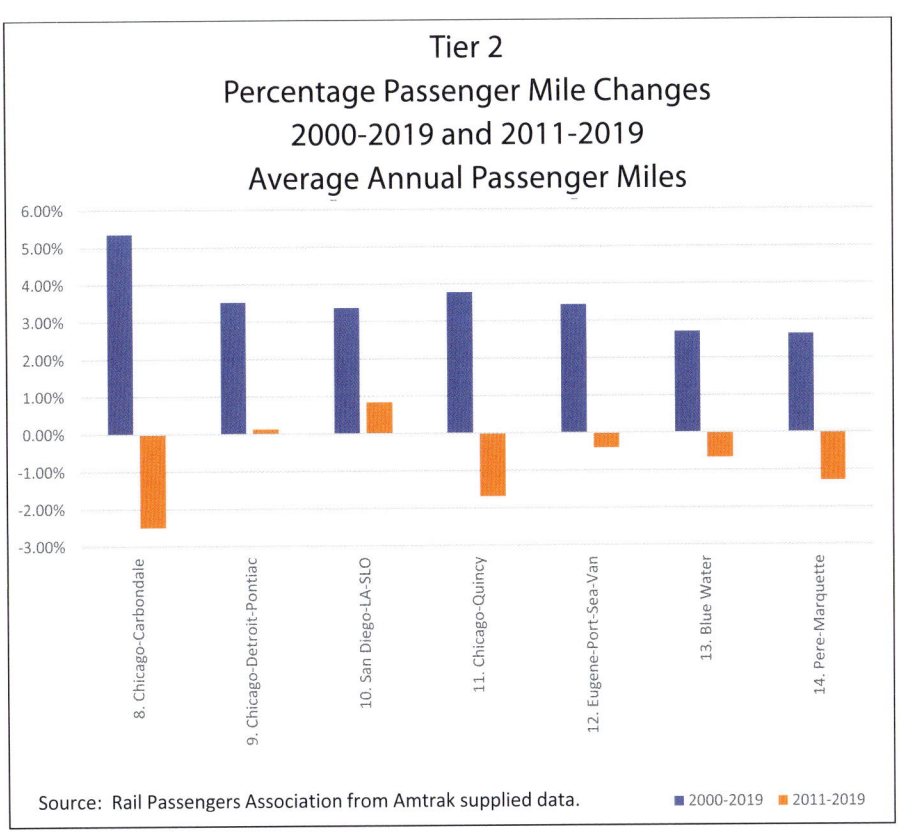

Tier 2 Percentage Passenger Mile Changes		
Service Name	2000-2019	2011-2019
8. Chicago-Carbondale	5.36%	-2.49%
9. Chicago-Detroit-Pontiac	3.53%	0.13%
10. San Diego-LA-SLO	3.37%	0.84%
11. Chicago-Quincy	3.78%	-1.68%
12. Eugene-Port-Sea-Van	3.44%	-0.40%
13. Blue Water	2.71%	-0.66%
14. Pere-Marquette	2.64%	-1.29%

The graphs displayed in tiers 1-4 show annual state-supported passenger-mile changes for two time periods. The data will be discussed in each of the state-sponsored services.

States chosen for discussion below both provide geographic diversity and demonstrate services ranging from clear successes to those in stasis or failure. Vermont takes first prize with passenger-mile growth, achieved with a routing change allowing service to a larger population along the "Knowledge Corridor" north of Springfield, Massachusetts. Washington and Oregon provide modest frequencies, Eugene/Portland/Seattle–Vancouver, featuring enviable onboard

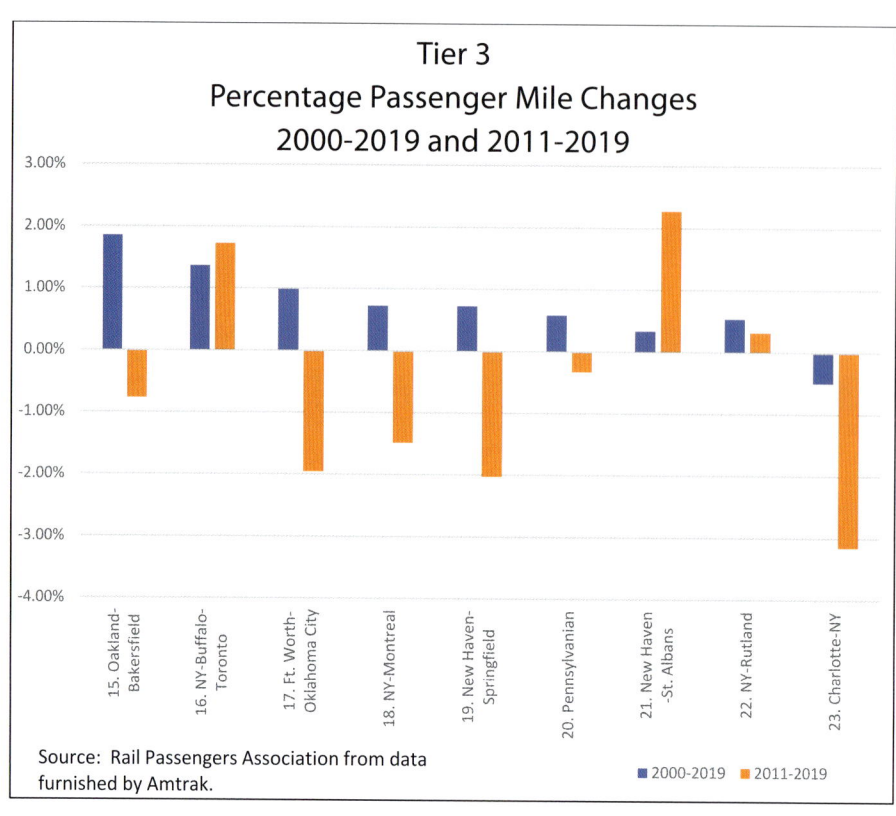

Tier 3 Percentage Passenger Mile Changes		
Service Name	2000-2019	2011-2019
15. Oakland-Bakersfield	1.86%	-0.76%
16. NY-Buffalo-Toronto	1.37%	1.73%
17. Ft. Worth-Oklahoma City	0.99%	-1.95%
18. NY-Montreal	0.73%	-1.48%
19. New Haven-Springfield	0.73%	-2.02%
20. Pennsylvanian	0.59%	-0.32%
21. New Haven-St. Albans	0.34%	2.28%
22. NY-Rutland	0.54%	0.32%
23. Charlotte-NY	-0.49%	-3.15%

cafe service and selection that could provide a model for Amtrak services. New York provides decent frequencies across the Water Level Route (Niagara Falls/Buffalo–New York City) with one daily train New York–Montreal and another New York–Toronto. Connecticut and Massachusetts recently rebuilt the New Haven–Springfield line and introduced greater frequencies and improved or rebuilt stations.

Connection with the NEC aids Pennsylvania's successful Keystone service east of Harrisburg, while the one daily train Pittsburgh–New York City enjoys ridership that suggests a second train on the route is needed. Oklahoma

Tier 4 Percentage Passenger Mile Changes		
Service Name	2000-2019	2011-2019
24. Missouri River Runner	-0.67%	-2.50%
25. Chicago-Indianapolis (a)	-1.77%	-4.80%
26. All State Supported	0.33%	0.31%
27. All Amtrak	0.95%	0.00%

continues efforts to improve its Heartland service (Oklahoma City–Fort Worth) but with seeming indifference on the part of Texas. Coordination across state lines can run up against differing degrees of politics, funding, and public needs, but markets for rail services seldom coincide with state lines. A nationally coordinated policy and organization could help achieve the best results for the public and enhance the investments made in the passenger rail network. Please see Part Four for policy recommendations.

State programs reviewed below are from west to east, beginning with California, arguably the most ambitious and successful.

California: An Overview

California has developed intercity passenger rail since 1991, with some southern California efforts dating to the 1970s.[6] Initial growth was

Table A.6

California rail passenger-miles growth and annual percentage change 2000–19 and 2011–19

Service	Passenger-miles growth 2000–19 (%)	Average annual change 2000–19 (%)	Passenger-miles growth 2011–19 (%)	Average annual change 2011–19 (%)
Surfliners San Diego-LA-San Luis Obispo	67.30	3.37	7.57	0.84
San Joaquins Oakland-Bakersfield	37.10	1.86	(6.85)	0.76
Capitol Corridor San Jose-Oakland-Sacramento-Auburn	116.03	5.82	9.65	1.07

impressive but slowed in later years. However, two services remain robust and well-patronized and are, by any measure, a success. The *San Joaquins*, however, are receiving some needed attention.

Long-term capital investment of about $3.8 billion through fiscal year 2019 has added network capacity, improved stations, and acquired equipment. The 2018 California State Rail Plan anticipates investing $119 billion by 2040 and hosting 1.3 million daily customers. Local, county, state, and federal sources will fund $5 billion in 2022 and $20 billion in 2027.[7]

The California Department of Transportation (Caltrans) seeks to accommodate both passenger and freight traffic on the rail network as efficiently as possible. Major investments are proposed for the San Diego–Los Angeles–San Luis Obispo route and for the Sacramento–Bakersfield line, with a new route Sacramento airport–Stockton. The Capitol Corridor will have capacity additions. At this point, California is furthest along among the states in intercity rail investment and may well be a model for policies that can work at the national level. The California Joint Powers Board agencies, which handle intercity rail management separate from Caltrans, recognize that the freight railroads also benefit the state economy, that adding passenger services eats up capacity, and that capacity is not free.

Pacific Surfliners

The Surfliners operate over 351 route-miles between San Diego, Los Angeles, and San Louis Obispo on the former Santa Fe Railway's San Diegan route and a portion of the former Southern Pacific Railroad's Coast Route north of Los

Angeles. In 2019, passenger-miles were second only to Amtrak's NEC, with 11.96 percent of NEC passenger-miles. It is the largest of the state-supported intercity services and also has the biggest challenges.

The Surfliners run twelve weekday San Diego–Los Angeles round trips, with five daily Los Angeles–Santa Barbara (Goleta) trips, two of those continuing to San Luis Obispo. Equipment consists of sixty-eight bilevel cars, including nine leased Amtrak Superliners, fourteen single-level Amfleet and Horizon cars, two cab and baggage cars,[8] and sixteen locomotives. Cars on order will add forty-nine coaches to the state fleet, with a portion intended for the Surfliners.

In 2015, oversight of the Surfliners went from Caltrans to LOSSAN (Los Angeles-San Diego-San Luis Obispo Rail Corridor Agency, formed in 1989). The track is owned by seven separate entities, so LOSSAN lives in a complex operating and legislative environment as it serves the large population living within fifty miles of the Surfliner route. LOSSAN seeks connectivity by coordination with Amtrak's Thruway bus services and multiple local transit agencies.

The main challenge for the Surfliners is the fact that two-thirds of the route is single track, which causes capacity constraints and operational delays. As of fiscal year 2020, $564 million in capacity, bridge, and station investment was underway. Additional work is needed to protect against rising sea levels and major storms, which are eroding some sections of the coastal right-of-way.[9]

The historic Los Angeles Union Station (LAUS, which has been the setting of many movies and TV ads) is a stub end rather than a through station. This slows turning of trains and limits capacity. However, a $950 million program will make LAUS a through station and will include a modern signaling system.

Table A.7

Comparison of Pacific Surfliners to Northeast Corridor (2019 fiscal year data)

Corridor	Population within 25 miles[a]	No. of stations	2019 customers[b]	Average population/ route miles	Miles of single track[c]
Surfliners 351 miles	18.7 million	37	2,777,000	53,276	232
NEC 457 miles	37.4 million	30	12,526,000	81,838	0
Surfliners % of NEC	50	123	22	65	X

[a] From Rail Passengers Association website.
[b] Intercity customers only, excludes commuters, approximate. From Rail Passengers Association website.
[c] Acela and Northeast regional from Amtrak data supplied to Rail Passengers Association.

Table A.8

Pacific Surfliner performance trends fiscal years 2012–19
(passenger miles, revenue, and state support in thousands)

	2012	2013	2014	2015	2016	2017	2018	2019
Passenger miles	233,501	232,295	231,877	246,451	251,650	259,160	253,461	248,232
On time[a] (%)	75	82	78	78	78	78	69	77
Revenue ($)	58,841	62,747	65,647	70,637	73,198	76,870	80,264	79,373
State support ($)	30.4	31.6	29.4	38.8	21.3	21.6	22.6	26.3
Fare-box ratio	56.0	57.6	61.7	67.1	70.5	78.8	79.2	77.3

Sources: Amtrak-provided data from Rail Passengers Association; LOSSAN Business Plans, fiscal year 2018–19 and 2019–20.

[a] On-time performance measured at end points.

An April 2020 agreement between the California High Speed Rail Authority and LAUS owner, Los Angeles Metro, will allow multiple uses of the reconfigured terminal, including Los Angeles–Palmdale commuter and high-speed services. Both the San Joaquins (at Bakersfield) and Surfliner services (at Los Angeles) could then become important connections for the California High-Speed Rail line that is now under construction.[10]

Surfliner feeders include Los Angeles subway, light rail, bus, and local commuter authorities offering both heavy rail and transit services. Such connectivity and coordination are critical for maximizing benefits from past and current investments. LOSSAN estimates $5 billion is needed to move to the next level of forecast demand, which by 2030 is expected to be 4.7 million customers per year on thirty-six daily trains.[11]

Table A.9

San Joaquin performance trends fiscal years 2011–12 and 2018–19
(passenger-miles, revenue, and state support in millions of dollars)

	2011–12	2012–13	2013–14	2014–15	2015–16	2016–17	2017–18	2018–19
Passenger miles[a]	166,337	170,076	165,539	164,250	155,936	155,196	147,747	145,716
On time[b] (%)	N/A	88.1	77.7	75.4	73.6	84.0	76.5	77.7
Revenue ($)	38,666	39,402	38,088	37,408	35,586	35,634	32,874	31,883
State support ($)	34,200	32,300	37,800	39,000	38,300	40,000	47,800	50,600
Fare-box ratio (%)	55.0	56.2	52.3	51.3	50.4	49.3	43.0	41.0

Source: San Joaquin JPA business plans for fiscal year 2013–14 through 2020–21.

[a] Data supplied by Amtrak to Rail Passengers Association.
[b] On-time performance measured at end points.

San Joaquins: Turnaround Candidate

The seven daily San Joaquins run through the Central Valley (Bakersfield–Oakland, five round-trips) and Bakersfield–Sacramento (two round-trips) over a 364-mile Y-shaped route. Management is by the San Joaquin Regional Rail Commission (SJRRC), which also has the San Jose–Stockton Altamont Corridor Express (ACE) under its wing. Sixty-eight percent of San Joaquin passengers continue on or come from a coordinated bus network, the primary route connecting Bakersfield with the Los Angeles area. Amtrak provides crews, reservations, ticketing, station, and cafe car services under contract. The fleet of 104 cars and 26 locomotives is owned by Caltrans (additional equipment is leased from Amtrak) and is shared with the Capitol Corridor.

One billion dollars has been invested in capacity improvements, facilities, and equipment for San Joaquin service. Most has been in track and signaling to improve the flow of both passenger trains and dense freight traffic of host railroads Union Pacific and Burlington Northern Santa Fe (BNSF). San Joaquin passenger-miles grew through fiscal years 2012 and 2013, but then reversed, and a 14 percent decline ensued through fiscal year 2019, with revenue declining 19 percent. This has required increased state support to maintain the service.

SJRRC business plans have not revealed causes of the ridership decline, though it may be due in part to mediocre on-time performance. There is also a possibility that immigration policies may have reduced business in recent years given the strong Latinx presence in the San Joaquin service area. In addition, a complete reevaluation of connecting bus routes and stops is needed. The failed experiment with a new Modesto to Sacramento train reduced passenger counts.[12] Management knows change is needed to provide better value for the public's tax dollars. Caltrans has authorized $500 million for a parallel route Stockton–Sacramento. This will shift growth from a route where current freight traffic is heavy. The new route will include six stations and two layover facilities and will allow better on-time performance. Additional frequencies will connect Fresno with a Sacramento airport bus transfer. Through these improvements, management seeks to reverse the ridership decline. The new service will add some stations on the east side of Sacramento but will not serve the main downtown station due to track configuration restrictions. Existing San Joaquin service will remain at the main Sacramento station.

The region has increasing air pollution, among the highest in the nation. One goal is to mitigate the pollution through investments in the San Joaquins. The en route cities of Fresno and Madera have consistently higher greenhouse gas measurements than other parts of the state, except for carbon dioxide in the Los Angeles area. It remains to be seen exactly when, but the expectation is that a better quality of the Valley's intercity rail service can divert enough highway traffic to reduce greenhouse gases significantly.[13]

The SJRRC is doing long-term planning for extensions such as feeding passengers to the California High-Speed Rail line currently under construction.

When completed, that service will fill the long-missing rail passenger route Bakersfield–Los Angeles now served only by buses. Other planning is for more services to the northern part of the state. California has determined that it cannot solve its mobility problems with more highways and that the San Joaquins is part of the answer.

Capitol Corridor: Award Winner

The Capitol Corridor Joint Powers Authority board (CCJPA) is made up of political appointees from the counties served by the Capitol Corridor. The board appoints senior management and leaves daily tasks to it. The corridor has strong public and political support, effective management, and a strategic plan for addressing the mobility needs of the region. Its Capitol Corridor service has eighteen stations on 168 route-miles San Jose–Auburn via Oakland and Sacramento.

Bus connections link Emeryville with San Francisco. Buses also connect at Martinez for the northern part of the state. One billion dollars has been invested since 1991, and the service has grown from six trains to thirty per weekday between Emeryville and Sacramento under the early leadership of Gene Skoropowski. Of these, fourteen operate to and from San Jose, and two trains serve Auburn on weekdays. Twenty-two trains operate on weekends. The corridor served 1,767,000 customers in 2019 and has demonstrated ridership growth since its inception, although the growth curve has flattened in the last few years, and, as throughout the country, the long-term impact of the coronavirus is impossible to predict. Amtrak provides crews, equipment maintenance, ticketing, and some equipment. Union Pacific is the host railroad. The fleet has 104 cars and 26 locomotives shared with the San Joaquin service. New low-level coaches for the San Joaquins and the LOSSAN services will allow high-level equipment to be transferred to Capitol Corridor.

Capitol Corridor management has worked closely with Union Pacific on investments benefiting both freight and passenger services. David Kutrosky, recently retired managing director, explained, "We do more listening and less talking. We search for common ground. We both need reliability. We address challenges and build trust. We shift schedules, enhance maintenance of way, give and take, restructure performance agreements."[14]

Investment by Union Pacific (UP) and Capitol Corridor to improve capacity has contributed high on-time performance on a heavily used freight route. Both Capitol Corridor and San Joaquins own capacity slots (time windows in which to run trains) in perpetuity. In all other state operations, Amtrak holds these slots. Capitol Corridor does not have claw-backs (penalties paid by host railroads to Amtrak for missing on-time goals). Instead, the Corridor separates its trains from Amtrak's long-distance services and has a $250,000 annual fund. Each time a train is late due to UP-caused problems, a deduction is made from the fund. At the end of the year, whatever is left goes to the UP.[15]

Table A.10

Capitol Corridor performance measures years 2010–11 through 2018–19 (revenue and state support in [$] millions, rounded)

Year FFY	Passenger miles	Revenue FFY ($)	State support ($)	Fare box recovery (%)	On-time (%)	Budgeted admin % of revenue
2010–11	101,251,000	27.2	29.2	48.0	95	14.0
2011–12	109,074,000	29.2	29.6	50.2	95	14.1
2012–13	111,191,000	29.2	29.1	51.0	95	14.1
2013–14	112,015,380	29.2	28.4	50.9	95	14.1
2014–15	96,160,598	30.1	32.6	52.0	93	13.7
2015–16	98,942,984	32.2	31.7	55.0	94	12.8
2016–17	104,135,023	34.0	31.7	57.0	91	12.1
2017–18	108,609,358	36.3	31.0	58.0	90	11.4
2018–19	113,798,088	38.1	28.7	60.0	89	12.8
Change (%)	11.03	40.07	–3	20.0	–6	–9
Annual avg. (%)	3.68	4.45	X	X	X	X

Source: All figures, except passenger-miles, from Capitol Corridor Joint Powers Board Annual Business Plans and reports fiscal years 2011–12 and 2018–19. Passenger-miles furnished by the Rail Passenger Association from data supplied by Amtrak.

Note: FFY is federal fiscal year.

Customer feedback is a critical part of the service's management. Questionnaires are handed out on trains, and management responds to online complaints. Kutrosky has observed that "passengers complain because they want to ride the service."[16]

Metrics for on-time performance (arrival within fifteen minutes of scheduled time) allow up to 325 minutes of delay per ten thousand train-miles. Efforts to meet schedules likely will be affected by the fact that UP and most other major railroads plan to run longer freight trains under the Precision Scheduled Railroading (PSR) concept, now current in the industry. This effort may well impact passenger operations across the country by reducing dispatchers' ability to integrate higher-speed passenger trains with longer and often slower freights. Intercity passenger services are unavoidably affected by host railroad policies and procedures. This may drive demand for additional public funding for physical improvements that will balance passenger and freight service demands.

The Capitol Corridor trains currently move between 3 and 5 percent of combined rail and highway passenger volume at peak periods. California currently commits about 7 percent of its annual transportation budget to commuter and intercity rail investment. This amounted to $2 billion in the 2020–2021 fiscal year, exclusive of the separately funded high-speed system. In its 2018 State Rail Plan, California estimated 6 percent of current statewide passenger-miles are by rail. The goal is passenger-mile growth of 15 to 20 percent by 2040, with a concomitant reduction of auto emissions by 80 percent in 2050 from the 1990 base.[17] The Capitol Corridor has a vision for investment needed by 2030 and beyond due to growth in mobility needs, limits on additional highway capacity, environmental concerns, and the ongoing need to better align affordable housing with jobs. Done well, intercity rail passenger service will tick all of these boxes, and the Capitol Corridor can provide useful guidance for state and federal government intercity rail policy formulation. One unsettled problem is determining a fair share of costs to be paid by the Capitol Corridor for use of Amtrak's Sacramento station.[18]

Two major investments in capacity will allow increased frequencies at each end of the route while protecting freight requirements. One is moving to a parallel route to avoid freight traffic between the Oakland area and San Jose. The other is adding a third mainline track past Sacramento to Roseville. These investments will shave transit times and improve schedule reliability. Longer term, Capitol Corridor is working with Bay Area Rapid Transit (BART) to add a tunnel beneath San Francisco Bay and eliminate the existing bus connection. It will then connect with the California High-Speed network. Capitol Corridor management also realizes it must seek dependable long-term funding to allow investment in additional capacity not restricted by freight requirements.

The Midwest: Bits and Pieces

Like a photographic darkroom image, a midwestern intercity network is gradually becoming visible. A confederation of twelve states,[19] the Midwest Interstate Passenger Rail Commission (MIPRC), has created the Midwest Regional Rail Plan with help from the Federal Railroad Administration (FRA). The MIPRC has a goal of creating a 3,000-mile, 110 mph (miles per hour) interstate network. There have been some proposals for a high-speed network (220 mph), but no serious work on that has occurred. What is emerging is bits and pieces of a higher-speed-than-usual network.

Laura Kliewer, director of MIPRC, described its role as fostering coordination among twelve state transportation departments (state DOTs), seeking consensus but not trying to manage the entire network. MIPRC also will help the state DOTs work with Amtrak. Each, however, will be expected to work independently with host railroads. Kliewer, her staff, and MIPRC commissioners meet with Congressional representatives and Amtrak annually to maintain communication, ask them to take action where needed, and promote intercity rail services.[20] When asked what would be the best long-term sustainable funding sources for intercity rail, Kliewer replied, "This is the million-dollar question! We don't have an answer or even a consensus." Long-term funding (as with Amtrak generally) is the critical missing link. Unpredictable year-to-year appropriations do not support large infrastructure projects and push their completion farther off into the future.[21]

Table A.11

Forecast annual economic impact, second train Milwaukee–St. Paul in millions (rounded)

Item	Minnesota ($)	WI-IL ($)	Total ($)
Induced visitor and employment spending	2.90	Not calculated	2.90
Reduced highway maintenance cost	20.80	32.50	53.30
Avoided traffic accidents	1.30	1.80	3.10
Pollution abatement avoided	0.09	0.12	0.21
Operations and maintenance	Included above	47.00	47.00
Total	25.09	81.42	106.51
Net state support	X	X	6.6
Annual benefit and annual state support estimates	X	X	16.14

Source: Victoria Transport Policy Institute, Transport Cost Analysis, www.vtpi.org/tca.

Illinois, Wisconsin, Missouri, and Michigan currently support intercity rail. Stakeholders include railroads, advocacy groups, government councils, planning agencies, and universities. The twelve states in MIPRC have more senators than the eight northeastern states that support the NEC, suggesting that the Midwest should have significant political heft when seeking sustainable state and federal funding. MIPRC objectives include developing a comprehensive vision for an integrated midwestern rail network; developing a governance model to be used by the states for planning, procurement, and operations; and building a strategic framework for passenger rail service, financing, and governance.[22]

MIPRC's vision, first articulated in 2002, is becoming real; the Chicago–St Louis line is farthest along, with Michigan routes progressing. MIPRC has estimated a two-dollar return over forty years for each dollar invested, but this study was done fifteen years ago and needs updating.[23] Some arguments for adding services—such as a second train between Chicago and St. Paul—are based on the expected reduction in highway maintenance funds that would result from travelers' choice of rail over highway travel. In Wisconsin and Illinois, for example, a 2015 study for Amtrak by the Victoria Transport Policy Institute and updated to 2019 found that customers converting from highway to rail will reduce highway expenditures by $32.5 million annually and will constitute 69 percent of economic benefits attributed to the proposed new service. The estimated benefit would be 16.14 times the cost of the service, net of customer fares.

Table A.12

Passenger-miles IL, IL-WI, MI, MO and IN (selected years, rounded)

	2003	2007	2010	2013	2016	2019
IL	75,796,000	147,910,000	188,140,000	214,643,000	186,643,000	193,777,000
IL-WI	34,444,000	47,619,000	62,739,000	65,822,000	64,963,000	70,932,000
MI	99,520,000	138,344,000	149,394,000	160,449,000	136,880,000	159,279,000
MO	28,613,000	22,537,000	36,112,000	37,945,000	31,648,000	27,979,000
IN	3,777,000	4,160,000	5,170,000	5,713,000	4,598,000	3,276,000
Total	242,147,000	360,570,000	441,555,000	484,613,000	424,733,000	455,243,000
% change period to period		49	22	10	0	7
% Change 2003–19		X	X	X	X	88
% Change 2007–19		X	X	X	X	26
% Change 2010–19		X	X	X	X	3
% Change 2013–19		X	X	X	X	–6
% Change 2016–19		X	X	X	X	7

Building support for needed investments should include measuring employment increases and investment multipliers by documenting real estate value increases around stations as passenger volumes build, particularly where multiple frequencies attract large numbers of customers. Governments are best positioned to make these long-term investments. MIPRC has tried since 2003 to get Congress to adopt policies to facilitate development of passenger networks, but our nation's complex, erratic, and politicized approach to rail investment has been a serious stumbling block. Currently, the twelve state DOTs operate independently but might find a louder voice if they banded together under MIRPC to support a Midwest rail network.

State Trends

Illinois, Wisconsin, Missouri, and Michigan's intercity rail services are provided by Amtrak under contract. Eight routes have up to twenty-two daily frequencies and produced 455,243,000 passenger-miles in 2019. The tables below summarize each state's performance for selected years 2003-2019. There is a separate listing for interstate service provided jointly by Illinois and Wisconsin. Indiana currently does not support rail service, having discontinued its one train in 2019 (the story behind this is discussed later).

Passenger-miles and revenue are used as measures. A separate line for Illinois and Wisconsin is due to their interstate service between Chicago and Milwaukee. Growth between 2003 and 2019 leveled off to single digits and then had a decline from 2013 to 2016 that has been reversed. Revenues, not surprisingly, followed a similar pattern. However, the 88 percent total growth between 2003 and 2019 suggests significant public support for these services.

Table A.13
Midwest intercity passenger revenues (selected years 2003–19 in millions)

	2003	2007	2010	2013	2016	2019
IL ($)	9.77	23.84	26.05	31.72	27.13	28.25
IL-WI ($)	7.57	12.83	14.55	16.86	18.48	20.47
MI ($)	14.34	23.24	24.56	8.78	27.03	32.15
MO ($)	2.95	3.25	4.07	5.62	5.14	5.07
IN ($)	0.35	0.67	0.80	0.89	0.97	0.70
Total	34.98	63.83	70.03	83.87	78.75	86.64
% change period to period	X	82	10	20	(–6)	10
% change 2003–19	X	X	X	X	X	148
% change 2007–19	X	X	X	X	X	36
% change 2010–19	X	X	X	X	X	24
% change 2013–19	X	X	X	X	X	3
% change 2016–19	X	X	X	X	X	10

Source: Amtrak data supplied by Rail Passengers Association.

There are headwinds, of course: equipment constraints, periodic flooding of some rail routes, and "pinch point" capacity issues on host railroads.

Illinois

The Chicago–St. Louis Lincoln Service route offers four daily round-trips and a long-distance Amtrak train to Texas and California. The service totaled 116,644,000 passenger-miles in 2019. Physical improvements would allow higher speeds (a goal of 110 mph would cut fifty minutes off current schedules), but technical issues and the current policy of track owner Union Pacific are limiting speeds to 79 mph. Renovated stations, right-of-way fencing, and improved grade crossing protections are in place. Remaining work includes improvements in track and terminals at each end, a Springfield bypass, and new passenger cars (due over time through 2023). Safety-enhancing Positive Train Control will allow 90 mph on the line.[24]

During the eleven years this project has been underway, it took multiple funding applications to receive $1.3 billion in federal funds, and frequency remains at four round-trips plus one long-distance train. In contrast, California's Capitol Corridor operates on the same host railroad (Union Pacific), and $1 billion in investment has resulted in twenty-four daily schedules and record growth.[25]

Table A.14

Illinois services performance

State	Route	Frequency	2011 passenger miles	2019 passenger miles	Change (%)	Annual average change (%)
IL	Chicago–Carbondale	2 RT daily	59,147,000	45,869,000	−22.45	−2.49
IL	Chicago–Quincy	2 RT daily	37,530,000	31,264,000	−16.70	−1.86
IL-MO	Chicago–St. Louis	4 RT daily	94,066,000	116,644,000	24.00	2.67
Total		X	190,743,000	193,777,000	0.016	0.002

Source: Amtrak data supplied by Rail Passengers Association.

Table A.15

Chicago 2018 ridership and population
(adjacent to state-supported routes)

Midwestern service	Chicago on and off riders	Population within 50 miles of route
Chicago–Quincy	137,913	11,179,000
Chicago–Carbondale	188,809	11,299,000
Chicago–St. Louis	455,663	13,719,000
Chicago–Milwaukee	785,476	11,402,000
Indianapolis–Chicago[a]	26,081	12,424,000
Chicago–Port Huron	164,228	17,006,000
Chicago–Grand Rapids	93,492	11,622,000
Chicago–Detroit–Pontiac	407,116	16,966,000
St. Louis–Kansas City	0	5,802,000
Total state-supported trains	2,258,778	Not additive
Total passengers of these routes and Amtrak long-distance services	3,300,000	X
Total Amtrak and commuter	41,400,000	X

Sources: Rail Passengers Association state data sheets at www.rpa.org.

[a] Indiana discontinued the Hoosier State on June 30, 2019.
 Amtrak continues to operate the Cardinal triweekly New York City–Chicago via Indianapolis.

Illinois had been supporting intercity passenger service prior to the advent of Amtrak. Many years subsequent to Amtrak's arrival, in 2006 service frequencies were increased from one train to two trains per day of the three Illinois routes. Ridership and passenger miles increased between 69 and 93 percent by 2009, proving once again the importance of increasing frequencies to attract customers. This effort was led by Joe Szabo when he served on various local Illinois government commissions.[26] He later served as the FRA Administrator between 2009 and 2015. Local government officials can play a vital role in advocating for improved train services.

The Chicago–Carbondale route has two daily round-trips, carried 269,000 passengers in 2019, and had a deplorable on-time record of 37 percent in 2018. Amtrak gave host railroad Canadian National (CN) a "D–" rating after eliminating Amtrak-caused delays. The state has allocated $100 million to CN for capacity improvements to reduce timekeeping problems, but timing of the improvements is uncertain.

Illinois also supports two daily round-trips Chicago–Quincy. It reached 31,264,000 passenger-miles in 2019 but has declined since 2011. Host railroad BNSF delivered a respectable on-time performance of 88 percent in 2018. It is not clear, though, how the slide in ridership should be addressed.

Chicago, the Railroad Capital

Chicago has always been the nexus of Amtrak long-distance operations and for the services supported by Illinois and other states. Except for the St. Louis–Kansas City line, all midwestern routes operate from Chicago Union Station (CUS), the beating heart of the current and future Midwest network. A key to achieving significantly increased intercity (and commuter) ridership is rebuilding of CUS track and facilities. Beyond that, intercity service expansion, capacity improvements on existing routes, and mitigation of freight and passenger conflicts have already advanced through an initiative called CREATE (Chicago Region Environmental and Transportation Efficiency).

Chicago's passenger and freight network has seen step-by-step improvements that eliminate choke points such as multitrack at-grade crossings. CREATE involves the railroads, Amtrak, and city, state, and federal entities. One completed project is the Englewood Flyover at the site of the former Sixty-Third Street Englewood station on the city's South Side. Freight traffic and trains of both METRA (the regional commuter operator) and Amtrak have benefited from elimination of a busy at-grade crossing. Other projects will improve speeds, separate at-grade lines, and improve alignments over several years.

Illinois/Wisconsin

In 2019, Illinois and Wisconsin shared up to seven round-trips of the Hiawatha service (Chicago–Milwaukee), totaling 70,932,000 passenger-miles, an 8.02 percent increase since 2011. On-time performance on host railroad Canadian Pacific reached 96 percent in 2018, giving it an "A" rating under Amtrak's on-time yardstick. Additional main line siding capacity would allow more trains, but the Illinois communities of Lake Forest and Glenview so far have blocked additional service despite strong regional support. An example of cooperation is demonstrated by the addition of a station adjacent to

Table A.16

Illinois–Wisconsin Hiawatha service

State	Route	Frequency	2011 passenger miles	2019 passenger miles	Change (%)	Annual average change (%)
IL-WI	Chicago–Milwaukee	7 RT Mon.–Sat. 6 RT Sunday	65,664,000	70,932,000	8.02	0.89

Source: Amtrak-supplied data provided by Rail Passengers Association.

Milwaukee's General Mitchell International Airport (with plenty of low-cost parking; this was a big attraction for those who would otherwise use O'Hare Airport). There also have been subsequent improvements to the station making it more accessible and improving freight flows. This has added 25 percent to the Hiawatha's passenger count and demonstrates the value of locating stations adjacent to airports.[27]

The Hiawatha service does not yet touch the "shining big sea water" of Lake Superior but one day may do so. For now, efforts by Illinois, Minnesota, and Wisconsin are under way to extend one Hiawatha run to St. Paul to augment the long-distance Empire Builder between Chicago and the Pacific Northwest. This added service would provide twice-daily connections at Chicago to and from some sixty-eight midwestern stations as well as to several Amtrak long-distance trains.

Illinois/Iowa

Illinois plans to add service Chicago–Moline via Rockford, with $775 million allocated for improvements. The original intent was to extend to Iowa City, for which FRA funds had been awarded. Iowa dropped out after a change in governors over concerns about providing matching funds and covering operating costs, so Illinois is working only on service to Moline. Service someday may reach across Iowa to Omaha, Nebraska, but being able only to reach Moline for now is an example of how changes in state politics can impede new services.

Michigan

Michigan supports five daily round-trips from Chicago to three destinations. The route to Detroit and Pontiac is the most robust, while the services to Grand Rapids and Port Huron have seen declines—not fatal but of concern nonetheless. The latter two have only one daily round-trip, which may be part of the problem. A further issue is a thirty-mile choke point on

Table A.17

Michigan services

State	Route	Frequency	2011 passenger miles	2019 passenger miles	Change (%)	Annual average change (%)
MI	Chicago–Detroit–Pontiac	3 RT Daily	107,606	108,827	1.13	0.13
MI	Chicago–Grand Rapids	1 RT Daily	16,548	14,628	11.60	1.29
MI	Chicago–Port Huron	1 RT Daily	38,076	35,824	5.91	0.66
Total		X	162,230	159,279	0.018	0.002

Source: Richard Rudolph, "Expanding Passenger Rail in Michigan," *Passenger Train Journal* 276, no. 3 (2018): 58–60.

host railroad Norfolk Southern (NS) between Porter, Indiana, and Chicago. All three Michigan services funnel through there, as well as heavy NS freight traffic which effects on-time performance, and there is a clear need for added track capacity.

Passenger-miles grew from 99,520,000 in 2003 to 159,279,000 in 2019 but have plateaued in recent years. Train frequency has not been increased, nor have routes been added. Studies have been made for a route to Traverse City, a resort area attracting about six million annual visitors estimated to grow to thirteen million by 2045. The state owns the rail route serving the area, but it requires extensive upgrading. Other rail supporters promote a "coast-to-coast" route linking Holland, Grand Rapids, and Detroit. Public hearings have been held and studies made but so far funding for this and other proposed services is not available. Mainly with federal funds, Michigan and Amtrak have invested in a higher-speed track on the Detroit/Pontiac route. Amtrak owns the line from Porter to Kalamazoo, Michigan, and the state has purchased the segment between Kalamazoo and Dearborn. Track improvements are being extended incrementally and will eventually provide speeds of 110 mph between Porter and Ypsilanti, Michigan. Adding through service to Toronto via Detroit and Port Huron and then across Ontario to Buffalo and its Empire Service connections could expand the appeal of the Michigan services.

Missouri

Missouri supports two daily trains St. Louis–Kansas City and experienced a 22.52 percent decline in passenger-miles between 2011 and 2019 in spite of investments in additional track capacity. Periodic floods due to location of tracks along major rivers affect on-time performance and cause cancellations. The state's rail services are managed by the Missouri DOT.

Table A.18

Missouri Services (figures in thousands, rounded)

State	Route	Frequency	2011 passenger miles	2019 passenger miles	Change (%)	Annual average change (%)
MO	St. Louis–Kansas City	2 RT daily	36,112	27,979	−22.52	(2.50)

Source: Amtrak-supplied data provided by Rail Passengers Association.

Indiana: Dead on Arrival

Indiana's attempt to establish intercity rail service between Indianapolis and Chicago was doomed by more-than-adequate existing competitive and time-efficient modes of travel, and thus, insufficient political and public support. Just because you want train service doesn't mean it makes sense.

Indiana's Hoosier State operated between Indianapolis and Chicago on the same schedule as Amtrak's triweekly Cardinal (New York–Washington–Cincinnati–Indianapolis–Chicago) on the four days that train did not operate. The five-hour schedule of the Hoosier State took it over several railroads, reflecting the fact that withering of the state's rail network over many years had eliminated the most direct routings. On-time performance was inconsistent. It was no surprise, then, that passenger-miles declined 43.18 percent between fiscal years 2011 and 2019. Its state funding cut off, the Hoosier State service ended June 30, 2019, leaving only the Cardinal on the route to Chicago.

What happened and why? The 2008 Passenger Rail Investment and Improvement Act required states outside the NEC to provide full funding for routes fewer than 750 miles. In Indiana, there was little support for intercity rail passenger service, with the exception of the smaller communities along the route: Lafayette, Crawfordsville, and Rensselaer. The Indiana DOT was charged with managing the Hoosier State.

Robert Zier, who had retired in 2008 from a nontransportation career, took a position as chief of staff at the state DOT. In an interview, he said that "the DOT is all about roads and bridges," but he felt it should be proactive in all transportation modes. Thomas Hoback, founder and now retired CEO of the prosperous freight-hauling Indiana Rail Road, introduced Zier to what passenger rail could do for the state's citizens and its economy, although Zier found that "economic arguments do not persuade highway engineers."[28]

Zier quickly grasped the importance of a rail passenger network with suitable train frequency, and a review of other states opened his eyes to possibilities for Indiana. He took an exploratory Hoosier State trip to Chicago that took six hours to get there and twelve to return. This was during a winter storm, and there also was freight train conflict, no food, inoperable bathrooms, and

Table A.19

Hoosier State performance (selected years 2000–19)

	2000	2004	2011	2015	2018	2019
Customers	25,908	17,934	37,200	29,703	27,900	20,900
Passenger miles	5,072,000	2,944,000	5,766,000	4,757,000	4,384,000	3,276,000
Revenue ($)	684,000	346,000	836,000	712,000	914,000	703,000
Revenue/train-mile ($)	4.75	3.68	10.20	8.72	11.19	8.60

Source: Data supplied by Amtrak to Rail Passengers Association; figures rounded.

delays due to traffic near Chicago. Zier knew that public support would come only with timely and reliable service and that the service needed to capture business as well as recreational travel.

He found numerous barriers. Track owner CSX wanted $150 million for capacity improvements that would enable four daily round-trips. Amtrak, on the other hand, fought any changes. Indiana's political leadership wanted nothing to do with rail passenger services and would not provide capital funding. Indiana's DOT was unwilling to seek federal grants and was concerned that highway funding would have competition from passenger rail efforts. In contrast, it is interesting to note that the Northern Indiana Commuter Transportation District (NICTD), which operates multifrequency electric interurban service between Chicago and South Bend, has excellent state and local support, including state funding. As a commuter operation, it has a customer base different from that of the Hoosier State, but the contrast between the two services is quite telling. Interesting also is the fact that long-distance Amtrak trains serving Indiana's northern tier receive no state support.

Indiana's US senators persuaded Governor Daniels to set aside $3 million annually for rail service in the state's $2 billion highway budget. Zier established a working relationship with CSX, but Amtrak remained uncooperative. When he examined line items in its bills to the state, Amtrak could not explain or justify the numbers. Zier learned that other states' rail managers found Amtrak's charges to be opaque, with many unsubstantiated and often excessive. Zier brought Indiana into MIPRC and contacted other states to learn how they dealt with Amtrak.

From Amtrak's viewpoint, at the corporate level, they wanted the Hoosier State but found little state-level support. When he was vice president–State Supported Services, Joe McHugh worked with Indiana officials, CSX, and state legislators to find solutions to the problems vexing the Hoosier State. CSX was willing to cut schedule time, and Amtrak offered to write grant requests for the state and alter the schedule. Amtrak also sought to add an airport stop for the Indianapolis International Airport (lower-cost parking would be available), and attempts were made to find a better routing via Thornton, Illinois, with the CN. There was some local Amtrak union resistance to Iowa Pacific. In the end, these efforts failed.[29]

Seeking to improve onboard services, Indiana contracted with Iowa Pacific Holdings. IPH provided fully restored heritage equipment and crews to serve Hoosier State passengers between July 2015 and February 2017. The train included a dome car with business class seating, high-quality food service, and enhanced coach accommodations.

But the headwinds were impossible to overcome. There was (and is) adequate air and bus service between Indianapolis and Chicago—175 miles. Transit times were more favorable by car, bus, and plane than a five-hour trip on Amtrak that could often be longer. The rail geography is just not there anymore that would make the train a viable option. An early morning departure from and late-night arrival in Indianapolis also was not helpful. In reality, the train corridor option was simply unrealistic and too costly to be successful.

North Carolina: A Tale of Three Cities

North Carolina's well-run program has had mixed results: the highly successful Piedmont (Charlotte–Raleigh) has outshined the Carolinian (New York City–Charlotte via Raleigh).

The Carolinian makes the same nine station stops as the Piedmont on the 172-mile Charlotte–Raleigh route. This suggests the problem is mainly between Raleigh and Washington, DC. Jason Ortner, director of North Carolina DOT's Rail Division, believes added Megabus competition, dilution from other Amtrak services, and frequent annulments have hurt ridership.[30] Southwest Airlines service has been introduced between New York and Raleigh, but Ortner feels this has not affected the Carolinian—though that train clearly needs attention. Ortner says the Carolinian topped all Amtrak long-distance services during the pandemic, retaining between 40 and 50 percent of its 2019 ridership. Schedules, fares, and marketing are under review, but changes will likely come after the pandemic subsides. North Carolina provides funding for

Table A.20

Comparing Carolinian decline and Piedmont growth

Item	Carolinian 2003–19 (%)	Carolinian 2011–19 (%)	Piedmont 2003–19 (%)	Piedmont 2011–19 (%)
Passenger-miles	41.23	(5.20)	394.01	52.79
Revenue/train-mile	(9.88)	(28.37)	162.80	28.82
Passenger-miles/train-miles	27.36	(25.93)	60.98	No change

Source: Amtrak-supplied data provided by Rail Passengers Association.

the Carolinian, but Virginia does not, even though there are stops in that state. Amtrak covers costs north of Washington.

The Piedmont, however, has been an outstanding success. North Carolina provides equipment and maintenance in a state-owned and state-staffed shop. The Rail Division works closely with communities to provide top-ranked stations, and capital investments have gone into grade separation and double-tracking. Amtrak provides crews and supports the website, but the operation clearly is the state DOT's. And the state owns the railroad, not only Charlotte–Raleigh but also to Selma and Morehead City. The entire 314-mile North Carolina Railroad is leased to Norfolk Southern, which operates its freight services and performs maintenance. Heavy freight traffic on the Piedmont route caused delays, but federally assisted double-tracking and passing sidings have improved on-time performance. The state DOT and NS meet regularly to resolve any issues that arise.[31]

The Piedmont has bipartisan political support. One billion dollars has been invested in the service to add capacity and improve facilities. Fourteen coaches and five lounge cars, all heritage cars from the pre-Amtrak era, have been rebuilt; the state is now looking for replacements of this aging equipment. Grants of $157 million will fund twenty-six coaches and six locomotives and will enable maintenance shop improvements. Thirteen grade separation projects have been completed, and forty grade crossings have been eliminated—a great improvement in public safety. The goal is to create a "sealed corridor" Charlotte–Raleigh without grade crossings. At this writing, a fifth round-trip on the route is on hold due to the pandemic but could be launched in 2021.[32]

North Carolina plans to participate in the 110 mph Southeast Corridor (Washington–Jacksonville) via Richmond and Raleigh with an extension (Raleigh–Atlanta). In anticipation of this, a new $110 million station has opened in Raleigh with capacity and parking to handle much larger crowds than the former station. In addition, negotiations are underway with CSX to acquire the former Seaboard route between the Virginia state line and Raleigh. When linked with Virginia's acquisition, this route will provide a through line from Richmond to Raleigh. Joe McHugh stated, "If they are successful, this would be a game-changer allowing dedicated passenger service over a high-speed line . . . from DC to Raleigh . . . that is faster than driving and [could] extend [the] Piedmonts to Richmond."[33]

The Piedmonts connect with local transit services, Amtrak Thruway buses, and Amtrak's Silver Star and Crescent long-distance trains. The Silver Star (New York City–Miami) service stops in Raleigh, while the Crescent (New York–New Orleans) stops in Charlotte, Salisbury, and Greensboro. Bicycles, by reservation, are carried on the Piedmont at no charge. Cafe service uses vending machines and offers table seating. Ticketing is through local stations and the Amtrak website. Wi-Fi is available on trains, and baggage can be checked at major stations.[34]

The Piedmont service has been built gradually with consistent bipartisan political support and ongoing public support. North Carolina's approach assures reliable equipment supply and maintenance and stations either built or rebuilt to meet the needs of a modern rail passenger service. Buses currently feed Amtrak long-distance trains, but the state may, in time, replace these with added rail services. At the same time, Ortner states clearly that only long-term funding can support such long-term projects.

Virginia Is for (Rail Travel) Lovers

Virginia exploits its location at the south end of Amtrak's NEC, partnering with Amtrak since 2009 to add new routes and frequencies. It has made strategic new investments in CSX track to ease traffic bottlenecks and lay groundwork for major growth. Amtrak Virginia has three routes: multiple frequencies of Washington, DC–Newport News via Richmond; Washington–Norfolk via Petersburg; and a once-daily service Washington–Roanoke via Lynchburg. All are extensions of NEC schedules, and many offer single-seat service to Boston. In addition, several long-distance trains cross Virginia, including the Cardinal to Chicago, the Silver Star to Tampa and Miami, the Silver Meteor to Miami, the Crescent to Atlanta and New Orleans, the Palmetto to Savannah, and the Carolinian to Charlotte. The state's Virginia Railway Express commuter service has two local routes from Washington Union Station. Virginians have shown support for intercity services as frequency and reach have improved. The figures shown exclude local NEC customers but include travelers to and from the NEC and to and from Virginia destinations. The next table shows the dramatic growth in Virginia's services.

The following table compares Virginia's services with a variety of other state-supported services and Amtrak's NEC Regionals.

Richard Rudolph, PhD, chairman of the Rail Users' Network, has noted increasing involvement of Virginia state government in intercity rail, helped by local advocates. Supporters in Charlottesville, for example, spent two years promoting service to Washington through press releases, public events, and

Table A.21
Virginia intercity metrics

	2005–19	Change (%)	2011–19	Change (%)
Passenger-miles, net change	101,366,000	117.04	35,886,000	23.60
Passenger-miles/train-miles	186 to 240	29.00	165 to 240	45.00
Revenue/train-mile	$45.38 to $74.90	65	$42.81 to $74.90	75

Source: Data supplied by Amtrak to Rail Passengers Association. Virginia services were added in 2009, 2013, 2014, and 2018.

Table A.22

Virginia 2019 metrics (compared to other services)

Services	Passenger-miles per train-mile	Revenue per train-mile ($)
Northeast regionals	255	124.19
Amtrak Virginia	240	74.90
Carolinian (NYC–Charlotte)	200	48.69
Surfliner (San Diego–LA–San Luis Obispo)	143	45.67
Lincoln Service (Chicago–St. Louis)	141	20.03
Average all state services	133	35.82
Heartland Flyer (Ft. Worth–Oklahoma City)	80	12.31

Source: Data supplied by Amtrak via the Rail Passengers Association.

outreach to communities on the route. This effort evolved into the Piedmont Coalition, gained political support, and obtained a trial operation that within three years attracted over three times the estimated ridership. Since 2013, Virginia has invested $467 million of state sales tax revenue in intercity rail, bipartisan support of which has enabled service expansion. There is interest, but no action yet, in extending service from Roanoke to Christiansburg or possibly Bristol in southwestern Virginia with extension into Tennessee, if that state was interested. CSX Transportation and Norfolk Southern host both Amtrak and Virginia services. Recent changes in freight operations have resulted in longer trains that do not mix well with short and frequent passenger trains. While there is a state fund to assist with capital improvements benefiting freight carriers, both of these railroads have shown declining interest in this form of incentive.[35]

However, a truly notable initiative is the December 2019 announcement that CSX and the state have agreed to a dramatic alteration of track access. Virginia, Amtrak, and federal agencies will purchase 350 miles of CSX right-of-way and 225 miles of track. In addition, a new bridge will be built adjacent to the Long Bridge across the Potomac River at Washington, currently a severe choke point for freight and passenger traffic. Virginia will add 37 miles of new main line to reduce other choke points between Washington and Richmond and will secure a route between Doswell and Clifton Forge, now run by a short line railroad. The state will own the New Bridge and also the former Seaboard Air Line Railroad route from Petersburg to the North Carolina state line for future use as a high-speed route. The $3.7 billion price tag ($1.9 billion is for the new Potomac bridge) will be financed one-third each by state and local and federal entities, including Amtrak, which has pledged to contribute $944 million equal to 24 percent of the total cost. This will allow the next stage of growth as Virginia deals with 2019's 230 million hours of highway delay that cost $6.5 billion annually, a number only expected to increase yearly. Widening

I-95 by one lane would cost an estimated $12 billion.[36] Virginia's strategic moves speak to the critical need for investment in rail passenger services to allow for growth of both passenger and freight traffic. The state recognizes the positive environmental effect of shifting passengers from autos to rail and also acknowledges the importance of rail freight to its economy. Rail passenger and freight services removed three million tons of carbon dioxide emissions, 6.4 percent of the state total, in 2017.[37]

Unusually, given the fraught politics in America, Virginia has achieved continuity in transportation policy in spite of term limits of four years for governors. Keeping partisan politics out of the transportation arena is allowing Virginia to obtain better long-term mobility results for the public.[38] This lesson would do well to be duplicated at the federal level.

Commuter operator Virginia Railway Express has suggested it can better coordinate with Maryland's MARC Train Service once the new Potomac bridge is built. This would mark the first time two commuter agencies cooperated to improve their respective services. It would increase frequencies and offer interstate service without having to change trains at Washington. Before this can happen, however, complicated operational issues must be overcome, including Washington Union Station's layout, lack of electrification on some routes, and high-level MARC platforms are incompatible with VRE equipment. In the meantime, work can proceed more quickly on third and fourth main tracks and other capacity enhancements on the CSX routes between Washington and Richmond. Other states might consider emulating Virginia's bold moves to further unlock the value of intercity and commuter rail mobility while enhancing the freight segment as well.

Maine: Rising Fast

The Downeaster has risen like a phoenix on a Boston–Portland–Brunswick route that had no intercity rail service in 2000 but boasted six daily round-trips in 2020. This success grew from a grassroots citizen effort: TrainRiders/Northeast secured ninety thousand signatures of residents seeking restoration of rail service. The effort went back thirty years; in 1995, the Maine legislature passed the Sensible Transportation Act authorizing state funding for rail service between Portland and Boston (later extended to Brunswick) under the aegis of the Northern New England Passenger Rail Authority (NNEPRA). It took another six years to start the initial service, and now, customers can travel by rail between ten intermediate stations on the 116 miles between Boston and Brunswick.

The next table shows the results, a clear message that the Downeaster is a well-patronized service. It has made remarkable progress in revenue per train-mile as well as a doubling of ridership for the period covered, all without a direct connection to Amtrak's NEC at Boston. In fiscal year 2019, farebox recovery was 51 percent, and on-time performance was 87 percent. Customer satisfaction

Table A.23

Maine's Downeaster performance (select periods, Amtrak fiscal years)

	2004	2010	2013	2015	2018	2019
Customers	250,028	478,600	559,977	420,742	540,000	557,200
Passenger-miles	20,886,000	38,197,000	45,557,000	34,267,000	43,973,000	45,166,000
Revenue ($)	3,585,000	6,712,000	8,212,000	7,254,000	10,087,000	10,510,000
Train-miles	332,000	420,000	504,300	421,468	470,584	473,984
Revenue/train-mile ($)	10.80	15.98	16.28	17.21	21.44	22.17

Source: Data supplied by Amtrak to Rail Passengers Association; figures rounded.

surveys consistently hover around 90 percent. The NNEPRA coordinates with Pan Am Railways, the Massachusetts Bay Transportation Authority (MBTA), online communities providing station services, and contractors providing cafe and maintenance services. Amtrak provides equipment, crews, reservation services, and an agent in Portland. TrainRiders/Northeast provides train hosts. Connections via Concord Coach Lines buses to northern Maine points are made in Portland.[39]

Patricia Quinn, NNEPRA's executive director, came from the hospitality industry. She noted that there were no government policies to help NNEPRA begin the Downeaster service. Like Amtrak, the service was expected to have a three-year life and then cease, further confirming the fact that rail passenger naysayers consistently underestimate the public's desire for well-run passenger rail. Even today, Quinn has no official government roadmap, vision, or policy under which she and her small staff can expand services. There is no reliable long-term funding source, so she has obtained financing from state grants, FRA grants, passenger fares, congestion mitigation fees, and Maine DOT funds. (New Hampshire has decided not to participate even though it has three stations on the route.) At first, MBTA did not participate but is now helping by dropping track access fees over its thirty-six miles of the service, and it also permits use of its North Station and two other local stations in Boston.

There are challenges. New locomotives are needed for the three train sets, and it is currently uncertain whether Amtrak will provide them from future locomotive purchases. Relocation of the Portland station is being studied, as is expansion of service north of Brunswick, but funding has not been secured. On the other hand, NNEPRA has obtained grants for capacity expansion and station and platform reconstruction. Furthermore, Positive Train Control was financed with a $50 million Defense Department set-aside, and the FRA funded six miles of double track that have helped relieve congestion. Still, no long-term funding has been secured for other projects or for future needs.

Regular, reliable, and adequate funding would obviate having to prepare time-consuming grant applications, which are not always successful. Uncertainty makes year-to-year planning difficult at best. Multiyear projects often require several grants to reach full implementation, yet such grants frequently allow for only portions of projects to be accomplished with no commitment for further funding. One major improvement would be physical connection of the Downeaster service to Amtrak's NEC at Boston's South Station—but that 1.5-mile track would require massive investment.

NNEPRA has only anecdotal evidence of the economic and environmental impacts on the communities it serves and has no standards or methods for collecting and evaluating data. Were it able to gain more reliable data, the case for funding would likely be much easier to make. Maine's US senators Susan Collins and Angus King have been supportive of the Downeaster, and Governor Janet Mills is studying how the service can promote economic development. Local representatives Chellie Pingree and Jared Golden are also supportive. One of Quinn's major efforts is to maintain and improve communications with federal, state, and local officials to build awareness and support for the Downeaster. She believes transportation is not a partisan issue but saw no champions for rail in the Trump administration. Relations with host railroads Pan Am (which provides track maintenance and construction) and MBTA are working well.[40] The State of Maine provided nearly $11 million in funding for fiscal year 2019, $19.49 per passenger carried. An imperfect comparison but interesting nonetheless: in 2017, Maine spent nearly $258 on its highway programs for each of its 1.335 million citizens.[41]

The Downeaster runs in a transportation policy void, so its handlers have had to use multiple tactics to create lasting value for passengers, communities, and the region. NNEPRA has built ongoing relationships with all levels of government, host railroads, and local communities. It has delivered consistently reliable service with the exception of 2015 when track and bridge replacement and bad weather disrupted schedules. Recovery from that low point has been rapid. The Downeaster shows how grass roots initiatives can achieve great things. The Downeaster is the only Amtrak service using outsourced food and beverage service. Perhaps future legislation will allow state-supported services to experiment with getting the best balance between customer needs and service costs. Overall, the Downeaster achieves customer service ratings in the 90 percent range.[42] The Downeaster can be expected to continue its bootstrap growth against the coronavirus and other headwinds, such as competing modes and uncertain funding. In 2019, 557,000 people voted for it with their travel dollars, helping support what truly is the Maine Phoenix.

Ohio: No Thank You

Ohio has to be counted as a failure for never trying. In 2010, it received some $400 million in federal funding to provide capital improvements and equipment for the 3-C Corridor (Cleveland–Columbus–Cincinnati) early in 2011. However, incoming governor John Kasich refused the funding (which other states were happy to receive) because he opposed providing the annual $17 million needed to support the service. And the state has created its own catch-22 that will keep it from joining any future Midwest passenger rail projects, such as the Pittsburgh–Columbus–Chicago route. A state law provides that Ohio cannot participate in any other initiatives until the 3-C service is up and running—which the state refuses to get up and running.[43] The last train serving Columbus quit in 1979, leaving the fourteenth largest US city devoid of rail passenger service.

Annoying Details

The rising cost of liability insurance is another problem. Coordination between Amtrak, the states, and the freight railroads is required for service expansion, yet the current piecemeal approach hinders development. This matter, along with access to freight railroads, poses huge hurdles for existing and potential service providers. Some freight carriers such as CSX (e.g., New Orleans to Jacksonville) and CN (e.g., efforts to improve Hoosier service into Chicago using a new route via Thornton) obstruct service expansion even when concessions are made on access charges and new investments.[44] Others, such as BNSF, have worked cooperatively (e.g., Southwest Chief track improvement between La Junta and Albuquerque only to be derailed by the Anderson administration). The liability and service expansion matters point directly to the need for strong continuity of leadership from the Amtrak board, CEO, and president in cooperation with the freight railroads and Congress.

Conclusions

By any measure, most state-supported programs have been successful and are likely to remain so. What do they tell us about passenger rail service in the United States?

- Although there are fluctuations in yearly passenger-miles due to occasional short-term problems with the services themselves, ups and downs in the national or regional economies, crises such as the coronavirus, and so on, overall, there is an upward trend in states with well-managed and well-funded services—up in passenger counts, passenger-miles, and ticket revenues.
- The state-supported services need Amtrak's national network, and Amtrak needs the state-supported services. Connectivity between the two is critical and must be continued so passengers can rely on, even if they have to change trains at some point, finding transportation to the greatest number of possible destinations. Similarly, state services feed passengers into Amtrak's long-distance trains. Current Amtrak management's 2020 reduction in long-distance frequencies, if continued after the coronavirus crisis subsides, can only weaken the state services that connect with them.

- Persistent grassroots efforts work if done slowly and with herculean effort. Local, regional, and state-level political support for starting, improving, and paying for rail services is the only way get such services.
- Long-term, reliable funding for state services is the only way to guarantee they will continue. Needless to say, the same is true for Amtrak. It and every state supporting passenger rail need a permanent dedicated fund so the uncertainty of unpredictable annual funding, and the political machinations that accompany it, do not threaten the viability of the services. However, money is not everything. The programs that run well are generally better managed.
- As a group (with the exception of the NEC), the states supporting intercity passenger services are collectively ineffective when it comes to influencing how Amtrak functions. They are usually acting individually, often in competition with each other, for grants rather than in concert and by marshaling political and public support. The states could leverage the $767.7 million (fares plus state support equaling 33 percent of Amtrak's total revenue) paid in 2019 to Amtrak by coordinating efforts to build a stronger national network. Except for Virginia, the state routes are managed as individual segments. Most connect with Amtrak's long-distance or NEC services, but most state efforts are directed toward local needs. By achieving better cooperation and coordination between the state-supported programs and Amtrak, we can have better mobility offering more city pair connections and frequencies.

Finally, some thoughts on managing our federally- and state-supported rail passenger system. In 1960, as the national "passenger problem" was peaking, Theodore Levitt wrote in the *Harvard Business Review* a fascinating and controversial piece entitled "Marketing Myopia." In it he described where the buck stops—with management:

> Every major industry was once a growth industry. But some that are now riding the wave of growth enthusiasm are very much in the shadow of decline. Others which are thought of as seasoned growth industries have actually stopped growing. In every case the reason growth is threatened, slowed or stopped, is not because the market is saturated. It is because there has been a failure of management. The railroads did not stop growing because the need for passenger and freight transportation declined. That grew. Railroads are in trouble today not because the need was filled by others (cars, trucks, airplanes, even telephones), but because it was not filled by the railroads themselves. They let others take customers away from them because they assumed themselves to be in the railroad business rather than the transportation business. The reason they defined their industry wrong was because they were railroad oriented instead of transportation oriented; they were product oriented instead of customer oriented.[45]

Many would disagree with Levitt—at least in part—and point out that government-subsidized competing modes put the railroads at a disadvantage they were unable to overcome, but he had a point: skilled and intelligent management is critically important, and it must focus on the right goal—serving the needs of the customer in a way that earns loyalty and an increasing customer base. In a very real way, the states supporting passenger rail are in the railroad business and are railroad oriented. This is necessary; they must know how railroads and rail services work. At the same time, we have seen that several states have succeeded in moving beyond, from running trains (product orientation) to providing mobility (service orientation) that appeals to and attracts passengers. And this applies to Amtrak's national network as well. Both regional and national passenger rail services focused on the traveling public's wants and needs can make those services an essential and permanent part of our transportation infrastructure.

Appendix 1 Notes

1. Bureau of Transportation Statistics, 2018, www.bts.gov/content/us-passenger-miles.
2. Telephone interview with David Kutrosky, retired managing director Capitol Corridor Joint Powers Authority, June 2020.
3. Amtrak 2019 Annual Report.
4. Equipment availability, seasonal, and schedule fluctuations played a role. Telephone interview with Robert VanderClute, October 7, 2020.
5. Trading Economics, United States Population, www.tradingeconomics.com, accessed July 17, 2020.
6. California Department of Transportation, California State Rail Plan 2018, https://dot.ca.gov/programs/rail-and-mass-transportation/california-state-rail-plan.
7. California Department of Transportation, California State Rail Plan 2018, https://dot.ca.gov/programs/rail-and-mass-transportation/california-state-rail-plan.
8. These are locomotives from which the engine, generator, and traction motors have been removed but whose cabs and controls remain to permit push-pull operation. The empty bodies behind the cab have rolling doors to accommodate passenger baggage. Rail enthusiasts have dubbed these units "cabbages."
9. LOSSAN Business Plans, 2013–2020.
10. LOSSAN Business Plans, 2013–2020.
11. LOSSAN Corridor Strategic Implementation Plan, April 2012 revised, https://www.sandag.org/uploads/projectid/projectid_260_14371.pdf.
12. Telephone interview with Joe McHugh, January 13, 2021.
13. Greenhouse gas emissions data from the California Air Resources Board, website at www.arb.ca.gov/resources.
14. Telephone interview with David Kutrosky, June 12 and 17, 2020.
15. Kutrosky interview.
16. Kutrosky interview.
17. California 2019–2020 Caltrans budget and California State Rail Plan 2018 Executive Summary and Appendices.
18. Telephone interview with Rob Padgette, June 23, 2020.
19. Illinois, Indiana, Iowa, Kansas, Michigan, Minnesota, Missouri, Nebraska, Ohio, North Dakota, South Dakota, and Wisconsin.
20. Email correspondence with Laura Kliewer, July 1, 2020.
21. Kliewer email.
22. Midwest Interstate Passenger Rail Commission (MIPRC) website, www.miprc.org.
23. Kliewer email.
24. Email interviews with David Randall, Rail Passengers Association, May 2020.
25. MIPRC website, www.miprc.org.
26. McHugh, email January 10, 2021, and telephone interview of January 13, 2021.
27. McHugh email.
28. Information about Robert Zier's efforts is from telephone and email interviews, October 2019. Additional sources include MIPRC website and telephone and email interviews with Sharon

Negele, MIPRC treasurer and State Representative of Indiana's District 13.
29. McHugh interview.
30. Telephone interview with Jason Ortner, July 28, 2020.
31. Ortner interview.
32. Ortner interview.
33. McHugh email.
34. Information from Kevin McKinney, *Passenger Train Journal* 277, no. 4 (2018), 24–33 and telephone interview with Kevin McKinney, June 2020.
35. Richard Rudolph, "The Commonwealth's Record of Success," *Passenger Train Journal* 278, no.1 (2019): 58–59.
36. Greater Greater Washington website, accessed December 20, 2019, https:/ggwash.org website; Virginia DOT, www.drpt.virginia.gov.
37. Virginia State Rail Plan, Executive Summary, September 2017, 5, http://www.drpt.virginia.gov/media/2345/varailplan_execsummary_final_011818.pdf
38. Includes observations from the McHugh email and telephone interview.
39. NNEPRA annual reports, 2010–2019.
40. Information in this section came from a telephone interview with Patricia Quinn, NNEPRA, September 9, 2019; the NNEPRA website, https://www.nnepra.com; and TrainRiders Northeast, www.trainridersne.org.
41. NNEPRA website; *Bangor Daily News* website, https://bangordailynews.com; Maine Development Foundation website, www.mdf.org.
42. Includes observations from the McHugh email and interview.
43. Telephone interview with William Habig, PE, Certified Planner, former director of the Mid-Ohio Regional Planning Commission, September 8, 2020.
44. McHugh email and interview.
45. Levitt, Theodore, "Marketing Myopia," *Harvard Business Review*, July–August 1960, 45.

Appendix 2: Amtrak Presidents and US Secretaries of Transportation

Amtrak Presidents

Roger Lewis	1971–1974	Alexander Kummant	2006–2008
Paul Reistrup	1974–1978	Joseph Boardman	2008–2016
Alan Boyd	1978–1982	Charles "Wick" Moorman	2016–2017
W. Graham Claytor Jr.	1982–1993	Richard Anderson	2017–2020
Thomas Downs	1993–1998	William Flynn	2020–2020
George Warrington	1998–2002	Stephen Gardner	2020–
David Gunn	2002–2005		

Secretaries of Transportation

Alan Boyd	1966–1969	Andrew H. Card	1992–1993
John Volpe	1969–1973	Federico F. Peña	1993–1997
Claude S. Brinegar	1973–1975	Rodney E. Slater	1997–2001
William T. Coleman Jr.	1975–1977	Norman Y. Mineta	2001–2006
Brock Adams	1977–1979	Mary E. Peters	2006–2009
Neil E. Goldschmidt	1979–1981	Ray H. LaHood	2009–2013
Drew Lewis	1981–1983	Anthony R. Foxx	2013–2017
Elizabeth Dole	1983–1987	Michael Huerta	2017–2017
James H. Burnley IV	1987–1989	Elaine Chao	2017–2021
Samuel K. Skinner	1989–1991	Peter Buttigieg	2021–

Bibliography

Books, Newspapers, Magazines, Pamphlets, and Other Published Sources

Association of American Railroads. *Yearbook of Railroad Facts*, 1970 Edition. Washington, DC: Association of American Railroads, 1970.
Anderson, Craig T. *Amtrak: The National Railroad Passenger Corporation*. San Francisco: Rail Transportation Archives, 1978.
Ball, Don Jr. and Rogers E. M. Whitaker. *Decade of the Trains: The 1940s*. Boston: New York Graphic Society, 1977.
Borkin, Joseph. *Robert R. Young: The Populist of Wall Street*. New York: Harper & Row, 1969.
Doughty, Geoffrey H. *New York Central's Lightweight Passenger Cars, Trains and Travel*. Lynchburg, VA: TLC Publishing, 1997.
Dubin, Arthur D. *Some Classic Trains*. Milwaukee: Kalmbach, 1964.
———. *More Classic Trains*. Milwaukee: Kalmbach, 1974.
Dulles, Foster Rhea. *The United States Since 1865*. Ann Arbor: University of Michigan Press, 1959.
Edmonson, Harold A., ed. *Journey to Amtrak*. Milwaukee: Kalmbach, 1972.
Fostik, John A. *Amtrak Across America*. Pepin: Enthusiast Books, 2017.
Frailey, Fred. *Twilight of the Great Trains*. Bloomington: Indiana University Press, 2010. First published 1998 by Kalmbach Books.
Goldberg, Bruce. *Amtrak: the First Decade*. Silver Spring, MD: Alan Books, 1981.
Goodwin, Doris K. *No Ordinary Time*. New York: Simon & Shuster, 1994.
———. *Leadership in Turbulent Times*, New York: Simon & Shuster, 2018.
Grant, H. Roger. *Richard C. Overton, Railroad Historian*. Lexington Group in Transportation History, n.d.
Henry, Robert Selph. *This Fascinating Railroad Business*. New York: Bobbs-Merrill, 1943.
Herbert H. Harwood. "This Was the Train That Was (But Never Was)." *Trains*, July 1968.
Jones, Harry E. *Railroad Wages and Labor Relations, 1900-1952: An Historical Survey and Summary of Results*. Washington, DC: Bureau of Information of the Eastern Railways, 1953.
Kennedy, John F. *Presidential Papers*. April 4, 1962, Special message on transportation, Folder JFKPOF-050-015-p0001, JFK Library, Boston.
Kisor, Henry. *Zephyr: Tracking a Dream Across America*. New York: Random House, 1994.
Loving, Rush Jr. *The Men Who Loved Trains*. Bloomington: Indiana University Press, 2006.
———. *The Well-Dressed Hobo*. Bloomington: Indiana University Press, 2016.
McClellan, Jim. *My Life with Trains*. Bloomington: Indiana University Press, 2017.
McCullough, David J. *Truman*. New York: Simon & Shuster, 1992.
Morgan, David P. "Who Shot the Passenger Train?" *Trains*, April 1959.
Morgret, Charles O. *Brosnan: The Railroads' Messiah*. 2 vols. Great Barrington, MA: Vantage, 1997.
Nupp, Byron. *National Transportation Policy in the United States—An Analysis of the Concept*. Denver: Transportation Law Journal, 1970.
Overton, Richard C. *Burlington Route*. Lincoln: University of Nebraska Press, 1965.
———. *Perkins/Budd: Railway Statesmen of the Burlington*. Westport, CT: Greenwood Press, 1982.
Parissien, Steven. *The Life of the Automobile*. New York: St. Martin's Press, 2014.
Perl, Anthony. *New Departures*. Lexington: University Press of Kentucky, 2002.

Plous, Fritz. "The Amtrak Era is Over. It's Time for a Replacement." *Railway Age*, October 4, 2018.
Pocari, John D. *Statement of Deputy Secretary of Transportation before the Senate Committee on Commerce, Science and Transportation*, September 15, 2010, https://www.commerce.senate.gov/services/files/0D11E47B-614B-4950-8E6F-EDEF90EE2B8B, accessed July 8, 2020..
Rae, John B. *The Road and the Car in American Life*. Cambridge, MA: MIT Press, 1971.
Randall, W. David. *From Zephyr to Amtrak*. Park Forest, IL: Prototype, 1972.
———. *Streamliner Cars*. 3 vols. Godfrey, IL: RPC, 1981.
Sanders, Craig. *Amtrak in the Heartland*. Bloomington and Indianapolis: Indiana University Press, 2005.
Schafer, Mike, Bob Johnston, and Kevin McKinney. *All Aboard Amtrak*. Piscataway, NJ: Railpace, 1991.
Stevers, Martin D. *Steel Trails, the Epic of the Railroads*. New York: Minton, Balch, 1933.
Stover, John F. *The Life and Decline of the American Railroad*. New York: Oxford University Press, 1970.
Taylor, William E. "When the Railroads Say 'Let's Go.'" *Popular Mechanics* 84, no. 1 (July 1945), 1–5, 160, 162.
Vranich, Joseph. *End of the Line*. Washington, DC: AEI Press, 2004.
What can be done to solve . . . THE Railroads' Passenger Train Problem, Recommendations of the Interstate Commerce Commission. Washington, DC: Association of American Railroads, 1959.
White, E. B. *Essays of E. B. White*. New York: Harper Perennial, 2006.
———. *One Man's Meat*. Gardiner: Tilbury House, 1997.
Wilner, Frank N. *Amtrak Past, Present, Future*. Omaha, NE: Simmons-Boardman, 2012.

Index

Note: Page numbers in *italics* refer to illustrations. Page numbers followed by a *t* refer to tables.

"above the rail" costs, 47, 93, 121
accidents on Amtrak routes, 79, 146, 147
accounting of Amtrak, recommendations for action, 178
Acela: Black on, 146, 147; customer experience on, 150; first year of service, 79; Gore's support of, 123; introduction of, 77–78; and Moorman, 129; pandemic's effect on, 171; passenger miles per train mile, 187*t*; revenue per train mile, 188*t*; success of, 78, 165; and Warrington administration, 109, 112, 137, 140
Adams, Brock, 223
Adirondack (New York City–Montreal, P.Q.), 72
advertising, recommendations for action, 178
AEM-7 locomotives, 72, 83
airline industry and air services: airports, 7; air traffic control system, 5, 32; and amenities, 168; Budd on role of, 91; competitive pressures from, 24, 26, 48, 50, 168; customer experience on, 8–9, 148, 149, 150, 168; and Department of Transportation, 142; and dress standards while flying, 10; and Essential Air Service Program, 7; freight competition of, 15; government support for, 30, 33–34; growth of, 19; Gunn on, 116; and intercity travel, 28, 28*t*; as "investments," 87n17, 92; and mail contracts, 19, 37; marketing of, 68; origins of passenger services, 40n50; public fascination with, 20; safety problems with, 26; service standards in, 142; share of passenger-miles, 189*t*; speed as advantage of, 148, 168; subsidies for, 5, 6–7, 19, 31*t*, 32, 38–39, 87n17; tax-exempt status of, 6, 39; transformative innovations in, 25–26; Young on threat of, 48, 50, 168
air pollution, 197
Air-Rail Travel Plan, 75
Albany-Rensselaer, New York, station, 80
alcohol on trains, 83, 149, 152
Alpert, George, 33–34
Alton, Illinois, station in, 83
amenities: challenges associated with, 141–42; cutbacks/reductions in, 43, 53, 83–84, 166–67, 171; perceived as extravagant, 93; recommendations for action, 177; resurrection of, 67; in sleeping cars, 152, *153*, 171. *See also* food and beverage services
American Car & Foundry (ACF), 24, 51, 115
Amfleet cars, *72*; acquisition of, 71; Business Class, 83; maintenance of, 114; "refreshment program" for, 83; and Reistrup administration, 103, 105; success with, 72, 159
Amfleet II cars, 72, *72*, 129, 161n26
"Amshacks," 72
Amtrak: in the seventies, 67–73; in the eighties, 73–76; in the nineties, 76–79; in the aughts, 79–81; in the teens, 81–85; Day One of, 62–63, 65–66, *65*; founding legislation of, 59–62, 85, 86, 161n25, 174, 176, 178; reauthorization legislation, 84, 103, 120, 141, 162n66, 176; saving, 173–78, 181–85
Amtrak 2.0, 183–84
"Amtrak Bloodbath," 72
Amtrak Police Department, 137
Amtrak Reform and Accountability Act, 94
Amtrak Thruway buses, 211
Anderson, Richard: administration of, 223; Black's perspective on, 145, 147; Boardman's criticisms of, 123, 139; and bureaucracy of Amtrak, 128; cost-cutting focus of, 123, 170, 183; damage done by, 170–71; and dining services, 162n66; efforts to reduce federal subsidies, 131; employees' perspectives on, 144; Gunn on leadership of, 114; lack of railroad experience, 170; and long-distance routes, 182, 183; management personnel hired by, 171; Moorman's recruitment of, 130–31; and on-board experience, 129; Reform Board abolished by, 178; and Southwest Chief, 139; termination of employees, 151; and Trump administration, 118
Arrowhead (Minneapolis–Duluth/Superior, Minnesota), 72
Association of American Railroads (AAR), 5, 59–60
Atchison, Topeka & Santa Fe, 58
Atlantic City service, 79
automobile, travel by: Budd on role of, 91; and car ownership, 27; competitive pressures from, 15, 18, 24, 25, 51; dominance of, 8; emissions from, 156, 200, 214; golden age of, 27; government support for, 33; and intercity travel, 28, 28*t*; mundane experience of, 9; and paved roads, 15; postwar trends, 23, 24; trends in percent share of passenger-miles, 189*t*. *See also* roads and highways
Auto Train, 75, 83, 165, 183, 187*t*, 188*t*

baggage cars, 146
Bagley, Stan, 137
Bakersfield–Los Angeles, 198
Bakersfield–Oakland, 197
Baltimore & Ohio Railroad: ICC survey on passenger trains of, 58; marketing campaigns of, 43; proposed merger, 41n54; and Reistrup, 100–101; and transcontinental services, 48
Bangor & Aroostook Railroad, 138
bankruptcies of railroads: New Haven bankruptcy, 7–8, 21, 33, *34*, 35–36; Penn Central bank-

ruptcy, 7–8, 36, 58–59, 61; and Whitman Commission, 33–36
Barthes, Roland, 27
Batory, Ronald L., ix, 166
Bay Area Rapid Transit (BART), 200
Bayh, Birch, 102
Beech Grove, Indiana, car shops, 71, 79, 82, 114, 161n26
benefits of passenger train travel, xi, 148–51
Biden, Hunter, 123
Biden, Joseph, 81, 143, 171, 184
Black, Robert Cliff, IV, 132–47, *133*; on attributes of good presidents, 97–98; background of, 133–34; on Boardman's leadership, 123; on board's plans for NEC and long-distance trains, 181–82; on business vs. service question, 169; on Claytor's leadership, 106; and core values of Amtrak, 147; on credibility, 135–36; on employee morale, 146–47; expectations of, 134–35; on future of Amtrak, 144; on greatest accomplishment, 145; on lack of coherent policy, 173; on Laney's plan to privatize Amtrak, *119*; long-term perspective of, 135–39; mission of, 139–41; motivations of, 134; on need for Amtrak, 143; on Obama's support, 122; on political support, 142; regrets of, 145–46; on service standards, 141–42, 144; and "subsidy" issue, 139
Black Hawk Chicago–Dubuque, Iowa, 72
Blue Water (Chicago–Port Huron, Michigan), 72, 191*t*, 204*t*, 207*t*
B&M commuter lines, 110–11
Boardman, Joe, *122*; administration of, 118, 122, 123, 170, 223; Black on, 138–39, 146; and Coscia's agenda, 162n58; as favorite of employees, 151; on Gunn administration, 116; and long-distance routes, 139; and Moorman, 126, 132; ousting of, 124, 126; safety emphasis of, 139, 140

board of directors, Amtrak's: appointments to, 8, 131, 140, 174, 175–76; Black's perspective on, 139–40, 181–82; and Boardman, 124; Bush's replacement of, 112; chairmen of, 8, 66, 94–95, 112, 174; challenges stemming from, 94–95, 116; composition of, 174–75; failure of Amtrak sought by, 112–13, 174, 181; fiduciary responsibility of, 139, 140, 174, 175; and Gunn administration, 112–13, 114, 116; Gunn on qualifications for, 95, 117–18; under Lewis's leadership, 102; and long-distance routes, 85–86; Moorman on, 131–32; political nature of, 8, 108, 174, 185; and presidential administrations, US, 139, 175–76; public access to meetings of, 140; and recommendations for action, 174–75; selection/nomination process, 174, 176; and TRAIN Act, 183
Boston & Albany, 111
Boston–Portland–Brunswick (Downeaster), 79, 188, 190*t*, 214–16
Boston's South Station, 216
Boyd, Alan: administration of, 106, 132, 170, 223; advocacy for rail passenger service, 172; Black's respect for, 135, 136; and committee addressing passenger crisis, 37; missions/agenda of, 140–41; railroad history understood by, 95; and Superliner cars, 140, 141
Bricker, John, 28
Brightline service in Florida, 182
Brinegar, Claude S., 223
Broadway Limited, xi, 44, *70*, 71, *71*, 79
Brotherhood of Maintenance of Way Employees (BMWE), 108, 137
Budd Company: Amfleet cars of, 71, *72*; closure of shop, 105, 115; El Capitan and Denver Zephyr delivered by, 87n6; postwar car orders, 24; Santa Fe's Hi-Level fleet, *74*; stainless steel self-propelled Rail Diesel Car of, 43; Train X prototypes of, 51; Viewliner prototypes, 161n26
Budd, Edward, 91
Budd, Ralph, 9; on cultivating return passengers, xiii; on passenger experience, 9–10, 129, 156; on regulation of competing industries, 20; on threat of nationalization, 16
Buffalo Central Terminal, 73
bureaucracy of Amtrak, 128, 134
Bureau of Transportation, 31
Burlington Northern, 64
Burlington Northern Santa Fe (BNSF), 130, 155, 197, 205, 217
Burlington Route, 14, 16–17, 54, 87n6, 203
Burnley, James H., IV, 223
buses: Budd on role of, 91; in combination with long-distance trains, 128; customer experience on, 148, 151; and government policies, 6; and intercity travel, 28*t*; promotional materials of, *92*; subsidies for, 7, 33; train travel compared to, 9; trends in percent share of passenger-miles, 189*t*; and Yellow Coach Company, 27
Bush, George H. W., 109
Bush, George W., 109, 112, 122
Bush (G. W.) administration, 120
business and industry, reliance on passenger trains, xi
business model of Amtrak, 127, 141
Buttigieg, Peter, 223
BWI Airport station, 73

café cars/service, 130, 148, 150, 197, 211
California, 193–200; Bay Area Rapid Transit, 200; Capitol Corridor, 78, 190*t*, 194, 194*t*, 197, 198–200, 199*t*, 203; funding for commuter/intercity rail in, 199; High Speed Rail Authority,

227

196; High-Speed Rail Line in, 196, 197–98; history of intercity passenger rail in, 193–94; long-term capital investment in, 194; Los Angeles Union Station (LAUS), 195–96; Pacific Surfliners, 194–96, 194*t*, 195*t*, 196*t*; passenger-miles by rail in, 189, 194*t*, 199–200; San Joaquins, 196*t*, 197–98
California Cars, 78
California Department of Transportation (Caltrans), 194, 195, 197
California State Rail Plan, 194
California Zephyr, xi, 75, 78, 148, 150, 153, 187*t*, 188*t*
Calumet, 79
Canada: routes serving, 188; VIA Rail of, 143, 158, 159, 167, 179n9
Canadian National (CN), 205, 210, 217
Capitol Corridor (San Jose–Oakland–Sacramento–Auburn), 78, 190*t*, 194, 194*t*, 197, 198–200, 199*t*, 203
Capitol Corridor Joint Powers Authority board, 198
Capitol Limited, xi, 84, 115
Card, Andrew H., 223
Cardinal (New York–Washington–Cincinnati–Indianapolis–Chicago), 79, 81, 149, 187*t*, 188*t*, 208, 212
Carolinian (New York City–Charlotte via Raleigh), 75, 192*t*, 210–11, 210*t*, 212, 213*t*
Carper, Tom, 143, 171–72
"Carter Cutbacks," 72
Carter, Jimmy, 109, 123
Centralized National Operations Center, 145
Chao, Elaine, 116, 130, 223
Charlotte–Raleigh, 190*t*
Cherington, Paul, 10n1
Chesapeake & Ohio Railway: and Baltimore & Ohio Railroad, 43; and Chessie cars, 50; and Deegan, 50; ICC survey on passenger trains of, 58; and Reistrup, 100; and transcontinental services, 48, 49; and Young's empire, 45
Chessie, 48–50, 52, 100
Chicago: as railroad capital, 205; ridership and population, 204*t*; Union Station, 149, 205
Chicago, Aurora & Elgin, 40n32
Chicago–Carbondale, 191*t*, 204*t*, 205
Chicago–Detroit-Pontiac, 191*t*, 204*t*, 207*t*
Chicago–Grand Rapids, 204*t*, 207*t*
Chicago–Indianapolis, 79, 102, 193*t*
Chicago–Milwaukee (Hiawatha), 159, 190*t*, 204*t*, 205–6, 206*t*
Chicago, North Short & Milwaukee, 40n32
Chicago & North Western, 101
Chicago–Port Huron (Blue Water), 72, 191*t*, 204*t*, 207*t*
Chicago–Quincy (Illinois Zephyr), 67, 191*t*, 204*t*, 205
Chicago Region Environmental and Transportation Efficiency, 205
Chicago, Rock Island & Pacific, 64
Chicago–Seattle, 67

Chicago, South Shore & South Bend, 64
Chicago–St. Louis (Lincoln Service), 190*t*, 201, 203, 204*t*, 213*t*
Chicago–Toronto, 80
Chicago Union Station, 149, 205
Chief, 54
children as passengers on trains, xi
Cincinnati Union Terminal, 72
civility of travel, 182
Civil War, American, 13
Claytor, W. Graham, Jr., 106–8, *107*; administration of, 118, 170, 223; advocacy for rail passenger service, 88n40, 172; Black's perspective on, 135, 136; and board, 140; death of, 77; mission of, 140; railroad experience of, 76–77; railroad history understood by, 95; Reistrup on leadership of, 104; on saving Amtrak, 185; work scrapped by successor, 175
Clinton administration, 108–9, 137
Clinton, Bill, 109, 122
C&O/B&O, 37, 43, 58, 100, 165
coal trains, 103
Coast Starlight, 148, 183, 187*t*, 188*t*
coast-to-coast/transcontinental services, 48, *49*, 73, 78, 87n3
Coleman, William T., Jr., 223
Collins, Susan, 156, 216
Colorado, 155
Committee on Appropriations Subcommittee on Transportation, Treasury, and Independent Agencies, 121
Committee on Commerce, Science and Transportation, US Senate, 171
Commodore Vanderbilt, *16*
commuter services: crisis facing, 52–53; and discontinuance of trains, 64; discontinued by Amtrak, 79; financial burden of, 23, 35–36; funding for, 93; ICC recommendations on, 29; Morgan's article addressing, 39; and New Haven bankruptcy, *34*, 35–36; and participation in Amtrak, 64; subsidies for, 7, 35–36
Competition for Intercity Passenger Rail in America Act, 81
competition proposal for Amtrak, 182
complexity of railroads and train travel, 9, 12
Concord Coach Lines, 215
Connecticut, 192
Connecticut Department of Transportation, 36
Conrail, 32, 67, 72, 105, 125
consolidation of railroads, 19, 21
Conte, Silvio, 143
Contract Air Mail Act, 19
coronavirus pandemic, 10, 85, 147, 181, 210, 217
corporate structure of Amtrak, for-profit, 127
corridor rail passenger services, funding for, 93. *See also* Northeast Corridor
Coscia, Anthony: and Anderson administration, 171; Boardman pushed out by, 118, 162n58; and control of NEC, 162n46, 181–82; on mission of Amtrak, 85–86; Moorman recruited by, 126; on profitability question, 86; on subsidies, 7
credibility, Black on, 135–36
Crescent (New York–New Orleans), 187*t*, 188t, 211, 212
Crosbie, Bill, 120, 121–22
CSX Transportation: and Indiana's rail program, 209; and North Carolina's rail program, 211; and Reistrup, 105; service expansion obstructed by, 217; and Virginia's rail program, 212, 213, 214
Cumberland Road, 18
customer orientation, 218–19

Davis, Jeff, 10n1
Deegan, Thomas, 50
Delzeit, Brian, 155
Denver, Colorado, Union Station, 83
Denver–Ogden route of Rio Grande, 64
Denver & Rio Grande Western, 64
Denver–Salt Lake City, 75
Denver Zephyr, xi, 87n6
Desert Wind, 79, 136
Detroit–Grand Rapids corridor, 48
Detroit/Pontiac route, 207*t*
Dingell, John, 141
dining cars: advertisement for meals on Pennsylvania Railroad, *44*; and Anderson administration, 162n66; and Black's administration, 136; challenges associated with, 158; china used in, 70, *71*; and civility of travel, 182; customer expectations in, 151; egalitarian nature of, 182; elimination of, 43; menus for, xii, *56*, *70*, 83, 165; and millennial generation, 136, 166; and Moorman administration, 128, 130; personnel of, 69, 150; pride of service in, *xii*, xii; and Pullman's standard of service, 156; and Reistrup administration, 100, 102; seating by stewards in, 148; service cutbacks in, 83–84; on the 20th Century Limited, 166. *See also* food and beverage services
discontinuance of trains: "Amtrak Bloodbath"/"Carter Cutbacks," 72; Amtrak trains in the eighties, 75; Amtrak trains in the nineties, 78–79; commuter services, 64; and growing passenger problem, 36; and Hartke legislation, 60; and ICC formula, 47; ICC's control of, 14, 29, 38, 53–54, 58–59, 60; New York Central Railroad on regulation of, 4–5; Pacific Parlour Cars, 84; and Penn Central's bankruptcy, 58–59; and Transportation Act (1958), 29; of the 20th Century Limited, 26
Dodge City, Kansas, 155
Dole, Elizabeth, 223
dome cars, 182
Downeaster (Boston–Portland–Brunswick), 79, 188, 190*t*, 214–16
Downs, Thomas: administration of,

108–9, 170, 223; on Anderson's administration, 170; Black's perspective on, 136–37; on board's fiduciary responsibility, 175; and Claytor, 107–8; on customer loyalty, 173; fiduciary responsibility of, 136; on lack of national transportation policy, 173; on lack of rail advocates in leadership, 172; loss of job, 108–9, 137, 140; and Mercer, 136–37, 140; on necessity of metrics, 93; on need for Amtrak, 182; on political aspects of presidency, 107–8; on president's role, 96; on qualities of good leaders, 97; railroad experience of, 76–77; railroad history understood by, 95; safety emphasis of, 108; on saving Amtrak, 185; on status of passenger trains, 91; and subsidy-free demands of White House, 108–9; on three-day-a-week service, 180; work scrapped by successor, 175

dress, standards of, 10
Dreyfuss, Henry, 17
drug use/testing, 152
Dukakis, Michael, 111

E60C locomotives, 73
Economist, 9
Edmonson, Harold A., 87n15
egalitarian nature of rail travel, 182
Ehrlichman, John, 68, 96
Eisenhower, Dwight D., 7, 25, 28–29, 51–52
El Capitan, 87n6, 159
electric interurban railroads, 18
electrification of railroads, 22, 108, 214
Electro-Motive Division of General Motors, 35, 69
Emergency Railroad Transportation Act, 16, 19
"Emerging Corridors Initiative," 102
emissions, reduction of, 156, 200, 214
Empire Builder: alcohol consumption on, 152; and declining passenger behavior, 152; dining services on, 75, 115, 149; and Gunn administration, 115; and Hiawatha, 206; passenger interviews aboard, 148, 149; passenger miles per train mile, 187t; and political support for NEC, 116; revenue per train mile, 188t; schedule cutbacks on, 79; and "3 percent" argument about, 169; and vacation/leisure travelers, xi
Empire Service, 165, 188
employees of railroads/Amtrak: and Anderson administration, 170; and behavior of passengers, 152; and Black's administration, 136, 141; and costs of labor, 37, 46, 52, 53; and crisis in railroads, 53; diversity in, 69; and drug use/testing, 152; and effects of insecure funding, 94; expectations for competence of, 141; and Gunn, 114, 121; and hiring challenges, 152; interviews conducted with, 151–54; job insecurity of, 146, 151; job losses of, 79, 114, 135; and labor agreements, 37–38; and labor board, 19; and management, 153–54; Moorman on, 128; morale of, 98–99, 146–47, 151, 170; and Pullman's standard of service, 158; reactions to cutbacks in services, 142; and regulation of railroads, 16, 19; retirement funds for, 19; turnover in, 152; unauthorized media comments from, 145; unemployment insurance for, 19; workloads of, 152

energy crisis of 1973, 68, 97
engineering department of Amtrak, 128
Englewood Flyover, 205
environmental concerns: air pollution, 197; auto emissions, 156, 200, 214; Black on, 147; rising sea levels, 195; in Virginia, 214
equipment: Acela, 77–78, 79, 109, 112, 123; Amtrak's acquisitions of, 63–64, 71, 74, 77, 78; and Anderson administration, 114, 170; Black on, 143, 146, 147; and Boyd administration, 106; and budget cuts, 160; as cost center of railroads, 46; costs of renovating/purchasing, 38; employees' responsibility for onboard failures, 153; foreign-built, 77; fragility of interior components, 159–60; and funding for Amtrak, 75; and Gunn administration, 114, 115; heritage fleet, 70, 80, 158, 159–60, 162n67; innovations introduced in, 43; and Lewis administration, 68; maintenance deferred/delayed, 43, 68, 72, 75, 114; maintenance procedures/schedules, 68, 160; maintenance shops, 64, 71, 79, 114; mixed/incompatible cars, 67, 101, 158–59; Moorman on state of, 129; and passenger experience, 165; postwar car production, 23–24; problems with, 103; recommendations for action, 177; and Reistrup administration, 101, 102, 103, 105; replacement of, 158–59

Erie, Chicago & Eastern Illinois, 45
Essential Air Service Program, 7
Eugene/Portland/Seattle–Vancouver, 191–92, 191t
"experiment," Amtrak as, 62, 101, 161n25

F40 locomotives, 101, 105
F40PH locomotives, 69, 71, 76, 77
"farebox recovery," 80
fares of railroads: incentive fares, 44, 100; regulation of, 4–5; tax on tickets, 25, 29, 53
Farley Post Office complex, 83
"FAST Act," 129, 156, 176
Federal Aid Highway Act, 25
Federal Aid Road Act, 18
Federal Aviation Act, 26
Federal Aviation Administration (FAA), 6, 26
Federal Highway Administration, 86
Federal Railroad Administration (FRA): Black on support from, 142; and committee addressing passenger crisis, 37; funding for Maine rail program, 215; lack of support from, 104, 116; and Moorman administration, 130; and Nixon administration, 60; relationship with Amtrak, 112; and route structure of Amtrak, 63

financial health of railroads: effect of regulation on profits, 14, 18; factors affecting, 15; financial strain of passenger service, 3, 7, 29, 52–54; and government support, 91; and Gunn administration, 112–13; and income problem of Amtrak, 181; Morgan's article addressing, 38–39; Murphy on low margins of passenger service, 14; overhead costs of railroads, 46–47; postwar struggles of, 23; revenue of Amtrak, 79, 188t; during World War II, 14–15, 17; and Young's reform efforts, 45. *See also* funding; subsidies for transportation industries

Firestone Tire and Rubber Company, 25, 27
first-class passengers, 83, 129, 149, 152
Florio, Jim, 143
Flynn, William, 86, 171, 183, 223
food and beverage services: and Anderson administration, 170; Black on economics of, 142; boxed meals, 84, 149–50, 165–66; café cars, 130, 148, 150, 197, 211; challenges associated with, 153; continued provision of, 73; cutbacks in, 70–71, 81, 84, 142, 162n66, 165–66, 170, 171; declines in quality of, 149–50, 152; and demeanor of staffers, 150, 158; employees' perspectives on, 151; on Eugene/Portland/Seattle–Vancouver, 191–92; and first-class passengers, 129; "flexible dinners," 84, 149–50, 166; Gunn on economics of, 115; high-quality, 70, 71; improvements made in, 75, 82; inconsistent quality in, 165; on long-distance trains, 142, 177; mandate on elimination of losses in, 84, 115, 129, 141, 162n66, 176; menus for, 70, 81, 82, 115, 145, 149, 153; and millennial generation, 136, 166; Moorman on, 128, 129–30; passenger expectations for, 142, 151, 152, 158; recommendations for action, 176, 177; and Reistrup administration, 102, 103

Ford, Henry, 15
Fort Worth–Laredo, Texas (Inter-American), 72
Fort Worth–Oklahoma City (Heartland Flyer), 80, 192t, 193, 204t
Foxx, Anthony R., 223
free market economics, ix
freight carriers and transportation: competitive pressures felt by, 4; coordination with state rail programs, 217; declines in, 15, 23, 30, 84; failure of Amtrak hoped

for by, 161n25, 169; financial struggles of, 84; and ICC formula, 46–47; and leadership of Amtrak, 76; Moorman on, 131; of northeastern railroads, 33; on the Piedmont, 211; preservation of, with Amtrak's creation, 61, 62; and railroad experience of Amtrak leadership, 76; regulation of, 4, 16; and revenue deficits of passenger services, 7, 33, 46; track capacity required by, 85

Fullam, John P., 58–59
"full crew" laws, 16
funding: and budget cuts, 109, 122, 134–35, 167; for commuter services, 93; competition with other transport modes for, 94; and Congress, 61, 73, 87, 142, 183; effects of insecure, 94; and Gunn administration, 113, 115–16; and hiring challenges, 152; and history of public funding for transportation, 91–92; inadequate levels of, 70, 73, 75, 87, 176; initial funding of Amtrak, 61–62; and Midwestern intercity network, 200; Moorman on, 131; political aspects of, 93; recommendations for action, 176, 177; and Reistrup administration, 104; state and local sources of, 93, 123, 139, 140, 190; trust fund option, 93–94, 177. *See also* subsidies for transportation industries

Gallagher, John S., Sr., 5
Gallamore, Robert, 10n1
Gardner, Stephen, 171–72, 182, 184, 185, 223
General Electric, 71
General Mitchell International Airport, 206
General Motors, 25, 27, 35, 69
Genesis locomotives, 77, *77*
Georgia Railroad, 64
GG1 locomotives, 71
Golden, Jared, 216
Goldschmidt, Neil E., 223
Goode, David, 125
Goodwin, Doris Kearns, 92
Goodyear, 25
Gore, Al, 123
Gould, Jay, 13
Graham, Hal, 68
Grand Central Terminal in New York City, 78
grassroots efforts, effectiveness of, 218
Gray, John, 5
Great American Stations initiative, 80
Great Depression, 15, 16–17, 19
Great Steel Fleet of NYC, *16*, 17
Greenwood, Mississippi, 154
Greyhound, 27
Gulf Breeze Birmingham-Mobile, Alabama, 79
Gunn, David, 109–21, *110*; administration of, 170, 223; background of, 109–11; Black's perspective on, 137, 138, 144; on Boyd's leadership, 106; on chairman and board, 174; consultants fired by, 135; and

equipment, 114, 115; expectations of, 111–13; as favorite of employees, 151; and funding for Amtrak, 61–62, 115–16; on greatest accomplishment, 117; on lack of rail advocates in leadership, 172; leadership style of, 115; mission of, 113–14, 140; Moorman on leadership of, 132; motivations of, 111; on myths about Amtrak, 121; on need for Amtrak, 116; on political support for long-distance and NEC trains, 85; railroad experience of, 81; railroad history understood by, 95; and service, 114–15; termination of, 118–21, 138, 140; work scrapped by successor, 175

Haldeman, H. R., 68, 96
Hamburg Industries, 64
Harley's Hornet, 67
Harrison, Hunter, 116
Hartke legislation, 60
Hartke, Vance, 60, 61, 102
Harvard Kennedy School, 32
Haswell, Anthony, 57
head-end power, 74, 101
Heard, Bruce, 68, 99, 134
Heartland Flyer (Ft. Worth–Oklahoma City), 80, 192t, 193, 204t
hedge fund investments in railroads, 115
Henry, Robert Selph, 13, 14–15
Hiawatha (Chicago–Milwaukee), *159*, 190t, 204t, 205–6, 206t
High-Speed Ground Transportation Act, 21–22
high-speed trains, *22*; Black on, 143, 146, 147; in California, 196, 197–98; and Clinton administration, *122*; Southeast Corridor (Washington–Jacksonville), 211; subsidies for, 21–22. *See also* Acela
Highway Trust Fund, 7, 32
Highway Users Federation, 25
Hill, James J., 13
Hoback, Thomas, 208
Hocking Valley, 45
Hodges, Luther, 35
Holton, Linwood, 112
Hoosier State, 208–10, 209t
Horsman, Thomas, 154
host railroads: Amtrak's relationships with, 76; bad track of, 67, 93, 101; and Capitol Corridor's claw-backs alternative, 198; establishing a trust fund for, 177; impact on intercity services, 199; limited capacity of, 84; poor financial condition of, 101; recommendations for action, 177, 178; and safety considerations, 88n33; Supreme Court on priority of Amtrak, 85; and on-time performance of Amtrak, 84, 130
housekeeping standards, 160
House Transportation & Infrastructure Committee, 81, 156
House Transportation & Infrastructure Subcommittee on Railroads, Pipelines and

Hazardous Materials, 86
Howard, Pamela, 155
Howes, William: and committee addressing passenger crisis, 37; on lack of mission, 172; on lack of transportation policy, 42, 172–73; on the passenger problem, 38, 59; on service standards, 165, 166; on uniforms, 68–69
Huerta, Michael, 223
Hughes, David, 120, 121, 138, 140
Hutchinson, Kay Bailey, 143

ICC. *See* Interstate Commerce Commission
ICE. *See* intercity express
Illinois, 201, 202, 203–5, 204t
Illinois/Iowa, 206
Illinois/Wisconsin, 205–6
Illinois Zephyr (Chicago–Quincy, Illinois), 67, 191t, 204t, 205
Indiana, 208–10, 209t
Indianapolis–Chicago, 204t
Indianapolis International Airport, 209
Indiana Rail Road, 208
"Inland Route" Boston–New York City, 6
Inter-American (Fort Worth–Laredo, Texas), 72
intercity express, 77
intercity travel: decline in rail's market share, 28, 28t; funding authorized for, 80; growth rate in, 190t; in the Midwest, 200–210, 201t, 202t, 203t, 204t, 206t, 207t, 208t, 209t; by mode, 28t; as overlooked service, 165; and population trends, 190; potential loss of, 54; and Precision Scheduled Railroading, 199; and Pullman Company, 47; service standards on, 53
Intermodal Transportation Center, 80
international passenger trains, 188
Interstate and Foreign Commerce Committee, Senate, 29
Interstate Commerce Act, 14, 18
Interstate Commerce Commission: and competition between industries, 28; and discontinuance of trains, 14, 29, 38, 53–54, 58–59, 60; establishment of, 14, 18; and financial health of railroads, 30; and financial reporting of railroads, 4; formula of, 38, 46–47; and labor costs, 38; and merger cases of the 1960s, 21; Morgan's article addressing, 38–39; original purpose of, 18; and passenger deficit problem, 29; and Penn Central merger, 36; and Penn Central's bankruptcy, 58–59; ratemaking jurisdiction of, 4, 20, 38, 53; report/recommendations of (1959), 29–30; and Senate subcommittee report (1951), 28; transportation study (1915), 18–19; and Young's reform efforts, 46–47
intrastate trains, 54
INVEST (Investing in a New Vision for the Environment and Surface Transportation) Act, 183, 185n5

investment banks, 45
Iowa Pacific, 154, 210

Jackson, Michael, 112
James Whitcomb Riley (Chicago–Indianapolis), 102
Joliet, Illinois, station in, 83
Jones, Milton Williams, 81
Journey to Amtrak (Edmonson), 87n15

Kansas, 155
Kansas City, Missouri, Union Station, 80
Kasich, John, 216–17
Kelleher, Herb, 9
Kelly Act, 19
Kelly, M. Clyde, 19
Kendall, David W., *66*
Kennedy, John F., 20–21
Kentucky Cardinal, 78
Kerley, David, 168
King, Angus, 142, 155–56, 170, 216
Kliewer, Laura, 200
Kratz, Chuck, 70
Kuhler, Otto, 17
Kummant, Alex, 121, 138, 140, 170, 223
Kutrosky, David, 198, 199

labor brotherhoods, 4. *See also* unions
LaHood, Ray H., 223
Lake Shore (now Lake Shore Limited), 67, 84, 148, 149, 187*t*, 188*t*
Laney, David, 112, 113, 114, 118–20, *119*, 138
Langdon, Jervis, Jr., 58–59, 100
LaTourette, Steven, 143
Lautenberg, Frank, 143
Lawrence, Kansas, station, 83
leadership of Amtrak: Black on attributes of good leaders, 97–98, 144; bonus structure for top management, 93; and difficult start of Amtrak, xiii, 62; fiduciary responsibility of, 144; governance versus, 94–95; lack of rail advocates in, 172; and Levitt's perspective on management, 218–19; personal problems of members of, 97; political nature of, 8; and presidential appointments, 175–76; process of selecting, 144; railroad experience of, 76–77; and stewardship, 95–98. *See also* board of directors, Amtrak's; presidents of Amtrak
Leahy, Patrick, 143
leisure travelers, xi
Levitt, Theodore, 218–19
Lewis, Drew, 223
Lewis, Roger, 223; administration of, 170; on Amtrak as experiment, 62; appointed first president of Amtrak, 62, 88n34, 96; and company morale, 99; damage done by, 99; and funding for Amtrak, 68; lack of railroad experience, 77, 96; life after Amtrak, 97; and maintenance of equipment, 68; Reistrup on service of, 102
Lincoln, Abraham, 91–92
Lincoln Service (Chicago–St. Louis), 190*t*, 201, 203, 204*t*, 213*t*

Lindbergh, Charles, 20
Loewy, Raymond, 17
logos of Amtrak, 65, 69, 79
long-distance trains/service: and Amtrak 2.0, 183; and Anderson's cost-cutting measures, 183; anticipated demand for, 181; and Biden's election as president, 184–85; Black on, 139, 143, 144; and Boardman, 139; and bus options, 128; cutting amenities on, 166–67; discussions about eliminating, 169, 183; food services on, 142, 177; Gunn on myths associated with, 121; improving financial performance of, 167; Moorman on, 127–28, 131; pandemic's effect on, 171; passenger-miles changes, 189*t*; regional services that complement, 188; service standards on, 165; state and local funding of, 139; and state rail programs, 188; Superliner cars of, *74*, 159; and "3 percent" argument, 169; three-day-a-week service, 183–84; as valued service, 169, 182
Los Angeles Metro, 196
Los Angeles–Palmdale, 196
Los Angeles–San Diego–San Luis Obispo Rail Corridor Agency (LOSSAN), 195, 196, 198
Los Angeles Union Station, 195–96
Lott, Trent, 108, 116, 143
lounge cars, 43, 67, 182
Lovell, Jim, 169
Loving, Rush, 61, 95, 174
Luna, Charlie, 101
luxury trains, 48–50

MacAnanny, James, 60
mail contracts: Amtrak's termination of, 80; loss of, 15, 19, 37, 54; Morgan's article addressing, 39; and origins of passenger aircraft, 40n50
Maine, 214–16, 215*t*
MARC Train Service of Maryland, 214
marijuana use, 152
"Marketing Myopia" (Levitt), 218–19
marketing of Amtrak, 67–68, 69–70, 71, 178
Massachusetts, 192
Massachusetts Bay Transportation Authority (MBTA), 36, 105, 110, 215, 216
mass transit, subsidies for, 31*t*
Mathews, James, 86
Maybach engines, German, 87n5
McAdams, Carolyn, 154
McCain, John, 120
McClellan, Jim: advocacy for rail passenger service, 172; and Amtrak's startup, 62; committee to address passenger crisis, 37; and Gunn, 110; on leadership of Amtrak, 85; and marketing of Amtrak, 68; on need for pro-passenger management, 173; on preservation of freight railroads, 61; on "for profit" status of Amtrak, 60; and route structure of Amtrak, 63
McGinnis, Patrick B., 33
McHugh, Joe, 118, 209, 211

McKinney, Kevin, 57, 63, 67, 183
McPherson, Harry, 135
Mechanical Department, 63–64, 160, 170
media relations, 135, 136, 137, 138
Megabus, 210
Menk, Louis, 96
mergers of railroads, 19, 21, 36–37, 41n54
METRA (Chicago), 36
Metroliners, 22, *22*, 39, *72*, 75, 147
Metro North (New York and Connecticut), 36
Mica, John, 81, 141, 145, 162n66
Michigan, 201, 202, 206–7, 207*t*
Michigan Central station in Detroit, 75
midwestern intercity network, 200–210; Chicago ridership and population (2018), 204*t*; emergence of, 200; and funding, 200; Hiawatha (Chicago–Milwaukee), *159*, 190*t*, 204*t*, 205–6, 206*t*; Illinois, 201, 202, 203–5, 204*t*; Illinois/Iowa, 206; Indiana, 208–10, 209*t*; Michigan, 201, 202, 206–7, 207*t*; and Midwest Regional Rail Plan, 200; Milwaukee–St. Paul, 201*t*; Missouri, 201, 202, 207, 208*t*; passenger-miles by rail in, 202*t*; public support for, 202; revenues of, 203*t*; Wisconsin, 201, 202
Midwest Interstate Passenger Rail Commission (MIPRC), 200, 201, 202, 209
military's role in transportation, 40n50
millennial generation, 136, 142, 166
Mills, Janet, 216
Milwaukee airport station, 80
Milwaukee–St. Paul, 201*t*
Mineta, Norman Y., 112, 118, 120, 223
Minneapolis–Duluth/Superior, Minnesota (Arrowhead), 72
mission of Amtrak: to attack passengers, 71; and Black's administration, 139–41; and board of directors, 175; Coscia on, 86; and Gunn administration, 113–14; and Moorman administration, 127–28; and Reistrup administration, 102–3; and succession of Amtrak presidents, 8; TRAIN Act's clarification of, 183
Missouri, 201, 202, 207, 208*t*
Missouri Pacific, 15
Missouri River Runner, 193*t*
Modern Railroads, 57
monopolies in railroad industry, 13–14
Montrealer, 79
Moorman, Charles "Wick," 124–32, *125*; administration of, 223; background of, 124–26; on board's fiduciary responsibility, 174; on changes needed at Amtrak, 131–32; employees' perspectives on, 151; expectations of, 126–27; on funding, 131; on greatest accomplishment, 130–31; on lack of coherent policy, 173; mission of, 127–28; motivations of, 126; on

Index 231

need for Amtrak, 130, 132; on "for profit" status of Amtrak, 60; Reistrup on leadership of, 105; on safety considerations, 128; on service, 129; on support, 130
Morgan, David P., 38–39, 91
Morgan, J. P., 13
motel chains, 27
Motor Bus Lines of America, 92
Mountaineer Norfolk (Virginia–Chicago), 72
Moynihan, Daniel Patrick, 143
Moynihan Train Hall, 83
Munoz, Oscar, 168
Murphy, Harry, 14

Nadler, Jerry, 81
National Association of Railroad Passengers (NARP), 57, 64, 101
National City Lines, 27
National Interstate and Defense Highways Act, 25
nationalization of railroads, 15–16, 19, 35, 54
National Park Service, 170
National Railroad Passenger Corporation, 3, 10n1, 61, 88n18
National Road, construction of, 18
national transportation policy. See transportation policy, federal
NEC. See Northeast Corridor
Neel, Roy, 123
New Deal initiative, 19, 23
New England States, 16
New Hampshire, 215
New Haven–Hartford, 188
New Haven Railroad, 7, 16–17, 21, 33–36, 111
New Haven–Springfield, 188, 192, 192t
New Haven–St. Albans, 192t
New Jersey Transit, 36, 113
New Mexico, 155
New Orleans–Los Angeles, 78
New York–Buffalo–Toronto, 192t
New York Central Railroad (NYC): aesthetic improvements in mid-1930s, 16–17; Great Steel Fleet, 16, 17; and Gunn, 110, 111; merger with Pennsylvania, 21, 22, 36–37; proposed merger, 41n54; reductions in passenger service, 5, 6; and regulation of railroads, 4–5; sale of passenger stations, 6; service standards of, 166; taxes on terminal in Toledo, Ohio, 6; and transcontinental services, 48; 20th Century Limited, xi, 26, 166; and Young, 45, 50, 52
New York City–Buffalo, 188
New York City–Buffalo–Niagara Falls, 165
New York City–Charlotte via Raleigh (Carolinian), 75, 192t, 210–11, 210t, 212, 213t
New York City–Chicago, 67
New York City metropolitan region, crisis facing, 52–53
New York City–Miami (Silver Star), 74, 79, 84, 211, 212
New York City–Montreal, P.Q. (Adirondack), 72
New York City–Toronto (Niagara Rainbow), 78

New York City/Washington–Chicago, 71
New York–Montreal, 192, 192t
New York–New Orleans (Crescent), 187t, 188t, 211, 212
New York, Ontario & Western, 40n32
New York–Pittsburgh–Indianapolis–Kansas City, 72
New York–Rutland, 192t
New York State, 192
New York–Toronto, 192
New York–Washington–Cincinnati–Indianapolis–Chicago (Cardinal), 79, 81, 149, 187t, 188t, 208, 212
Niagara Falls/Buffalo–New York City, 192
Niagara Rainbow (New York City–Toronto), 78
Nickel Plate, 48
Night Owl, 101
Nixon administration: anticipation of Amtrak's failure, 68, 88n34, 96, 161n25; appointment of Lewis, 62, 68, 88n34, 96; and creation of a national rail passenger entity, 63; and Hartke legislation, 60; opposition to subsidies, 59, 60, 61; and route structure of Amtrak, 63
Nixon, Richard: anticipation of Amtrak's failure, 68, 88n34; and conservatives' views of Amtrak, 174; elected president, 60; and postmaster general appointment, 161n12; and Rail Passenger Service Act, 61; resignation of, 97
Norfolk Southern (NS), 124–25, 207t, 211, 213
North by Northwest (film), 148
North Carolina, 210–12
North Carolina Railroad, 211
North Coast Hiawatha, 67, 72
North Coast Limited, xi
Northeast Corridor, 73; and Acela, 77–78; Amtrak's acquisition of, 72; Black on management of, 144; BWI Airport station on, 73; coal trains on, 103; and Coscia's agenda, 162n46; crisis facing, 52–53, 59; and Downeaster, 214; focus of Amtrak governance on, 181; funding for, 22, 93, 131, 142, 183; and Gunn, 113, 121; maintenance of, 72, 128; Moorman on, 131; myths associated with, 121; and on-time performance, 130; Pacific Surfliners compared to, 195t; passenger-miles changes, 189t; passenger miles per train mile, 187t; and Pennsylvania's Keystone service, 192; political support for, 85; and privatization movement/plans, 75–76, 81; proposals to split NEC from Amtrak, 81, 118–19, 119, 162n46, 176; reequipping services on, 77–78; regional services that complement, 188; and Reistrup, 105; revenue per train mile, 188t; ridership surge on, 78; sale of, proposed by Reagan, 75; and state rail programs, 188; Strategic Business Unit, 136–37; and threat of labor strikes, 109, 137; and TRAIN Act, 183; tunnels and bridges of, 176; and Virginia's rail program, 212
Northern Indiana Commuter Transportation District, 209
Northern New England Passenger Rail Authority (NNEPRA), 214, 215, 216
Nowak, Ed, 16

Oakland–Bakersfield, 192t
Obama, Barack, 81, 122, 162n46, 175
O'Brien, Lawrence, 37
observation cars, 67
ocean liners, 168
Oklahoma, 192–93
onboard services: challenges associated with, 141–42; cutbacks in, 80–81, 83–84; improvements in, 82; and Iowa Pacific, 210; and Moorman administration, 129; and Reistrup administration, 103. See also food and beverage services; passenger experience; sleeping cars/sleeper service
online reservations, 165
on-time performance: Black on, 144; challenges associated with, 84, 144; and communities being served, 154; and investment to improved capacity, 198; and passenger experience, 148–49; role of host railroads in, 84, 130; US Supreme Court ruling on, 85
optimism at Amtrak, 66
Oregon, 191–92
Ortner, Jason, 210, 212
overhead costs of railroads, 46–47. See also financial health of railroads
Overland Route, 18

P42DC locomotives, 159
Pacemaker, 16
Pacific Electric, 40n32
Pacific International, 71
Pacific Parlour Cars, 83, 84
Pacific Surfliners (San Diego–Los Angeles–San Luis Obispo), 191t, 194–96, 194t, 195t, 196t, 213t
package express service, 74
Palmetto, 79, 81, 212
Pan Am, 216
parlor cars, 43, 67, 83, 84
passenger experience: and boxed meals, 166; budget cuts' impact on, 70, 129, 167; decline in standards for, 10; expectations of customers, 141; and housekeeping standards, 160; inconsistent quality in, 158; interviews with passengers on, 147–51; and mechanical problems, 160, 165; Moorman's emphasis on, 129; onboard staffs' role in, 151, 165; and quality of service in early days of Amtrak, 57; and rattles on trains, 160; reasons people choose train travel, 148–51; Reistrup's emphasis on, 102–3; in sleeping cars, 152, 158; surveys used to gauge, 93; on the 20th Century Limited,

166; Young's emphasis on, 45, 50, 129
passenger-miles: in California, 189, 194*t*, 199–200; in Midwestern intercity network, 202*t*; percentage passenger-miles changes, 189*t*, 190*t*, 191*t*, 192*t*, 193*t*; by travel mode, 189*t*; trends in, 189, 190; in Vermont, 191
"passenger problem": about, 25; declines in ridership, 15, 23–24, 30, 44, 53; extent of crisis, 29, 52–54; federal intervention in, 59–62; financial strain on railroads, 3, 7, 29, 38, 52–54; and ICC cost survey, 58; and ICC formula, 14; and mergers option, 36; Morgan's article addressing, 38–39; Senate subcommittee investigation of, 28; and Young's innovative proposals, 45, 52
Passenger Rail Investment and Improvement Act (PRIIA), 80, 123, 208
passenger service: as civic obligation, 4, 14; freight revenues offsetting, 7, 33, 46; Murphy on low margins of, 14; near elimination of, 91; perceived as outdated, 39, 93. *See also* "passenger problem"
Passenger Train Journal, 57, 63, 166, 183
Peña, Federico F., 223
Penn Central (PC) Railroad, 22; and Amtrak's origins, 61; bad track of, 67; bankruptcy of, 7, 36, 58–59, 61; and coal trains, 103; and Gunn, 110, 111; merger creating, 21, 36–37; petition to discontinue trains, 58
Penn Station, 78, 83, 108–9
Pennsylvania, 192
Pennsylvanian, 72, 79–80, 188, 192*t*
Pennsylvania Railroad: advertisement for meals, *44*; aesthetic improvements in mid-1930s, 16–17; locomotives of, 71; merger with NYC, 21, 36–37; Metroliner program, 22, *22*; proposed merger, 41n54; and transcontinental services, 48, 87n3; and Young, 52
Pere Marquette, 45, 48–50, 191*t*
performance reports, recommendations for, 178
Perl, Anthony, 94
Perlman, Alfred, 26, 30, 166
Peters, Mary E., 223
Philadelphia–Harrisburg, 190*t*
Phillips, Don, 138, 162n63
Phillips Petroleum, 25
Piedmont (Charlotte–Raleigh), 210–12, 210*t*
Piedmont Coalition, 213
Pingree, Chellie, 216
Pioneer, 78, 79
Pioneer Trails, 136
Pittsburgh–New York City, 80, 192
Pittsfield Housing Authority, 6
Plous, Fritz, 60–61
politics and political agendas in transportation: and Biden's election as president, 184–85; Black on, 141; Gunn on, 95; Loving on, 174; and political appointments, 95; and Reistrup administration, 105; in Virginia, 214
Positive Train Control, 215
Precision Scheduled Railroading, 116, 199
presidential administrations, US, 95, 96, 108, 175–76. *See also specific presidents*
presidential election of 1948, 22–23
presidents of Amtrak, 223; attributes of best, 97–98; and chairmen of the board, 174; fiduciary responsibility of, 98; inconsistent quality in, 170; as interim or placeholders, 8, 98, 109, 121, 122, 123, 126, 129, 170; Lewis's undermining of Amtrak, 62; McClellan on challenges of, 85; and mission of Amtrak, 8, 175; Moorman on, 127, 132; and political nature of Amtrak's leadership, 8; recommendations for action, 175; and saving Amtrak, 185; shift away from railroad insiders, 141; support from federal bureaucracy, 142. *See also specific presidents*
pride in trains, railroads', xi, *xii*
privately run passenger service, 3
privatization movement/plans, 75–76, 81, *119*, 121, 172
profitability issue of Amtrak: Amtrak established as 'for profit' entity, 60, 65; and Amtrak's service model, 93, 169–70; Black's perspective on, 139, 143; and business model of Amtrak, 127; Coscia's statement on, 86; effects of expecting, 91, 94; Gunn on myth of, 121; Howes on failure of, 173; legislative language on, 60, 88n18; and Lewis administration, 62; modification of for-profit language, 160n10; and TRAIN Act, 183; and Warrington, 112
"Progress and Change" (White), 2, 12, 147
Progressive movement, 4
Progressive Railroading, 125
Providence, Rhode Island, station in, 75
public relations value of trains, 54
public transportation, need for, ix
public utility commissions, 4
Pullman, George M., 156
Pullman Company: child passengers of, xi; and death of Jones, M W., 81; efforts to attract riders, 15; and lack of competition, 15; and Sightseer Lounges, 141; standard of service in, 156–57, *157*, 158; and Young, 45, 47–48, 50
Pullman-Standard (P-S), 24, 51, 71, *74*, 105, 115

Quinn, Patricia, 215

racial diversity, 69
Rail Diesel Car, 43
Rail Passengers Association, 57
Rail Passenger Service Act, 61, 140, 169, 174, 183
"Railpax," 3, 10n1, 60, 88n24
"Railroad, The" (White), x
Railroad Retirement Act, 19
Railroad Valuation Act, 4
Rail Travel News, 57
Rail Users' Network, 212
Railway Age, 24, 57, 120, 125, 126, 171–72
Railway Labor Act, 38, 106
Railway Post Office cars, 37
rationalization of routes, 3
Raton, New Mexico, 155
Raymond Loewy–styled buses, 27
Reagan administration, 134–35
Reagan, Ronald, 75, 109
reauthorization legislation, 84, 103, 120, 141, 162n66, 176
recommendations for action, 173–78; for board of directors, 174–75; for governance of Amtrak, 174; for presidents of Amtrak, 175; for presidents of United States, 175–76; for US Congress, 176–77
"Red Circle" fares, 44, 100
Reed, John, 54, 103
Reform Board, Amtrak, 178
reform/restructuring proposals, 66, 72, 86–87, 121, 178
regulation of railroads: addressing monopolies, 14; Budd on negative effects of, 16; competition as focus of, 20; contrasted with other transportation industries, 4; expansion of, 4, 19; limiting ability to compete, 16; over-regulation addressed in 1980, 15; period of minimal levels of, 13–14; profitability impacted by, 15, 18; of rates/fares, 4–5, 14, 15, 19, 20, 26; and Senate subcommittee report (1951), 28; of services, 14; and Young's reform efforts, 45, 52
Reistrup, Paul, 98–105, *99*; administration of, 170, 223; and B&O's marketing campaign, 43; background of, 99, 100–101; and committee addressing passenger crisis, 37; and equipment, 67, 101, 102, 103, 105; expectations of, 101–2; on "experiment" of Amtrak, 101, 161n25; and funding, 104; on greatest accomplishment, 105; Lewis replaced by, 97, 99; mission of, 102–3; motivations of, 101; on need for Amtrak, 104; railroad history understood by, 95; and service, 103; and track issues, 103, 104
Rensselaer, Indiana, 154
reservations, modernization of, 165
revenue of Amtrak, 79, 188*t*
Richmond, Virginia, Main Street Station, 80
Riddell, Doug, 139
Rio Grande Railroad, 64, 75
roads and highways: congestion on, 21, 154, 156; and Department of Transportation, 142; Federal Aid Highway Act, 25; federal/state support of, 4, 18, 30; and financial reporting, 33; and golden age of automobiles, 27; Highway Trust Fund, 7, 32, 114, 131; impact on rail services, 4,

14, 15, 21; interstate system, 7, 21, 25, 27, 29, 33, 51–52, 156; and INVEST Act, 185n5; as "investments," 87n17, 92; National Road construction, 18; and national transportation policy, 29, 131; public preference for travel by, 8; subsidies for, 7, 25, 31t, 32, 39, 87n17; tax-exempt status of, 39. *See also* automobile, travel by
"Robber Barons" era, 13–14
Robert Heller & Associates, 41n54
Robinson, John, 60
Rochester, New York, station in, 83
Rocky Mountaineer, Canada, 182–83
roomettes, 150. *See also* sleeping cars/sleeper service
Roosevelt, Franklin D., 19, 22
Roosevelt, Theodore, 4
Rosen, Jeff, 112–13
Rosenwald, Brian, 83, 166–67
route structure/network: creating, 63–64, 65; expansion of, 165; service additions/extensions, 75, 78, 79–80; service cuts (*see* discontinuance of trains);
Rudolph, Richard, 212–13
rural communities and small towns, 86, 116, 154, 188

Sacramento airport–Stockton, 194
safety considerations: and accidents, 79; Batory on, ix; Black's emphasis on, 147; and Boardman, 139; Downs's emphasis on, 108; Moorman's emphasis in, 128; as paramount, 88n33; Reistrup's emphasis on, 102
San Diego–Los Angeles, 195
San Diego–Los Angeles–San Luis Obispo (Pacific Surfliners), 191t, 194–96, 194t, 195t, 196t, 213t
Sandusky, Ohio, 154
San Francisco Bay, tunnel beneath, 200
San Joaquin Regional Rail Commission (SJRRC), 197–98
San Joaquins (Oakland-Bakersfield), 72, 194t, 196t, 197–98
San Jose–Oakland–Sacramento–Auburn, 194, 194t, 198
San Jose–Stockton Altamont Corridor Express, 197–98
Santa Fe, 54, 56, 67, 87n3, 87n6
Santa Fe's Hi-Level fleet, *74*
saving Amtrak, 173–78, 181–85
SDP40F locomotives, *69*, 71, 101
Seaboard Air Line Railroad, 38, 213
Seaboard Coast Line, 54, 64
sea level, rising, 195
secretaries of transportation, 8, 95, 107, 117, 140, 172, 176, 223
Segotta, Neil, Jr., 155
Senate Commerce Committee, 61, 156
Sensible Transportation Act, 214
September 11, 2001, terrorist attacks, 137
service, Amtrak as, 169–70
service standards on passenger service: Amtrak's authority to set metrics for, 85; Black's perspective on, 141–42, 144; commitment to, 54–55, 56, 57; declines in, 53, 55, 70; inconsistent quality in, 158; recommendations for action, 177
Shaw, Pat, 138
Shuster, Bud, 81
sightseeing from Amtrak, 148
Sightseer Lounges, 141
Silver Meteor, xi, 148, 183, 187t, 188t, 212
Silver Palm, 81
Silver Star (New York City–Miami), 74, 79, 84, 211, 212
The $64 Billion Massachusetts Vehicle Economy, 32
Skinner, Samuel K., 223
Skoropowski, Gene, 198
Slater, Rodney E., 223
sleeping cars/sleeper service: acquisitions of, 78; amenity packs in, 152, *153*, 171; Black on, 146; cutbacks in, 83, 84; "heritage" cars, 80; inconsistent customer experience in, 152, 158; introduction of inexpensive, 43; and Pullman's standard of service, 156–57, *157*, 158; and Reistrup administration, 100, 103; roomettes, 150
small towns and rural communities, 86, 116, 154, 188
Smathers, George, 29
Smith, John Robert, 112
Smith, Rachel, 154
socialism, concerns about creeping, 3, 34, 96
Sorenson, Theodore, 20
Southeast Corridor (Washington–Jacksonville), 211
Southeastern Pennsylvania Transportation Authority (SEPTA), 36, 105, 113
Southern Crescent, 64, 88n40
Southern Pacific, 60
Southern Railway, 64, 88n40, 124, 125
Southwest Airlines, 9, 167, 210
Southwest Chief, 75, 148, 155, 187t, 188t, 217
splitting Amtrak, proposals for, 81, 118–20, *119*, 162n46, 176
Springfield, Massachusetts, station in, 83
Staggers, Harley, 67, 104
Staggers Rail Act, 6, 28
stainless-steel trains, *16*, 17, 43, 48
Standard Oil, 25, 27
Stanford study, 60
Starlight, 167
state rail programs, 187–220; Black on operation of, 144; coordination/cooperation of, 193, 217, 218; failures, 188, 216; funding of, 176, 190, 218; grassroots efforts in, 218; growth trends in, 189, 189t, 190, 190t; interdependence of Amtrak and, 217; international, 188; investments in passenger rail, 189; key indicators for, 189t; and liability insurance, 217; Maine, 214–16, 215t; North Carolina, 210–12; Ohio, 216–17; passenger miles per train mile, 187t; percentage passenger-miles changes, 189t, 190t, 191t, 192t, 193t; recommendations for action, 176; revenue per train mile, 188t; success of, 187, 217; and survival of Amtrak, 187–88; transfers between services, 188; Virginia, 212–14, 212t, 213t, 218. *See also* California; midwestern intercity network
stations and station operations: costs associated with, 5; Great American Stations initiative, 80; improvements made in, 75, 80, 83; modernization of, 6; replacing high-cost facilities, 72; taxation on value of, 5–6; ticket agents eliminated in, 83. *See also* specific stations
stewardship, standards of, 95–98. *See also* Black, Robert Cliff, IV; Gunn, David; leadership of Amtrak; Moorman, Charles "Wick"
St. Louis–Kansas City, 204t, 205, 207, 208t
Stockman, David, 134
stock market crash of 1929, 15
St. Paul, Minnesota, Union Depot, 83
subsidies for transportation industries, 6–8; Anderson's efforts to reduce, 131; Black's perspective on, 139, 144, 145–46; for commuter services, 35–36; Congress's consideration of, 59–60; and Downs, 108–9; general opposition to, 91; hidden, 30–33; for high-speed trains, 21–22; ICC recommendations on, 29; imbalance between industries, 5, 19, 28, 30–31, 31t, 32–35, 38–39, 87n17, 92; as "investments," 87n17, 92, 145–46; Mica's objections to, 81, 162n66; Morgan's article addressing, 39; Nixon administration's opposition to, 59, 60, 61; Perlman on inequities in, 30; and Senate subcommittee report (1951), 28; and Young's reform efforts, 45
Sunnyside Yards, 181
Sunset Limited, 78, 107–8, 116, 187t, 188t
Super Chief, xi, 54, 56
Superliner cars, *74*; acquisition of, 71; and Boyd administration, 106, 140, 141; delivery of last car in 1981, 74; Gunn on quality of, 115; maintenance of, 114; overall success of, 159; plumbing problems in, 160; postwar car orders for, 24; and Reistrup administration, 105
Superliner II cars, 77
Surface Transportation Subcommittee of the US Senate's Interstate and Foreign Commerce Committee, 29
Surfliners. *See* Pacific Surfliners
Szabo, Joe, 204–5

Talgo equipment, 77
taxation of railroads: and bankruptcies of railroads, 8; burden of, 5–6, 15; and commuter services, 36; and crises in railroads, 53; ICC recommendations on, 29; imbalance between industries, 5, 6, 39; Perlman on inequities in, 30; as source of state

revenue, 25; ticket tax, 25, 29, 53; and Young's reform efforts, 45, 46, 52
Teague, Walter Dorwin, 17
Texas Eagle, 79, 148, 187t, 188t
Thirtieth Street Station, Philadelphia, 78
three-day-a-week service, 180, 183–84
Three Rivers, 80
ticket agents, elimination of, 83
TIGER Grant awards, 155
Time magazine, 80
timetables of Amtrak, *67, 82*; and Amtrak's startup, 69; buried online, 184; discontinuation of printed, 152, 171; need to restore printed, 178
Topeka and Emerson, 64
Toth, Gary, 32
track: and Acela, 77–78; bad/rough track of host railroads, 67, 74, 93, 101, 102, 103, 104; Black on, 143; of NEC, 105; recommendations for action, 177; and Reistrup administration, 103, 104; on-time performance and capacity of, 84–85; and Warrington, 112
TrainRiders/Northeast, 214, 215
Trains magazine, 38–39, 91, 126
TRAIN (Transforming Rail by Accelerating Investment Nationwide) Act, 183
"Train X" of Young, 50–52, *51*
transcontinental passenger service, 48, *49*, 73, 78, 87n3
TransitAmerica, 161n26
Transportation Act (1920), 4, 19, 20
Transportation Act (1958), 29
Transportation, Housing, and Urban Development Appropriations Subcommittee, 156
Transportation in the US (Toth), 32
transportation policy, federal, 17–20; absence of, 8, 17–18, 19, 42, 117, 121, 131; Black on, 143–44; focused on highways, 29, 131; Gunn on, 117, 121; Howes on lack of, 173; ICC recommendations on, 29; imbalance in approach of, 91; of Kennedy, 20–21; Moorman on, 131; Perlman on inequities in, 30; and political pressure, 8; and regulatory policy, 18–20; and Reistrup administration, 104; trust funds as standard in, 94, 144; and Young's reform efforts, 45. *See also* subsidies for transportation industries
trucking industry, 4, 6, 20, 33, 152
Truman, Harry S., 20, 22–23
Truman-Wheeler Bill, 20
Trump, Donald, 140
Trump administration, 118, 216
tunnels and bridges, rebuilding of, 176
TurboTrain, 39
20th Century Limited, xi, *16*, 26, 166
Tyler, Clark, 135

uniforms at Amtrak, 69, *71*
Union Pacific Railroad (UP), 16–17, 54, 197, 198, 203
unions: and Amtrak's startup, 64; and political nature of Amtrak's leadership, 174; and repeal of independent labor board, 19; resistance to Iowa Pacific, 210; threats of striking, 108–9
US Congress: Amtrak's difficult relationship with, 81; Black on, 141, 143; Downs' advice on, 107–8; and funding for Amtrak, 61, 73, 87, 183; and funding for NEC, 142; King on Amtrak's relationship with, 156; and Midwestern intercity network, 202; modification of for-profit language, 160n10; and Moorman administration, 130; opponents of Amtrak in, 176; and preparing for Day One, 64; and pressure to aid railroads, 57; and proposed elimination of Amtrak, 185; and railroad crisis, 29; and reauthorization legislation, 141; and recommendations for action, 176–77; and Reistrup, 101–2; and route structure of Amtrak, 63; and subsidy proposals, 59–60; support from, 130, 135, 183
US Department of Commerce, 20
US Department of Defense, 19
US Department of Justice, 36
US Department of Transportation: addressing the passenger problem, 60; and "Amtrak Bloodbath"/"Carter Cutbacks," 72; and Amtrak's startup, 62–63; and committee addressing passenger crisis, 37; on emerging corridors, 72; emphasis on highways and airlines, 142; establishment of, 106; expectation of Amtrak's failure, 104, 120; and Gunn administration, 112, 113, 114, 116; inequitable allocation of resources among all industries, 115; and Reistrup administration, 104; secretaries of transportation, 8, 95, 107, 117, 140, 172, 176, 223
US Post Office, 19, 29–30, 37, 54, 161n12
US Senate, 29, 61, 171
US Supreme Court, 85

vacation travel, xi
value of railroads, ICC's determination of, 4
Vanderbilt, Cornelius, 13
Vanderbilt, William K., 13
VanderClute, Bob, 62, 68
Vantuono, William C., 90, 138, 164, 166, 167, 169
Vermonter, 79
VIA Rail Canada, 143, 158, 159, 167, 179n9
Victoria Transport Policy Institute, 201
Viewliner cars: acquisitions of, 74, 77; baggage cars, 82–83; Gunn on poor quality of, 115; maintenance of, 160; postwar car orders for, 24; prototypes of, 161n26; underutilization of, 166
Viewliner II cars, 83
Virginia, 212–14, 212t, 213t, 218
Virginia–Chicago (Mountaineer Norfolk), 72
Virginia Consolidated, 190t
Virginia Railway Express, 212, 214
Volpe, John, 61, 63, 223

Walnut Ridge, Arkansas, 154
Warrington, George: and Acela, 109, 112, 137, 140; administration of, 109, 137, 170, 223; Gunn on leadership of, 112; limited railroad experience of, 77, 137; mission/agenda of, 140; subsidy-free claims of, 108
wars, extensive use of railroads during, 40n50
Washington, DC–Cincinnati corridor, 48–50
Washington, DC–Newport News via Richmond, 212
Washington, DC, Union Station, 75, 83, 141, 212, 214
Washington–Norfolk via Petersburg, 212
Washington–Roanoke via Lynchburg, 212
Washington state, 191–92
Water Level Route, 192
Waterloo, Indiana, 155
waterways, 20, 92, 114
Watkins, Hays, 37
Watts, David, 100
website of Amtrak, 178
Weeks, Sinclair, 28
Weishaar, Noelle, 154
Westchester County railroad stations, 5
Western Pacific Railroad, 35
West Virginian Washington, DC–Parkersburg, West Virginia, 67
Wheeling and Lake Erie, 45
White, E. B., x, xi, 2, 12, 47, 147
Whitman, Frederic B., 35
Whitman, Reginald, 60
Whitman Commission, 21, 29, 33–36, 53, 59, 62
"Who Shot the Passenger Train?" (Morgan), 38–39, 91
Williston, North Dakota, airport financing in, 6
Wilner, Frank, 73, 75, 87
wine, complimentary, 83
Wisconsin, 201, 202
Wolverine, *16*
Wood, Stephen, 154
World War II, 14–15, 17, 20, 22–23

X2000 trainsets, 77
Xplorer of NYC, 87n5

Yellow Coach Company, 27
Young, Robert R., 45–52, *46*; on airlines' marketing, 48, 50, 168; on attracting customers, 48, 50, 51, 129; background of, 45; and the battle for Pullman, 47–48, 87n2; and the Chessie, 48–50; criticisms of industry, 29; death of, 52; end of passenger car industry predicted by, 24; and the ICC formula, 46–47; and Train X, 50–52; and transcontinental services, 48, *49*, 87n3

Zier, Robert, 208–9
Zimmermann, Karl, 83

Geoffrey Doughty joined the Operating Department of Maine Central Railroad in 1974. After stints in the Accounting and Engineering Departments, he was promoted to the Safety Department in 1982, following the railroad's consolidation with the Boston & Maine and the Delaware & Hudson under Guilford ownership. He was later a safety consultant and safety director for two New England trucking associations from which he retired.

Jeffrey Darbee has recently completed a forty-six-year career in historic preservation and is author of several books on historic architecture and railroad history. He resides in Columbus, Ohio.

Now retired, **Gene Harmon** worked for two major railroads in freight marketing, and he became an independent contractor in corporate restructuring, logistics management, and market development. He has worked in Thailand on passenger and freight marketing and strategic development. Gene has traveled by rail in four continents. He is a member of the Lexington Group where he has made a variety of presentations on logistics and transportation.